100 THINGS
PATRIOTS FANS
SHOULD KNOW & DO
BEFORE THEY DIE

Donald Hubbard

TRIUMPH
B O O K S

The Library of Congress Cataloging has catalogued the previously edition as follows:

Hubbard, Donald.
  100 things Patriots fans should know & do before they die / Donald Hubbard.
     p. cm.
  ISBN 978-1-60078-524-5
  1. New England Patriots (Football team)—History. 2. New England Patriots (Football team)—Miscellanea. I. Title. II. Title: One hundred things Patriots fans should know and do before they die.
  GV956.N36H83 2011
  796.332'640974461—dc22

                                                          2011009696

This book is available in quantity at special discounts for your group or organization. For further information, contact:
  Triumph Books LLC
  814 North Franklin Street
  Chicago, Illinois 60610
  (312) 337-0747
  www.triumphbooks.com

Printed in U.S.A.
ISBN: 978-1-62937-173-3
Design by Patricia Frey
Photos courtesy of AP Images unless otherwise indicated

To Malcolm Butler

Contents

1 Brady

Chosen in the sixth round of the 2000 draft, Tom Brady has since developed into one of the greatest quarterbacks in NFL history and probably the best "value pick" ever. Brady paled next to the platoons of workout warriors in his senior draft class, as evidenced by his since-released combine tapes; yet before any team had made its selection, he modestly but accurately estimated his worth to a suitor, stating "I think my best asset as a player is that in the fourth quarter, with the game on the line, I have the desire to win and the feeling that our team is not going to lose." Raised in Northern California, he idolized Joe Montana during his boyhood, and by the time that Brady had played his last down for the Michigan Wolverines, he had prepared himself as the stylistic heir to the even-tempered but intensely competitive former Fighting Irish and '49er legend.

Spawned from a Michigan program still tied to retired coach Bo Schembechler's rush-oriented "three yards and a cloud of dust" offensive mantra that had been more sold on Drew Henson as a starter, Tom Brady seemingly had fallen into another hapless situation, backing up another Drew, this one long-time starter Bledsoe in New England. In fact, during his rookie season, Brady only threw three passes the entire campaign, and while many fans had begun to sour on Bledsoe, most of them did not look toward the rookie from Michigan as the solution, but rather mobile second-year quarterback Michael Bishop, a star from Kansas State. Even before Rush Limbaugh had garbled his analysis of Donovan McNabb, knowledgeable fans and NFL executives and coaches had shed any reluctance to starting an African-American quarterback, and after

Bishop completed a 44-yard bomb for a touchdown against Indy, for many, his time had come.

It never did, as the Pats signed another quarterback, Damon Huard, and cut Bishop during the 2001 pre-season, and while Brady survived the ax himself, he appeared no closer than before to guiding the New England offense. Indeed, at the inception of the 2001, he held the clipboard and from the sidelines, patiently watched starter Drew Bledsoe bark out the signals. Until of course the Jets' Mo Lewis planted Bledsoe on the sidelines in the second game of that season, effectively ending Drew's status as team starter and as an elite NFL quarterback. False perspective has the young second-string quarterback running into the fray and immediately driving the club into the ranks of the league's preeminent franchises. It did not happen that way, at least not right away as the Pats lost that second game of the year against New York and then in the fourth week, Brady and his charges mustered only 10 points as the Dolphins blew them out.

But as Brady became more comfortable, the team became his team to run, and while a couple more hiccups remained (a loss to Denver and a 24–17 loss to the Rams), he kept his job even after Bledsoe had returned to health. Coach Bill Belichick made a very bold decision at this juncture, not permitting his season starter to return to his starting role, trembling little as the fate of Belichick as a coach and the Patriots as a club now rested in the hands of Tom Brady. And with a brief return by Bledsoe in the playoffs, it has stayed that way.

It all seems so obvious now, yet at the conclusion of the 2001 season, the young quarterback had to outduel the Rams' "Greatest Show on Turf" in the Super Bowl as an underdog. Kurt Warner had come to stardom in an even more improbable route than Brady had trod, excellence in the Arena League. Once there, though, Warner won a Super Bowl two years earlier with superstars such as Marshall Faulk and Torry Holt surrounding him. By this point

The 199ᵗʰ pick in the 2000 NFL Draft, Tom Brady has won four Super Bowls and two NFL MVP awards as quarterback of the Patriots.

Brady no longer had any talent of his own to hide, as television analyst Joe Theismann noted, "You know everybody talks about Brett [Favre] this, Brett that…Let me tell you, when Tom Brady wants to step back and cut it loose,, I'll match his arm with anyone in the league—but the thing is, he's accurate. When he sets to fire, he can fire."

In that 2001 title game, the Rams' Warner produced far better numbers than Brady, completing more passes than his Pats' opponent attempted and gaining 220 more yards for his team in the air. Of course, Warner also completed passes to Patriots' defensive backs Ty Law (ran back the other way for a 47 yard touchdown) and Otis Smith (culminating in a New England field goal), while Brady did not commit these game-breaking mistakes, as he led his team to victory in Super Bowl XXXVI. Thematically, Tom Brady had written the script for the remainder of his career, someone who only once (to date) has led the NFL in quarterback passing rating, but someone who helped his team achieve the ultimate goal of repeatedly winning the final game of the playoffs. He earned the Super Bowl MVP after the Rams' game and also saw action in his first Pro Bowl.

He had also entered the Pantheon of Massachusetts' sports heroes, buttressed not only by his game-winning heroics but by his common touch. He drove a beat-up truck around and stopped by local delis and pizza joints for his lunches, recognized by few at first, a star with a common touch.

Vexingly, though Brady played well in the next campaign, but 2002 proved a letdown as the team which only accumulated a 9-7 record. The club had traded away Drew Bledsoe in the off-season, so Brady had no controversy regarding his role as a starter, but his teammates sagged and failed to make the playoffs, due largely to a porous defense. They needed some tough defenders and Belichick and personnel director Scott Pioli, to their credit, obtained Ted Washington and Rodney Harrison after that disappointing experience.

Mythically, the Patriots fielded a fairly mundane defense in 2003, characterized by character players who overachieved based on their desire, a mischaracterization for a very talented congregation that shut out three opponents that season. In reality, the offense

Brady Behind the Plate

Almost everyone knows the essential facts concerning Tom Brady and his career, even non-football fans, to the extent that any such people exist. It is difficult to craft a book about things every Pats fan should know when so much is already known about the great Brady. But here is something very few people know and which goes to his prodigious athleticism: Tom Brady was an 18th round selection of the Montreal Expos in the 1995 major league baseball draft. As a catcher.

had lost some of its firepower as running back Antowain Smith sacrificed some effectiveness and Tom Brady lost the services of Troy Brown for four games, with Brown catching 57 less passes than the previous season. Brady's brilliance that year lay in distributing the ball to a number of eligible receivers, such as back Kevin Faulk, tight ends Daniel Graham and Christian Fauria and receivers such as Deion Branch and David Givens. While other clubs had transcendent talents like Randy Moss or Terrell Owens running deep routes for them, Brady prospered with the assets at his disposal, making his teammates better.

This ability to quickly read defenses and deliver the ball to the best receiving option served Brady during the tough playoffs and in the Super Bowl against Carolina, a 32–29 nailbiting win. While Smith ran for a touchdown for the Pats that day, Brady zeroed in for short TD passes to Branch, Givens and "tight end" Mike Vrabel. Thriving under pressure, he guided his team down the field at the end to permit Adam Vinatieri to lick the game-winning field goal. Tom Brady had also cemented his reputation as a classic playoff performer along with watching his teammates hoist another Lombardi trophy.

In that off-season, the club did not add much in the way of receiving weapons, but obtained Bengals' star running back Corey Dillon who rushed for 1,635 yards and a 4.7 yard per carry average, a very significant upgrade over the departed back Antowain Smith. They now had one of the finest offenses to book-end their stout defense, and won every regular season game in 2004 with the exception of a loss to the Steelers (15–1 that year before the playoffs) and a fluke loss to a poor Dolphins team.

The Patriots sailed through the playoff with embarrassing ease until they faced the Eagles in the Super Bowl, a 24-21 narrow win, again characterized by Brady's coolness under pressure. Subtly though, the star had changed off the field, the subject of glamorous magazine cover shoots.

Brady had another terrific year in 2005, but unfortunately the club did not as Dillon's production dropped off steeply, one factor in many that led to a 10–6 record heading into the playoffs. The Pats smoked the Jaguars in the first round of the playoffs, 28–3, but then uncharacteristically folded in the divisionals against the Broncos, led by Jake Plummer of all people. In that game, Brady committed one of his few notable faux pas in his career, intercepted in the end zone by Champ Bailey, who famously galloped almost 100 yards in the other direction before Pats' tight end Ben Watson tackled him. Final score, Broncos 27, Patriots 13.

Although their star quarterback had not thrown to a league-leading type of receiver since the last healthy years of Troy Brown, he excelled with some very useful players, whom the team had let walk in free agency, so much so that in 2006 he had to throw to unfamiliar veteran additions Jabar Gaffney and Reche Caldwell and one of their all-time busts, Chad Jackson from Florida. Fortunately, Corey Dillon rebounded on the ground and formed a threatening tandem with rookie Lawrence Maroney, while Kevin Faulk continued to do everything well. By now the team had become a victim of its own success, criticized despite its 12–4 record and two playoff wins. It had lost to Peyton Manning and the Colts during the season and in the conference championship, and while Manning had Reggie Wayne, Dallas Clark and Marvin Harrison to throw to, Brady simply did not have receivers who compared favorably to this arsenal. Too many Pats fans missed perceiving a good season that year, particularly along the offensive line, a fine group anchored by Matt Light at tackle, Dan Koppen at center, and Steve Neal and Logan Mankins at guard.

To their credit, the Pats management filled the void by picking up Randy Moss, Wes Welker and Donte Stallworth, and Brady took full advantage of this largesse, throwing for 4,806 yards with a record 50 touchdowns against only 8 interceptions. Moss caught 98 passes for a record 23 touchdowns while Welker accumulated

112 receptions, as their quarterback racked up a stunning 117.2 rating for the year, a league-leading rating and historically, the second highest single-season passer rating. Named the NFL's MVP and chosen for his fourth Pro Bowl, only one thing eluded him as the club lost only one game that season, the Super Bowl to the Giants.

An early season-ending injury against the Chiefs prevented Brady from the chance to avenge this momentous loss, and although replacement Matt Cassel played well, the team failed to make the playoffs in 2008. Brady returned to a fifth Pro Bowl nomination in 2009, with some fine performances by Moss and Welker at receiver, but Lawrence Maroney had not matured at back and the team lost five games by a touchdown or less. In the first round of the playoffs, the Ravens held the Pats to two touchdowns, both passes to Julian Edelman, and a one and out humiliation.

By this point, neo-theologians had begun to speak about how the Patriots had lost their soul, a Faustian bargain that apparently commenced with the addition of one Randy Moss to the roster in 2007, although superfans jumped on Brady too, for his marriage to model Gisele Bundchen and his perceived softening to a jet set lifestyle. Forget the near perfect season in 2007 and Moss' quiet

Late Picks

Bill Belichick often chooses a quarterback after the first round, generally as a back-up or a potential developmental project, but rarely selects one as low as the sixth round. In 2002 he picked Rohan Davey from LSU (4th) and later Kliff Kingsbury (6th), Matt Cassel (7th), Kevin O'Connell (3rd) and Zac Robinson (7th in 2010). Perhaps as a nod to Brady's mortality, the team did choose Jimmy Garoppolo with a second round pick before the 2014 season. While we are on the subject of NFL drafts, before the Pats selected Brady in the sixth round in 2000, they had first chosen Adrian Klemm, J. R. Redmond, Greg Robinson-Randall, Dave Stachelski, Jeff Marriott and Antwan Harris.

contributions to the team and Matt Cassel, by the beginning of 2010 he personified the quest for personal records at the expense of Lombardi trophies. Unfair to Moss in many respects, he actually fueled this speculation by staging a tirade after his team's opening season regular season victory over the Bengals.

Belichick traded Moss to the Vikings early season, one of the gutsiest in-season trades in the annals of local sports, comparable to the Red Sox shipping beloved shortstop Nomar Garciaparra to the Chicago Cubs in 2004. Brady's struggled a bit in initially with the absence of his friend and prime long route target, but the development appeared to galvanize the team, and he ended up with his second league leading passer rating by the end of the year.

Parenthetically, the quarterback passer rating has helped analyze performance, but particularly in the case of Brady, it has proven a limited tool. Only twice has Brady led the NFL in that rating index, but only Peyton Manning among his contemporaries seriously approached his performance. There is no statistic for stupid plays not made (if there was, it would be called "the Brett Favre factor"), but like Bob Dylan's John Wesley Harding, Brady was never known to make a foolish move. This quality of intelligent play, geared toward making his teammates better has made Brady and his teammates Super Bowl champions.

The humble sixth round draft choice has not changed all that much, but his life has. He clearly prefers to live in the West Coast or even...shudder... New York, and he married a supermodel well beyond the range of most male Patriots fans. Sometimes he rankles the purists in New England by wearing a Yankees cap or talking to Kobe Bryant before a playoff game against the Celtics, but honestly, Tom Brady has only conducted himself in a manner that most of us would have given his opportunities. He is as far from a Ben Roethlisberger type imaginable and has not once come remotely close to embarrassing his employers or his fans. And he has probably done so with a level of class and dignity most of us could only dream to muster. With perhaps one exception, his Beatles haircut from the fall of 2010.

The 2010 season did not end well, with a loss to the Jets in the playoffs. Brady had set the all-time mark in the regular season for passes attempted without an interception, but uncharacteristically he threw one during the first drive in that playoff game, a rare mistake. He distinguished himself in that regular season though, posting an MVP caliber season as he guided his teammates to a 14-2 regular season record.

In 2011, Tom Brady was a Wes Welker dropped pass and a Giants' fluke pass reception away from another Super Bowl victory. Afterwards, Tom's wife Gisele was overheard saying "My husband can not f------ throw the ball and catch the ball at the same time. I can't believe they dropped the ball so many times." For his part, Tom merely observed, "I think it was just the missed opportunities."

With a defense that was still evolving, and with Rob Gronkowski hurt through much of 2012 and 2013, Brady could not lead his team past the AFC Championship Game. In 2014, with more defensive balance and an improved running game, Brady no longer had to throw more than 600 passes a year. And this time he had a healthy Gronk to throw to in addition to Julian Edelman, and this time, he finally earned his fourth Super Bowl ring. And gave the truck he won as the MVP to teammate Malcolm Butler.

Belichick

The round terms of Bill Belichick's life story are probably more familiar to a Patriots fan than the tale of George Washington cutting down a cherry tree or Abe Lincoln splitting logs to build a log cabin. A coach's son, Belichick discovered his vocation about the same time he first opened his eyes as an infant. In pursuit of his own dreams to coach one day, he sought out every poor-paying go-fer job in the NFL, catching on with Ted Marchibroda and the Colts in 1975. After short stints with the Lions and Broncos, Ray Perkins hired him as an assistant in 1979 for the New York Giants, and after Perkins departed, Belichick stayed, becoming a protégé of successor head coach Bill Parcells. In 1991, his apprenticeship complete, the Cleveland Browns named Belichick their head coach.

Belichick led Cleveland for five years, mostly unsuccessfully, although his team did post an 11-5 record in 1995 with a playoff victory that year against the Patriots. Some of the trademarks of his later success became apparent there, particularly when he supplanted local favorite Bernie Kosar as the club's quarterback, but poor ownership and Belichick's own shortcomings doomed the experiment. He then went back to assisting Bill Parcells, first in New England in 1996 and then for the next three years with the Jets. Parcells, as is his custom, got either bored or frustrated with his job, and he anointed Belichick as the next head coach of the Jets for the 2000 season. At that juncture, Belichick balked and decided to take Bob Kraft's offer to lead the Patriots.

Less appreciated is that his introduction as the New England Patriots head coach could easily have been almost as disastrous as Clive Rush's near execution decades earlier. Bill Parcells had laid it out so that Belichick would become head coach of the Jets, in order that Parcells could screw the Patriots by proxy. Belichick did not mumble the lines set forth in the script though, and decided he liked Pats' owner Bob Kraft and so he decided instead to follow his destiny as the man who would bring the Lombardi trophy for multiple visits to Foxboro.

Since then, Belichick has led the Patriots to four Super Bowl titles and has often crafted a playoff contender out of a seemingly

Head coach Bill Belichick has presided over a golden era of Patriots football since taking the helm in 2000.

mediocre team. Some of his game decisions have come into question (going for it on 4th and 2 against Peyton's Colts in 2009 or the fake punt against the Jets in the first round of the playoffs after the '10 season), but he remains the most respected coach in the NFL.

Other clubs have tried to replicate the Belichick's level of excellence by hiring away his assistants: Romeo Crennel in Cleveland, Eric Mangini by the Jets and the Browns, Charlie Weis at Notre Dame and Josh McDaniels by the Broncos, and none of these teams have been blessed with success. Each of these erstwhile assistants stepped into programs in decline, but so did Belichick when he accepted the New England job.

These coaches could perform a number of tasks well, Bill Belichick performs all of them well. He has a good relationship with ownership, he works very hard, he recognizes and develops talent both in personnel and assistant coaches, he motivates players and he runs his offenses and defenses with imagination.

There is something missing for the taciturn coach: He has five fingers on his left hand but only four Super Bowl rings.

Four

It was time for Tom Brady to go, hang up his cleats, and pass the reins to rookie quarterback Jimmy Garoppolo. After four games, the Patriots had won twice and lost twice, most embarrassingly in the fourth game to the Kansas City Chiefs, 41–14. The Chiefs defense picked Brady off twice, returning one interception for a touchdown The offensive line, having lost its Pro Bowl guard Logan Mankins, was an Island of Misfit Toys. Brady needed more weapons and was getting sacked quicker than almost every other quarterback in the league. Gronk wasn't Gronk and no one knew who Danny Amendola was or why he had been chosen to replace Wes Welker. And the defense had been overrun by inferior teams. And hey, back to Brady, he was 37 years old, which translated to 259 years in dog years.

Radio talk-show listeners, both first-time callers and longtime offenders, meticulously broke down how Brady had irretrievably broken down. Scribes and commentators alike chided a blind devotion by management and the coaching staff to an obsolete System. Universal darkness covered all.

Former Patriot Rodney Harrison remarked, "I've never seen a team so unprepared." While expressing confidence in his team and observing that they still led their conference, Bob Kraft lamented, "Last night was one of the worst games since I've owned the team and it was very draining."

Protected against the shifting winds of public scorn by his hoody, Bill Belichick simply said, "We're getting ready for Cincinnati."

Then the Pats won 10 out of their next 12 regular season games, losing only to Green Bay in a very close away game, then to Buffalo in the final "don't get any of our players hurt" scrimmage, having by then won home-field advantage and a first-round bye in the playoffs.

What changed? Most notably, superstar tight end Rob Gronkowski, injured during large stretches of the past two seasons, regained his groove and the team regained some balance with an improved ground game with Shane Vereen, LeGarrette Blount, and Jonas Gray. Symptomatically, the improved ground game sprung from an improved line, with rookie Bryan Stork asserting himself at center, flanked by veteran guards Dan Connolly and Ryan Wendell and tackles Nate Solder and Sebastian Vollmer.

And though the team lost team leader Jerod Mayo on defense after the sixth game, the defense jelled around free agent cornerbacks Brandon Browner and Darrelle Revis and young players such as Dont'a Hightower, Jamie Collins, and Chandler Jones. Plus Rob Ninkovich became the second coming of Mike Vrabel. New England no longer had to rely on Tom Brady leading shoot-outs, as the defense now won games for the team.

It suited them well, as they enjoyed the bye in the first round of the playoffs before facing the Ravens. It was a bad match-up for New England; historically, Baltimore under coach John Harbaugh had defeated them twice in the playoffs. This time the Patriots turned the tables on their rival, but it was a close thing, having to come back on two occasions from 14-point deficits. Fittingly, the decisive moment occurred in the last play when Joe Flacco Hail-Maryed it into the end zone, but it was harmlessly batted back onto the field. Greatest comeback in Patriots' playoff history.

And the best pass of the day came not from Tom Brady, but from Julian Edelman, the erstwhile Kent State quarterback; Brady tossed the ball back to Edelman, who then completed a 51-yard touchdown pass to Danny Amendola to tie the score late in the third quarter. Observed a suddenly beloved Amendola, "It's a play we've been working on all year. Testament to Julian; has a great arm and is a great athlete. He put it on the money, that's for sure."

They thoroughly thrashed the Colts, after which a controversy arose concerning whether or not the Pats had deliberately deflated their footballs to provide them with an advantage against Indianapolis.

Finally, the Super Bowl against the Seahawks, a game deemed a toss-up by odds-makers.

First the good news, the Patriots won their fourth championship.

Like all Belichick/Brady Super Bowls, the nail-biting never stopped. Seattle's Marshawn Lynch easily provided Seattle with the edge on the ground, as LeGarrette largely ran into ruts all day. But Brady clearly outperformed Russell Wilson, and though Brady

Tricky

Julian Edelman may have had the best play of their first playoff game against Baltimore, but the trickiest play belonged to Belichick. Running back Shane Vereen declared himself ineligible to a referee before a play, then sat on the line of scrimmage, Baltimore's 24-yard line. Suddenly eligible "left-tackle" Michael Hoomanawanui shots out uncovered, received the ball, and ran to the 10. Angry Ravens' coach Harbaugh stormed onto the field and was penalized.

threw two interceptions to Wilson's one, Wilson's was the most telling.

It was a peculiar first quarter, Seattle possessed the ball for less than four minutes but the score was tied 0–0 at the end. The Patriots drove the ball relentlessly during their second possession, but with third down on the Seahawk's 10-yard line, Brady's pass to Edelman was intercepted by Jeremy Lane. Threat over, but so too was Jeremy Lane's day; the talented corner was injured after the pick after being tackled by Julian Edelman. Significantly, Seattle had lost one of its cornerbacks and Brady was not going to throw in the direction of the other one, Richard Sherman.

In the second quarter, New England largely ignored its running game, with Brady dealing to Amendola, Gronkowski, Edelman, and Brandon LaFell, with LaFell scoring his team's first touchdown on an 11-yard completion.

Each team punted away their next possessions, and then Seattle staged another drive. Wilson ran very little during the game, but Marshawn Lynch overran the Patriots, capping if off with three straight runs, the last for a touchdown.

New England answered with a touchdown of its own, a 22-yard pass from Brady to Gronkowski with Gronk holding up the football like a chalice in the end zone, with 36 seconds remaining in the half.

Improbably, Seattle tied the score 14–14, keyed by a 23-yard pass left to Ricardo Lockette, augmented by a 15-yard face-mask penalty called on Kyle Arrington. The drive culminated in a touchdown pass from Wilson to Chris Matthews and gambling coach Pete Carroll was vindicated.

Katy Perry regaled the fans during halftime, and Seattle promptly took the lead on a field goal after Wilson threw another beautiful pass to Chris Matthews, this one for 45 yards. On the next possession, Brady was picked off again and Seattle scored another touchdown for a 24–14 lead with 5:00 left in the third quarter.

On the Seattle sideline, an NBC camera caught Richard Sherman raising two fingers, then four fingers; either to call out No. 24 Darrelle Revis or to show that his team now led with 24 points.

The Pats went nowhere in their next two drives, the second time punting on their own 22 with 14:28 left in the game. But Seattle did nothing with this advantage, as the Pats stopped Lynch short twice, then Rob Ninkovich sacked Wilson for an eight yard loss.

Brady responded, completing two 21-yard passes to Julian Edelman and a four-yard touchdown pass to Danny Amendola. Seattle 24, New England 21, 8 minutes left.

Seattle answered with a five-yard run from Marshawn Lynch but inexplicably they went with the pass, and Wilson did not complete his two passes; they punted, having only burned one minute off of the clock.

Stopping Lynch

Another perspective to gauge the utter foolishness of not handing the ball off to Marshawn Lynch at the end of the Super Bowl? Lynch had only been stopped for no gain once, by Jamie Collins in the first quarter. Indeed, one of the best stops of the day occurred two quarters later when the Pats' contained Lynch to a two-yard gain. The tackler? Malcolm Butler.

New England took the ball back on its own 36 after Seattle punted and Shane Vereen resembled the next coming of Kevin Faulk with a seven-yard run and three receptions. Gronk caught passes for 13- and 20-yard gains and Julian Edelman caught a three-yard pass for the touchdown and the four-point lead with scarcely more than two minutes left in the game.

Seattle took over on its 20 and struck right away with a 31-yard pass to Marshawn Lynch, placing them in New England territory immediately. Wilson threw two incompletions then an 11-yarder to Lockette, Seattle needed a touchdown and was not going to get it with short passes.

So Wilson heaved a pass to Kearse deep on the right sideline. Malcolm Butler covered it beautifully, batting the ball away with his left hand after he had positioned himself in front of Kearse. On the way down the football pinballed off of Kearse's left leg, then his right leg, then off of his right hand, but it never hit the ground as he scooped the ball, got up, and was tackled by Butler on the New England 5-yard line.

With only 1:06 on the clock, Seattle took its second time out, but clearly New England had lost yet another Super Bowl on a fluke pass reception. Amani Toomer. Mario Manningham. David Tyree. Bizarro Wes Welker. Now Jermaine Kearse. On the sidelines Tom Brady looked like someone had hit his face with an ironing board.

Marshawn Lynch ran off tackle for four yards, to the 1-yard line, and Bill Belichick, incredibly, was not using his time-outs to provide Tom Brady with the semblance of one last drive after the inevitable touchdown.

Then Seattle called the worst offensive play in Super Bowl history, a pass in the middle of the field which Malcolm Butler jumped. The game got ugly once Tom Brady got on the field to kill the game, but it ended with Butler.

Cried commentator Cris Collinsworth, "I'm sitting here and I absolutely cannot believe that play call. If I lose the Super Bowl because Marshawn Lynch can't get it in from the 1-yard line, so be it. So be it. But there is no way…I don't believe the call."

Another analyst, Rodney Harrison, observed during the post-game report that "What happens when you play against the Patriots, you try to outsmart yourself and think you have to do something that you normally don't do. You can't tell me one defense in the National Football League that can keep Marshawn Lynch from getting one yard."

Even Richard Sherman was not silent, grasping the obvious, "I'm a little bit surprised; it was an unfortunate play."

The hero himself stated, "I knew they were stacked…it all comes with preparation. I knew they were doing a pick coming under…it was crazy."

The play was even crazier than first thought. Seattle had three tries to let its most talented player, Marshawn Lynch, score a touchdown. Instead they had him set up as a decoy. But even there, Seattle had Lynch and two receivers poised left, covered by only three Patriot defenders. Had Carroll called for Wilson to boot leg left, a Pats' defender would have been given the impossible choice of flushing out after Wilson and allowing a receiver free or covering his man, watching helplessly as Wilson crossed the plane.

Seattle had just handed New England the game and the keys to the duck boats for the victory parade though Boston.

4 The Greatest Guard

By August 1981, *Sports Illustrated* had already anointed John Hannah as the "Best Offensive Lineman of All Time" in its cover story of the great left guard. And to think, he still had five more Pro

Bowl selections remaining in his career. In the article itself, *SI* did hedge a bit, comparing him to Colts lineman Jim Parker while also sprinkling in a couple more handful of names of other worthies, but by mid-career, Hannah deserved at least consideration as one of the greatest blockers ever. Not mentioned enough, John Hannah, after terminating his playing days, merited consideration as one of the greatest football players in NFL history.

He certainly came from good bloodlines; his father Herb played for the New York Giants and his brother Charley divided a 12-year NFL career of his own equally between the Tampa Bay Buccaneers and the Los Angeles Raiders. And had injuries or other circumstances not intervened, undoubtedly other Hannahs would have populated pro football rosters.

Hannah himself excelled in other exploits besides football, wrestling competitively and heaving the shot put and discus in track and field. He amazed talent evaluators by his speed though, and other sports fell off as he devoted himself to football. Besides this anomalous quickness, he distinguished himself by his strength, a prerequisite for work on his father's large farm, and for his intelligence. He graced the University of Alabama and coach Bear Bryant with all of these gifts, starring in the early 1970s as the program integrated and entered one of its most glorious periods, leaving the Tide before it began accumulating national championships. He revered Bear, commenting later that the only shortcoming he ever found in his mentor was not dispensing good advice on how to deal with professional contracts, an issue that became a large part of his future struggles.

The Pats drafted him in the first round of the 1973 draft, the fourth player chosen overall, a standout in a particularly distinguished haul of players that year. Early in his career he got pushed around a bit by veterans, but Hannah became an early disciple of independent film study, dissecting peccadilloes of opposing linemen and linebackers. With experience, he dominated most of his tormentors and neutralized the rest.

His most formidable adversary may have been Billy Sullivan, the team owner who had signed him to some very frugal early contracts, promising him that with patience, he would receive remuneration commensurate with the finest blockers in the league. This proved illusory, and he actually received a yearly salary more in line with the marginally talented of his peers.

Along with tackle Leon Gray, Hannah staged a joint walkout before the 1977 season, a tactic that reaped financial benefits but incurred the wrath of local fans and various knights of the keyboard of the Boston dailies. He only sat out a few games, but it soured his relations with ownership (though he fared better than Gray, a player traded by the club after a decent interval had passed). Years after his friend had left the team, Hannah confessed, "I still haven't gotten over it."

Despite his discontent with how matters ended, Hannah only seemed to improve his performance, earning nine All-Pro

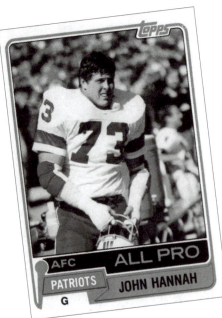

John Hannah was a nine-time All-Pro selection and was named "The Best Offensive Lineman of All Time" by Sports Illustrated *in 1981.*

selections during his career, a long one that finally saw him play in a Super Bowl at the conclusion of the 1985 season. Like his tenure at Alabama, Hannah helped bring the team to the mountain but never experienced a title-winning season as a player. After that penultimate contest, Hannah retired though still able to perform his job; a career in finance beckoned. John Hannah was no one's fool.

His nickname "Hog" diminishes a bit the total game of John Hannah, and thankfully it comes up as infrequently as the Celtics' Cedric Maxwell being called "Cornbread." He played much of his career between 260 and 270 pounds, not that heavy even then, and his technique did not center on brute pancake-blocking force. Legendary Pats personnel maven Bucko Kilroy described Hannah in motion thusly, "For all his size and explosiveness and straight-ahead speed, John has something none of the others ever had, and that's phenomenal, repeat, phenomenal lateral agility and balance, the same as defensive backs."

The quarterback he protected for so long, Steve Grogan, summed up Hannah as "powerful, smart, and hard-working...he was the most intense player I ever played with." Every down meant everything to Hannah.

Unlike skill position players, offensive linemen have very few statistical benchmarks to help gauge their contributions to the team. They may pick up a fumble now and then or catch an errant pass, but mostly they need to guard the quarterback and spring holes in the line for their backs. If they are good, it is akin to what Supreme Court Justice Potter Stewart once said about pornography, you know it when you see it. With Hannah, simply look at the improvement in the Patriots' running game during his 13 years of service with the team; succinctly he made everyone much better, and every Pats back wanted their great guard to run interference for him.

The classic footage of Hannah focuses on his pulling from his guard position to lead the blocks on the other side of the ball, knocking down defenders like so many candlepin bowling pins. No one did it better, and John Hannah is not only a member of the Patriots Hall of Fame, but also an obvious selection into the Professional Football Hall of Fame in Canton. Still not certain that this Hannah fellow was special? In 1994 he was selected to the NFL's 75th anniversary all-time team as a guard along with Jim Parker and Gene Upshaw.

5 When 14–2 is Not Good Enough

Zealots aside, most charitable New Englanders understood why the Patriots did not return to the Super Bowl after the 2008 season ended, having lost their star quarterback after precious few plays against the Chiefs in the season opener. Although the team did return to the playoffs in 2009 with a healthy Tom Brady, that campaign proved even less satisfying than the preceding one; there, at least a plucky Matt Cassel led his team to 11 wins. The 2009 edition only won 10 regular season games before the Ravens blew them out in the first round of the playoffs. Bah, humbug.

Trouble was, the team had traded Richard Seymour to the Raiders and Mike Vrabel to the Chiefs (with Cassel), while Tedy Bruschi and Rodney Harrison retired, so the 2009 team lost much of its leadership, toughness, and talent before the season began. Expectations dipped considerably before the 2010 season, and then stalwart defenders Ty Warren and Lee Bodden went on injured reserve in August, crushing blows to a young defense.

Despite winning the season opener against the Bengals, the club could not get out of the gate without controversy, as star receiver Randy Moss, in one of his rare speaking engagements, chose the postgame press conference to air his grievances at length, thereby avoiding the Festivus rush. Tired of seeing tailback Lawrence Maroney find fresh ways to underperform, Bill Belichick cut the disappointing back after the game. Things only got worse as the brash Jets defeated New England the next week, with Kevin Faulk injured and out for the year after sustaining a hit in the fourth quarter. Even when the team won, as it did the next week against Buffalo, it looked awful, as the team managed to surrender 30 points to an uncompetitive Bills team.

Then the Patriots began to transform into the champions of old, winning convincingly against divisional opponent Miami, despite Moss not catching one ball the entire contest. Afterward, the club dumped Moss, trading him and a future seventh-round draft choice to the Vikings for a third-round choice, and followed up this deal by acquiring receiver Deion Branch from the Seattle Seahawks. In short order, the front office had sent packing an increasingly dissatisfied and selfish player, replacing him with someone who knew how to win and had proven it during the team's glory years earlier in the decade.

Avenging themselves against the Ravens, the team then cut down a talented San Diego Chargers team to lead into a game against the Vikings and Moss, fittingly enough on Halloween. Brady spread the field with a 65-yard touchdown pass to Brandon Tate and led the team to victory. Afterward, Moss staged another bizarre press conference, expressing his undying devotion to the Patriots, an act that earned him a prompt release from Minnesota.

The Browns upset New England the following week, but the loss did not mark a regression, as the team went on to post convincing wins against the Steelers and then the Colts. In the latter contest, Peyton Manning had led his team back in the fourth quarter, poised to bring his team down the field one last time for either the opportunity to win with a touchdown or allow ex-Patriot Adam Vinatieri to score the tying field goal and send the game into

The Best-Laid Plans…

With 1:14 remaining in the first half of their 2010 playoff game against the Jets, Patriots defensive back Patrick Chung called for a fake punt from New England's 38-yard line with his team trailing 7–3. The center direct-snapped the ball to Chung, and the normally sure-handed special teamer handled the ball worse than Connie Chung would have. Tackled behind the line of scrimmage, Chung provided the Jets a final opportunity in the half to score, which they soon did on a Mark Sanchez–to–Braylon Edwards touchdown pass. Chung took full responsibility for the botched play, but it did raise questions in fans' minds concerning the role that Bill Belichick or the special teams coach played or should have played. Named Coach of the Year for having just molded a young team into a 14–2 juggernaut with the second-best turnover ratio in NFL history, Belichick received more press for this one faulty fake punt. Red Sox fans have mellowed after 2004 and 2007, but Patriots fans are greedy, expecting one of the finest coaches in football history to be infallible, and he isn't. As Patrick Chung found out, that's just how the ball bounces sometimes.

overtime. Belichick had little faith in his team defense the last time he faced Indy, but this time rookie Jermaine Cunningham pressured Manning into throwing an interception right into the hands of Pats free safety James Sanders. Brady took a couple of knees and New England prevailed, barely, 31–28.

The defense had improved significantly since the last season, as cornerback Devin McCourty starred almost immediately, and other rookies such as Cunningham and Brandon Spikes improved each week. Vince Wilfork continued to rule the line of scrimmage, but emerging younger veterans such as Jerod Mayo and Brandon Meriweather also stepped up. On offense, rookie tight ends Aaron Hernandez and Rob Gronkowski played well from the beginning, transforming a gaping team weakness into an area of strength and depth along with veteran acquisition Alge Crumpler.

The new-look Patriots concluded the season at 14–2, defeating most of the premier teams in the league (humiliating the Jets 45–3 in their rematch) and staking out home-field advantage up to the Super Bowl in Dallas.

And then in their first playoff game, the Patriots lost to the Jets by the score of 28–21. Jets coach Rex Ryan and his players had trash-talked the entire week leading up to the game while Belichick and his men largely stayed silent, the one exception being puckish Wes Welker who thinly and constantly alluded to Ryan's alleged devotion to feet.

The Patriots should have rolled over the Jets, the same team they had throttled a month earlier. The best regular season in the NFL meant nothing as the team ingloriously bowed out after its first playoff game. The team's defense will probably mature and improve, but the club needs another Rodney Harrison or a particularly quick and nasty pass rusher. If they find these types of men, the Patriots will win titles again.

14–2 is not good enough in New England any more.

6 The Forgotten Streak

Sadly, the Patriots' superb 21-game unbeaten streak hardly appears as even a footnote, buried underneath the almost-perfect 2007 season. It began with a 38–30 victory over the Tennessee Titans on October 5, 2003, and stretched through to the final day of October 2004, when they finally lost to the Steelers 34–20. This skein deserves particular mention, a period of excellence too often overlooked in the Bill Belichick era.

The 2003 season itself started poorly, with the Pats carrying a 2–2 record to start the season, including getting butchered in the opening game by the Bills 31–0. The club had just given up on longtime safety Lawyer Milloy, who started for Buffalo that day and no doubt enjoyed every click of the clock. The poor start mirrored the frustrating 2002 season itself, when the Patriots not only failed to defend their Super Bowl title but also failed to even sneak into the playoffs.

In retrospect it seems silly that anyone doubted the team, but it did appear that New England had experienced a single glorious moment in defeating the Rams for their first and apparently only title, at least for a while. The phrase "In Bill We Trust" had not yet been coined, yet the coach knew he had to turn over the roster to stay competitive, and the departure of mainstays like Drew Bledsoe and Milloy signified that past sentiments meant little to Belichick in assembling his team.

Having defeated the Titans in Week 5, the Pats did win their remaining regular season games but not by much in most cases, defeating six teams by six points or less, and defeating the Dallas Cowboys and Miami Dolphins by identical 12–0 scores. In fact, their only blow-out victory occurred in their final regular season game against Buffalo, when they symmetrically returned the favor from opening day and romped 31–0.

In the playoffs that year, the Patriots again did not overwhelm their foes, opening up against Tennessee and escaping with a 17–14 win. Their largest victory margin in the playoffs occurred when they defeated the Colts 24–14 to earn a shot at another Super Bowl title. There they eked out a victory over a very well-prepared Carolina team 32–29, a nail-biter fit for kicker Adam Vinateiri.

Offensively the 2003 Patriots possessed no 100-catch receiver and no one close to rushing for 1,000 yards, yet Antowain Smith and Kevin Faulk ran well, particularly in the clutch. Tom Brady distributed the ball generously in the air to a range of receivers such as Faulk, Troy Brown, Christian Fauria, Deion Branch, Daniel Graham, and David Givens. Branch led the team with 57 receptions but at least six receivers caught 28 passes or more. The defense is covered in more detail elsewhere in this book, but rather than it being peopled by an average bunch of lunch pail–toting overachievers, it actually fielded stars at nearly every position and the club eventually prospered in the absence of Milloy.

The 2004 Pats started off the new season with élan, defeating Peyton Manning and a very strong Colts team 27–24. This year, they did have a monster running back, having obtained Corey Dillon from the Bengals. The change did him good as he galloped to 1,635 yards, rushing for a 4.7 yards-per-carry average. Brady continued to distribute the ball to his receivers on a committee basis and the defense continued to excel on the way to another title.

They did have a hiccup against the Steelers in their seventh game, a tough loss against a very strong opponent, and they did somehow find a way to lose to a very weak Dolphins team (4–12) late in the season, but otherwise probably played better as a team than they had at any point in the past. They even had a chance to avenge their streak-breaking loss to Pittsburgh by defeating the Steelers to win the AFC. At the risk of another close title game, they won the Lombardi Trophy after defeating the Eagles.

The streak is remarkable for more than the obvious reasons. While the Colts later set a regular season unbeaten streak, the Patriots still hold the all-time record because their streak included the playoffs, with three stirring wins over tough opponents. Again, the 2007 season has caused fans to forget the Patriots' earlier streak, a shame because that effort helped lead the team to two titles.

7 The First Championship

On September 23, 2001, the Jets' Mo Lewis delivered a crushing hit along the sideline to a scrambling Drew Bledsoe, causing the Pats' starting quarterback serious internal injuries that took him out of the game and out of action for several ensuing weeks. Into the fray came little-used backup Tom Brady, and this is where modern New England Patriots history truly begins.

Despite signing the coach of their dreams, the 2000 New England Patriots rattled off a rotten 5–11 record in Bill Belichick's inaugural year as the team's head coach. Little had changed between the end of that bitter campaign and the commencement of the new season to suggest that New England had much chance of sneaking into the playoffs, never mind erecting a dynasty. Belichick had actually lost three more games than departed coach Pete Carroll, and his starting quarterback had begun his descent from one of the premier throwers in the NFL to just a solid performer. And good luck to the team if Bledsoe got hurt, his backup was a skinny sixth-round pick from Michigan.

In the second game of the season against the hated Jets, Bledsoe faded back to pass but ran to his right once he saw his receivers covered. He vectored for the sideline, trying to squeeze out of bounds just inside the first-down marker, when he met linebacker Mo Lewis, who delivered one of the most powerful hits in league history. Bledsoe hit the deck, downed by internal injuries so severe that he lost two liters of blood and might have died had he not received the immediate and effective medical attention that he did. He had to leave the game and much of the still-young season.

Of course Tom Brady replaced him, providing those missing elements in Bledsoe's game needed to transform New England into a perennial Super Bowl contender. Brady played so well that when Bledsoe returned for action, the baton of leadership had irretrievably passed and it was Brady's team. During the regular season, the Pats posted an 11–5 record, and while Brady provided a catalyst, the fine defense that Bill Parcells had helped install years ago with recruits like Willie McGinest and Tedy Bruschi excelled.

Still, this was New England and in the playoffs they had to face the Raiders in the first round in Foxboro, the same club that had denied them advancement in the playoffs so many years ago due to a disputed referee's call. The tables turned in the "Snow Bowl," as an apparent fumble by Brady late in the game was ruled an incomplete pass, as the referee invoked the "tuck rule." The Pats took advantage of the call and proceeded to win the game on an Adam Vinatieri field goal.

As Al Davis went screaming all the way back to the West Coast, the Pats prepared for their next obstacle, the Pittsburgh Steelers. The Steelers in some ways resembled the team that Parcells faced in his last run with New England, coached by Bill Cowher and heavily dependent on one of the greatest running backs of all time, Jerome Bettis. Yet in that interim, their versatile quarterback Kordell Stewart had developed and he had Hines Ward and Plaxico Burress to throw to.

Yet, New England struck first with a 55-yard punt return for a touchdown by the estimable Troy Brown. He astutely ran down the middle of the field rather than his planned route down the sideline due to some coverage irregularities that he perceived; although a magician is never supposed to reveal his tricks, Brown later admitted, "It was supposed to be a left return, but the guys overplayed it to the outside, and I saw the seam up the middle and we just hit it." Bruschi planted a Steeler who dared deter Brown on his run to glory, causing foreign sweatshops to go into overtime to produce new Bruschi jerseys to be sold throughout New England for his adoring fans.

Pittsburgh chipped a field goal, but its defense delivered the most telling blow when defender Lee Flowers rolled over Brady's ankle, twisting it and causing the quarterback to leave the game. Brady had passed quite well to that point, hitting on 12 of 18 attempts, but no more capable backup than Bledsoe existed in the NFL. Having chomped at the bit since his injury, he quickly found receiver David Patten for a 15-yard strike. On the next play, Bledsoe was forced out of the pocket and just before he found the sideline, the Steelers' Chad Scott delivered a stunning hit on him, one starkly reminiscent of the Mo Lewis delivery. Bledsoe sustained a cut on his chin, but pluckily returned to the game and promptly served two complete passes to Patten, the second for a touchdown, and gave New England a 14–3 lead at the half.

In the third quarter, Stewart drove his team down the field well, bringing the Steelers down to the Patriots' 16-yard line before settling for a field-goal attempt. They should have gone for the first down because their kicker, Kris Brown, never had a chance. The Patriots' Brandon Mitchell shook off the linemen ahead of him and raised his arms to block the kick. Troy Brown recovered, ran 11 yards with the ball, then lateraled to teammate Antwan Harris who ran the ball back the other way for a touchdown and a 21–3 lead.

Having just given the game away, the Steelers played well the remainder of the game, scoring two touchdowns, but New England had already scored enough points to win, and in his last active game as a Pat, Drew Bledsoe had just led his team to a 24–17 victory and a trip to the Super Bowl.

The team celebrated and Bledsoe received plaudits from media members and talk show callers throughout the next week, but in the upcoming Super Bowl, the team had to defeat the St. Louis Rams, then thought to be on the verge of becoming the NFL's next great dynasty. They had won the 1999 season's Super Bowl and still had the weapons available to them to blow out any opposing team: quarterback Kurt Warner, running back Marshall Faulk, and receivers Torry Holt and Isaac Bruce, collectively dubbed "The Greatest Show on Turf." Warner had passed for 4,830 yards for a quarterback rating over 100 for the season while Faulk rushed for more than 1,300 yards and caught 83 passes for the highest scoring offense in the NFL. The Rams defense had conceded its opponents few points, finishing seventh league-wide in that department. On paper, the Pats had no chance, although during the regular season the two teams met in Foxboro and the Pats only lost by a touchdown. Still, the oddsmakers had the Rams winning the final game of the playoffs by two touchdowns.

Some football insiders may have intuited it at the time, but very few fans in any section of the country yet appreciated one important fact: Bill Belichick was and always will be a far superior head coach than the Rams' counterpart, Mike Martz, and probably most everyone else, before or since. Belichick and his assistants devised a game plan on defense—neutralize Faulk and let the Rams try to win in the air—and they stuck to it. On offense, Bill trusted Brady to do the right thing, not a bad decision in retrospect, although one that Bledsoe understandably loathed.

Little things mattered, too. Before the start of the game, the Rams offense was announced, but when it came time to let the Patriots starters run out one-by-one, a peculiar event occurred; the entire Patriots team came out as one cohesive unit. Now everyone does it this way, but Belichick's men set the standard.

Symbolism did not save the Carter Administration, and it would have done little for New England if not for some very opportunistic defensive play. Ahead 3–0 on their second possession of the second quarter, the Rams had begun to hum on offense, thanks to a five-yard run off left tackle by Faulk and then a 15-yard scamper in the opposite direction. Then Warner dropped back to pass to Bruce, but Ty Law picked him off for a 47-yard touchdown return. Similarly, Warner completed a pass to Ricky Proehl that took the ball down to the Patriots' 45-yard line, but Antwan Harris induced a fumble which his teammate Terrell Buckley recovered. Brady marched his teammates forward and found receiver David Patten for a touchdown before halftime, allowing the underdog Pats to take a 14–3 lead.

Keeping Faulk at bay had worked, but Warner had passed very well, and his total of 28 passes completed for 365 yards stands out among the finest Super Bowl performances by a quarterback, marred by the turnovers. The irritating Patriots defense had negated much of his efforts, as Otis Smith intercepted Warner to silence one Rams drive, and when Adam Vinatieri booted a field goal from 37 yards out, the Pats had extended their lead to 17–3.

It looked all sewn up for New England in the fourth quarter when the Rams fumbled on the Pats' 3-yard line and Tebucky Jones apparently ran it back for the game-ending coup de grace. But a Pats penalty nullified everything and Warner subsequently rushed for a two-yard touchdown to narrow New England's lead to a precarious-looking touchdown margin.

Much of the rest of the quarter remained quiet until very late, when Warner hit receiver Ricky Proehl for a 26-yard touchdown pass. With the score tied and just over a minute left in the game, commentator John Madden announced to the world that he thought the Patriots should let time run out and take their chances in overtime.

Belichick and Brady did not concur. Brady swiftly connected on three dink-and-dunk passes to back J.R. Redmond to maintain the drive. Then he bled the Rams with a 23-yard completion to Troy Brown and a six-yard completion to tight end Jermaine Wiggins, a native of East Boston. The next pass was incomplete, and with time expiring, Vinatieri serenely booted the 48-yard field goal for the first championship in Patriots history.

All New England had the opportunity to celebrate with the team as the players and coaches later paraded through downtown Boston on amphibious sightseeing tour "Duck Boats" on a particularly chilly day that deterred few. The patterns of the team's greatness through the decade had emerged: a genius coach assembled dominant teams which, with the exception of Tom Brady, would field relatively few Pro Bowl players and even fewer future Hall of Fame candidates.

8 Larry Eisenhauer Goes for a Swim

The Patriots had just won the most monumental game in their young franchise's history by defeating the Bills in Buffalo for the chance to play the Chargers for the American Football League championship in December 1963. The victory over the Bills in frigid temperatures proved the high point of the team's fortunes, because by the time they had finished all of their flying the team members had little energy left for the title game itself. They ended up losing by the massive score of 51–10, and did not have an opportunity to vie for a title again until they faced Mike Ditka and the juggernaut that was his 1985 Chicago Bears.

No matter, the 1963 club came away with one of the most notable incidents in team history. While staying at San Diego's Stardust Hotel, some of the team members repaired to the lounge where over the bar area there was a glass partition, separating the patrons from some modern-day mermaids performing synchronized routines in the water.

Having just come from the pool set aside for visitors, lineman Larry Eisenhauer decided to access the area where the female swimmers were performing. Before long, he and his father had jumped in and had begun to entertain his teammates who were sipping down their beers and cocktails. For a while the story kept getting

After attending Boston College, defensive lineman Larry Eisenhauer became a member of the Boston Patriots in 1961.

better and better, with practically the whole team jumping in and some members mooning the remaining bar patrons, but these events probably did not happen.

The story without embellishment is good enough, and does hark back to a more relaxed time in team history where big football players danced with mermaids and lost title games. Lest one believe Eisenhauer was a frivolous footballer, his teammates dubbed him "the Wildman" in part due to his intensity before and during games, often denting his locker with his head or his arms as he psychologically prepared himself for the upcoming contest. Inarguably though, then-coach Mike Holovak tolerated characters on his team, many of whom housed much less devotion to winning than Eisenhauer.

Had Bill Belichick coached this team, he would not have been amused. And his team would have defeated the Chargers.

9 Bob Kraft

Beloved now both as the team owner who brought championships to New England and a generous philanthropist, few remember that for many years, Bob Kraft had to fight off some very biting press from the Boston media. Bill Parcells fanned a lot of the resentment, departing the team after its second Super Bowl appearance and leaving the impression that meddlesome owner Kraft helped drive him out of town.

Kraft's image continued to suffer in the three post-Parcells years, even though under new head coach Pete Carroll the club actually compiled better regular season records than those posted by the Big Tuna. The criticism of Kraft probably reached its nadir after the 1998 NFL Draft when the Pats drafted Tebucky Jones, a strange pick as the club touted him as a potential star cornerback. Some in the press openly mocked Kraft when he spoke of the possibility of Jones becoming an effective press corner, implying that Kraft had no inkling of what a press corner was or how Jones might possibly fulfill that function in the NFL.

The tribulations of Bob Kraft receded rapidly once he lured Bill Belichick to New England, with three titles quickly coming to town from 2001 to 2004 and a fourth in 2014. No longer seen as some glorified fan who did not know how to run a team, Kraft became the region's savior and an architect of the Patriots' ascent into the highest rung of excellence as an organization. Parcells drifted thereafter from team to team with the recurring theme becoming that he did not sit long or age well with any organization, providing affirmation that this Kraft fellow knew what he was doing from the time he purchased the team in 1994.

In fact, Kraft had more than a clue years before he owned the team, outsmarting everyone who thought he knew better how to run the franchise or where to maintain the team. The key to Kraft's ultimate success rested in his keen appreciation of the ugly duckling, the unimaginative slab known at various times as Sullivan/ Foxboro or Schaefer Stadium. An eyesore and a structure born to be razed, Kraft purchased the stadium, and by extension the lease thereto, in 1988 for $25 million (he had snapped up some adjoining land a few years earlier).

Clueless owner Victor Kiam evidently felt little love for the stadium and much less appreciation for the value of actually owning the venue where the team practiced and played. In effect, every time he cheered for his team or said something stupid to the press, Kiam was doing so as Kraft's guest.

Since Bob Kraft purchased the Patriots in 1994, the team has played in 36 postseason games. The team played in 10 playoff games during the previous 34 seasons combined.

When a much more cunning individual, James Busch Orthwein, wrested control from Kiam, fully intending to move the whole operation to St. Louis, this new owner still had to face off against Kraft. Orthwein had hired Parcells as head coach, certainly a development that later caused Kraft palpable anguish, but he could not pull up the franchise from its roots because Kraft had the roots in his hand in the form of the lease.

Orthwein tried, reportedly offering Kraft $75 million to free the club from its onerous lease, quite a potential return on an investment, but Kraft did not blink, holding on to the unattractive impediment. Orthwein might have huffed and puffed a bit, but he soon recognized that Kraft controlled the destiny of the local 11, a team that was not going to relocate to Missouri. Orthwein gave in, ceding the franchise. Kraft now possessed total control of the team he once so fervently rooted for. Kraft and New England had won.

Other than threatening to move the club to Hartford, the Kraft ownership of the Patriots has been blessedly short of melodrama. Kraft hired the finest coach in football, Bill Belichick, and when the club is not winning Lombardi Trophies, it almost always contends. Bad ownership has cost Boston's sports franchises as far removed as the 19th century, but Bob Kraft has provided the Patriots with stable ownership, a huge ingredient in their success.

10 The Snow Bowl

To fully savor the 2001 AFC Divisional Playoffs, a Patriots fan must remember or discover the 1976 playoff game between the Patriots and Raiders, which Oakland won due to an extremely controversial and inaccurate call by an official. The Pats had outplayed their opponent all day in that contest, and Oakland quarterback Ken Stabler had just thrown an incompletion on third down.

Enter Ben Dreith. This official called a roughing-the-passer penalty on Pats lineman Ray Hamilton, a phantom call if there ever was one. This mistake ensured that the Raiders received the gift of a first down deep in New England territory, and soon after they capitalized on the largesse with the game-winning touchdown.

Dreith continued to officiate NFL games for several years after the infamous 1976 playoff game, but he never served again in any game involving the Patriots. His call might not have even been the worst one of that game. Earlier, with the Patriots facing a third-and-five on the Oakland 32-yard line, quarterback Steve Grogan looked for tight end Russ Francis but could not place the ball to him; Raiders linebacker Phil Villapiano had Velcro-ed himself to Francis.

While not as intense as the club's rivalry with the Jets, the Patriots and their fans do not cherish or harbor any respect for their opponents from Oakland. The Raiders had always courted an outlaw image, no more so than when Jack Tatum hit Darryl Stingley in a meaningless exhibition game and paralyzed him for life. No, the teams do not like each other, and Patriots fans have long memories.

Stuff like that always happened to the Patriots during the snake-bit Sullivan years of ownership. In 2001, however, the Patriots fielded Tom Brady at quarterback at home in the snow.

As the new millennium has ripened into its second decade, most fans might have trouble believing that the Raiders ever fielded a playoff team, never mind a serious Super Bowl contender. But this club had a terrific coach in Jon Gruden on January 19, 2002, and an offense skillfully guided by its quarterback, Rich Gannon. Explosive Tim Brown and the still-stellar Jerry Rice caught passes and returned punts and Charlie Garner fronted an effective running

Tom Brady's apparent fumble in a 2001 playoff game against the Oakland Raiders was ruled an incompletion. The Patriots went on to win what is now known as the "Tuck Rule Game."

game. On defense, Charles Woodson starred in the defensive back-field, although most of his counterparts did not perform at his level.

At game time, temperatures were freezing and snow had already laced the field. Adam Vinatieri kicked off to dangerous Raiders return man Terry Kirby (the author of a 90-yard touchdown earlier in the season), but the inclement weather precluded such heroics on this day. The game settled into a low-scoring event, as New England trailed Oakland 13–3 after three quarters of play. In all honesty, Tom Brady had not played well.

Legends must begin somewhere, however, and with Brady, he founded his own with 12:29 left in regulation, relentlessly driving his team downfield and at one point completing nine straight passes to four different receivers. Uncharacteristically, Brady capped the drive with his own six-yard touchdown run. Oakland still led 13–10, but when the Raiders failed to score or devour what remained on the clock, the Pats had one final chance to either win or tie the contest.

The Patriots possessed no timeouts when Oakland punted to them with 2:19 remaining in the game. Fortunately, returner Troy Brown sprinted the ball to just short of midfield…and then fumbled. Alertly, teammate and special teams star Larry Izzo recovered, but with snow coming down heavily now, the near fiasco only highlighted the difficulty of the task awaiting the Patriots.

Brady went right to work, first completing a seven-yard pass to back Kevin Faulk. On the next play, seeing no open receivers, the quarterback ran the ball to the sideline for a first down. Then things went wrong, as the Raiders sent Woodson on a blitz to Brady's right. As Woodson arrived, Brady had either just begun to throw the ball, had not seen the defender and still held onto the ball, or had just begun to tuck the ball into his gut. In any event the ball came loose, and while Brady stretched out his right leg to try to prevent Raiders linebacker Greg Biekert from recovering it, Biekert scooped it up and had apparently just sealed the visitors' victory.

But then a review was called and referee Walt Coleman went off to the sideline to look at tape of the play. When he returned, Coleman cited NFL Rule 3, Section 21, Article 2, Note 2, now known as the "tuck rule," and called the play an incomplete pass as the Patriots' offense jogged back onto the field.

The Rules states, "When [an offensive] player is holding the ball to pass it forward, any intentional forward movement of his arm starts a forward pass, even if the player loses possession of the ball as he is attempting to tuck it back toward his body. Also, if the player has tucked the ball into his body and then loses possession, it is a fumble."

A Supreme Court Justice or a Canon Law Scholar would have experienced profound discomfort making sense of this rule. As Brady said later, "I knew I was throwing the ball. I was trying to get rid of the ball. I'm glad they ruled it the way they did." Regardless, he immediately exploited the situation with a first-down pass to receiver David Patten, and now his team had the ball at the Raiders' 28-yard line.

After three non-productive plays, the Patriots had to attempt the field goal, at least a 45-yarder for kicker Adam Vinatieri, who had missed on four of his last five attempts from that distance. At this point, the Pats may have wanted to bring out the snow plow as they had against the Dolphins 19 years earlier. Instead, they received a gift from Jon Gruden—a timeout designed to "ice" Vinatieri—which allowed the cool kicker time to clear more snow away from his area. On the kick, it appeared that Vinatieri had immediately and irretrievably sliced the ball to his right, but it remained barely between the uprights for the tie. Overtime.

After winning the coin toss, the Pats had apparently stalled on fourth down with four yards to go on the Raiders' 28-yard line. Belichick did not like his kicker's chances with the inclement conditions and a possible field-goal attempt exceeding 40 yards, so he ordered Brady to convert the fourth down. After taking the snap, Brady dropped and pumped right, then drilled a pass up the middle to Patten for six yards and the first down. This time Vinatieri had a chip shot compared to his last attempt, and he drove home the winning field goal. The Pats had just avenged their unfair loss to the Raiders in 1976 with an arguably unfair victory of their own. New England went on the next week to face the Steelers in the AFC Championship Game while the Raiders went home cursing their fate.

After the winning kick went through the uprights, Pats holder Lonnie Paxton ran into the end zone, dropped on his back, and began to make a snow angel. The final game in the Patriots' old stadium had ended well, but controversy continues to this day. Some fans call this epic the "Snow Bowl" while others have tabbed it the "Tuck Rule Game."

11 Visit the Professional Football Hall of Fame

One of the joys of penning this book was not only interviewing sports figures, reading old game accounts and revisiting cherished venues, but in seeing interesting things for the first time. Having never visited the Pro Football Hall of Fame in Canton, Ohio, I looked forward to my trip there and also approached it with some trepidation because had I not enjoyed it, I would not have recommended it.

Particularly since it is so far away from some of the bases of Patriot Nation, a conservative eleven hour drive from Boston or Providence, it might not get as much attention as it deserves, a most unfortunate development. Due to the spatial factors of time and distance, the Hall attracts mainly aficionados of the more localized Steelers, Bengals and Browns, but given the passion of most Patriots supporters and the massive contributions made by the team to the professional game, it is more than time to alter this trend and bring some more New Englanders to Canton, Ohio.

After you have purchased your tickets, the first thing that greets you is a large bronzed likeness of Jim Thorpe, apparently bound to drive through the line of an opposing defense. Nearby, the decision to locate the Hall in Canton is based on the facts that the lineal descendant to the NFL was founded in Canton in 1920, the Canton Bulldogs were a founding professional team and Jim Thorpe played for Canton and helped to popularize the fledgling league. While the claim for Fame is not as solid as that of the Basketball Hall of Fame sitting in Springfield, Massachusetts (how do you beat Naismith and peach baskets at the local YMCA?), it does have a more legitimate claim than does the Baseball Hall of Fame in Cooperstown, New York.

Anything but a musty old museum, the Hall caters to all ages and interests, with a ball-throwing exhibit and an x-box section for younger footballers, to some of the more conventional fare, such as Dick Butkus' helmet for those old enough to remember him playing. In the Super Bowl Theater, a twenty four minute film is shown on a very large screen, effectively bringing to the fore truer sounds and sights than experienced at home or at the local sports bar. At one point the screen shifts to the right and then out of view as another much larger screen appears, adding a bit of Disney or Universal Studios to the experience.

Specific to the Patriots' audience, there is a "Teams of the NFL" room, with New England's helmet and game day jersey on display along with a narrative of the club's history. There is also a listing of retired numbers, a fairly arcane fact, with Gino Cappelletti, Mike Haynes, Steve Nelson, John Hannah, Bruce Armstrong, Jim Lee Hunt and Bob Dee having received this honor and this most honorable mention in the Hall itself.

It does not end there. In another wing, the tale of competitors to the NFL is chronicled, with a generous dollop of the Pats' contribution to the development of the American Football League; the exhibits may have changed, but when I last visited I saw a helmet once worn by Bob Dee and credit extended to him for scoring the first touchdown in the AFL, during a pre-season game. There are some program covers regarding the early team and mention given to Houston Antwine and Nick Buoniconti for making the All-Time AFL team.

In the Super Bowl display, you will find more than enough to keep any Patriots' fan happy, particularly if you arrive after they receive and display their latest Super Bowl ring.

In addition to the team artifacts, the Hall has set out enticing and informative exhibits for NFL fan in general, covering officiating, coaching and most importantly the contributions of the players in the post-season. You will see how helmets and cleats developed, but there are numerous stations showing parts of games, the action that draws patrons to the sport that has arguably supplanted baseball as America's pastime.

The relatively few players and other contributors to the pro game are honored by a long and winding room with the busts of each man. Unlike the Baseball Hall of Fame, where roughly half of the early likenesses on the plaques look like your Dad, the busts in Canton actually look like the Hall of Famers. An astute Pats' fan would have little problem identifying John Hannah, Mike Haynes, Nick Buoniconti and Andre Tippett from their well-crafted statuary, with no need to look at the name underneath.

For true students and archivists of the sport, the Hall also houses an impressive archives containing over 18 million documents and over 2 million photographs. Unlike the exhibits open generally to patrons, one must set up an appointment in advance to meet with the archives staff to conduct serious research. In the event that you believe you might also get to see some relics not available to the ticket buying public, you will most likely be disappointed as over 95% of the tangible memorabilia and artifacts are housed upstairs

Getting There

Depending on how you plan your trip, you can arrive at the Hall either by taking the highway almost up to the front doors or by taking the back roads for the last 15 miles or so. I preferred driving through the country, because like the trip to Cooperstown, you can enjoy a more rural America, scenes that have almost entirely disappeared from southern New England. You can also appreciate a bit of NFL history, as some of the early franchises sprung from such small towns as Canton or Green Bay, unspoiled by any surrounding sprawl. Particularly if you are driving from New England or from a relatively faraway Midwestern destination, ending the last part of the trip in a less hectic manner helps provide a segue to a more relaxing stroll through the Hall itself.

Amongst the wealth of information in the archives are team files dating back to the 1920's old Walter Camp books and rule books from as early as 1866, back when the football game better resembled rugby and the football itself looked like a miniature medicine ball.

It is rare to commend any museum or attraction for its gift shop, but the one in Canton stands out because each team has its own section for jerseys and other memorabilia, everything from throw-back bobbleheads to mini helmets. If you cannot come to Canton, visit the Hall of Fame's on-line store.

One misconception about the Hall is that it only contains a small boxed-in area with half of a giant football bursting to the top. That design always reminded me of a device my mother stored in her kitchen to extract juice pulp-free from an orange half. Extensive renovations have created much more space than what most of us believe constitutes the whole physical plant of the Hall of Fame. The architectural design is unique, a fitting tribute to both the Hall and the game it honors.

12 Cherished Myths

We all know people who love spinning tales, stories so good that their creators forget that they have at best partial basis in fact, and yet unfortunately the myths become believed just as fervently by innocent listeners. After more than 50 years in existence, a fabric of folklore has enveloped the New England Patriots, an unsurprising development since the original Boston Patriot, Paul Revere, is the subject of a batch of nonsense himself. We love our myths, in fact, one of our country's presidents once uttered something to the effect that he loved the tale of Paul Revere's ride whether it was true or not. At the risk of desecrating revered misconceptions, here are some of the more revered myths in Pats history:

1. **Randy Moss ruined the team.**

Of relatively new vintage, the plot goes like this: before Randy Moss came to New England, the team had recently won three Super Bowls with less-than-stellar receivers, and after he arrived, the club chemistry changed for the worse.

Despite some unsavory moments in Minnesota and Oakland, Moss was one of the greatest receivers in NFL history before he came to New England. Matched with Tom Brady, records were set as the Pats won every regular season game and every playoff game leading into the Super Bowl. There they narrowly lost to the New York Giants, and have not returned to the Super Bowl since.

So naturally it is Moss' fault, even though Wes Welker came to the team the same year and has avoided criticism. As disappointed as every Patriots fan was with the final result in 2007, in considerable part the team just missed an undefeated season *because* of Moss, not in spite of him. In 2008, Brady was hurt in the first game, and even though Matt Cassel played well, the team missed the playoffs that year. Again, Moss served as a productive player and good clubhouse citizen. In 2009 the team also failed to win a Super Bowl, but at this juncture, the accumulated effects of several bad drafts and a defense that collectively aged overnight overtook the team.

The team did not decline because Randy Moss came to New England, and in fact a stronger argument can be made that his presence kept the club relatively competitive. By the 2010 season he had become a pest and a distraction and Bill Belichick correctly shipped him out, but before then he was a popular teammate and a very productive receiver.

2. The Patriots stunk until Bill Parcells came to New England.

Under team owner Billy Sullivan, the Patriots ebbed and flowed, but still managed to have a number of notable seasons long before the Big Tuna led them. In 1963, Boston played for the AFL championship against San Diego and otherwise enjoyed some winning seasons under Mike Holovak that decade.

After Sullivan sacked Holovak, stability vanished contemporaneous with the franchise's move to Foxboro, as a number of mercurial and some downright awful coaches walked into this coaches' graveyard. Although he is now mainly remembered for how he left rather than for what he accomplished, Chuck Fairbanks led his charges to some very good records in the late 1970s; in the 1985 campaign, Ray Berry squired his team to its first Super Bowl. So while Parcells laid the foundation for future excellence under Bob Kraft, Bill Belichick, and Tom Brady, the Pats had some very good seasons interspersed with embarrassing ones. They more closely resembled the Boston Red Sox before 2004 than a perennial also-ran.

3. The Patriots knew what they were doing when they drafted Tom Brady.

The 2000 draft cemented the Patriots' destiny as the team of the new millennium. They drafted Tom Brady in the sixth round with the 199th overall pick, but most of the pickings that year were very slim, and the six players chosen before Brady were mostly stiffs. J.R. Redmond gave them some good efforts, but try naming the others.

The 2000 quarterback class was weak at the time and more than 10 years later that evaluation has been borne out, except for Brady. Paucity of players aside, the Pats needed a backup quarterback, and if their brain trust was so smart they would have selected Brady with their first pick and laughed away the remaining rounds.

Simply put, the Patriots got lucky, and have been riding that run of luck ever since.

4. **Curtis Martin left town because of money.**

Money is not the root of all evil, though axiomatically the love of money is, and equally taken as a matter of sacred truth to many if not most Pats rooters is the belief that the club allowed stinginess to intercede between it and superstar back Curtis Martin.

A third-round pick out of Pitt, Martin spun New England on its ear during his rookie season, rushing for 1,487 yards. When a local boy asked the popular back to his birthday party, Curtis actually attended, charming all of the invited guests and most of the folks who heard about it. He continued to excel in his next two seasons in New England, but one very important thing changed along the path when head coach Bill Parcells left the club to helm the New York Jets.

The Patriots did not turn the other cheek as Parcells shot his way out of town and ruined Super Bowl week, extracting draft picks from the Jets before they could sign him as their Big Tuna. Ensconced in New York, Parcells plotted his revenge.

Enter Jets front office guru Mike Tannenbaum. Having seen firsthand the talent and class possessed by Curtis Martin, Parcells naturally coveted the back for his new team. In order to make Martin's journey from Foxboro to the Meadowlands more certain, the Jets bid on his services as a restricted free agent by inserting a "poison pill" into the contract. The Patriots organization did not balk at paying Martin more money, but the poison pill would have forced the club to sign him with a provision that in one year he would become an unrestricted free agent without compensation.

In essence, not only would the Patriots have to pay him the additional money, which they had no problem doing, but also after renting him for one year they would lose him without picking up draft picks or other compensation after another team (read: the Jets) signed him. Instead, New England swallowed the slightly less-bitter pill and let Martin depart to New York, receiving first- and third-round picks in return.

Parcells and Tannenbaum had staged a coup, obtaining one of the greatest backs of his generation for basically an uneven trade, one made worse when the Jets took off and the Patriots continued to decline until Bill Belichick and Tom Brady came aboard. Thereafter, Curtis Martin starred but did not earn a single Super Bowl ring, a cautionary tale to the effect that when inserting a poison pill, make certain it is the other fellow who ends up choking on it in the long run.

13 The First Camp

Traditionally, fans love to hear the tale of the Patriots' first pre-season camp in 1960 in comedy-of-errors fashion, with a hopelessly disorganized club rifling players in and out of its training facilities with senseless abandon. Some of the confusion surrounding the first training sessions is quaintly well-documented, but it is at once hyperbole and oversimplification. It also fails to account for some of the major obstacles facing each of the eight new AFL franchises and also leaves out some of the sweeter parts of the overall experience.

Having secured a Boston franchise in November 1959, Billy Sullivan and company had less than one week to participate in the new league's first draft. With no scouting staff in place and having no concept of how many of its draft selections intended to bypass the NFL to sign with the Pats, the club gamely made its choices. The new clubs had territorial picks, and in total the process extended through 53 rounds over two days.

Unfairly, some teams like the Houston Oilers became immediate powerhouses because they chose well and their prime pick, Heisman Trophy winner Billy Cannon, decided not to play in the NFL. The Pats lucked out when Ron Burton signed with them, but too many of their other choices either did not sign with them or were poor players who did. There might also have been some hesitancy to draft a player who had little interest in the upstart NFL, a point made in the second NFL draft when Boston unsuccessfully attempted to lure Fran Tarkenton to its cause.

By necessity, when head coach Lou Saban called his first camp to order on July 4, 1960 (what better day to start a franchise named the Patriots than July 4?), he started off with 12 quarterback candidates and eight potential centers. That evening, some local Amherst residents staged a barbecue for these new recruits, an unremembered neighborly gesture. Some estimates have the club eventually auditioning as many as 350 players, some of whom only saw one day of action before Saban concluded that they possessed insufficient talent or conditioning.

Under Center

Who were the first 12 quarterbacks who came to camp that historic first day of Patriots camp? Bob Anastas, Bob Cox, Harry Drivak, Frank Hall, Durel Matherne, Bob Mears, Les Plumb, Tom Schwalbach, Dick Soergel, Ed "Butch" Songin, Robert Spoo, and Harvey White. Only Songin and White saw any time with the team that season at quarterback, and yet for those players cut, much of their most productive work in life lay ahead. For example, in his later incarnation as a Wayland (MA) High School coach, Bob Anastas, reacting to the deaths of some of the students, founded Students Against Drunk Driving and has spoken to millions of young people since that time.

One recruit, a marginal player on a 1950s major college team, famously never took showers after practices or games, and he received an early pink slip. Too bad, had Saban slotted him on the offensive line he may have helped the new franchise win some games based on the potential player's potent offensive capabilities. On another occasion, "After the morning workouts, five players decided (A) it was too hot, (B) the pace was a bit beyond them, and (C) maybe they could get the afternoon's All-Star Game on the air. So the quintet took its airplane tickets and departed."

But butchers, bakers, and candlestick makers continued to run in and out of Amherst, most for their final curtain call as football players. Mike Holovak wrote about it, and Gino Cappelletti to this day tells a funny story about all of the recruits sitting around a single television during their free time. One player walked up to the television and changed the channel. From across the room another player apparently took umbrage and changed the channel back again. This went on for a bit until the two channel surfers started fighting each other, a most unwelcome development for their teammates who were all worried about their individual chances of making the roster. Turns out it was a pre-arranged joke among the two pugilists, a development undoubtedly more entertaining than whatever black-and-white fare they had just seen on the networks.

By necessity, the cash-strapped management had to keep costs down, and worse, due to some league mandate, the team members had no separate training table and ate at the university cafeteria. One player, dismissed from the team, continued to hang around for the free food until an assistant pointed him out and asked him to leave camp forever. The players each received $50 for participating in a preseason exhibition game and "a little spending money" for planned intersquad workouts throughout the Commonwealth of Massachusetts.

Growing pains aside, the club successfully began cultivating a local fandom with exhibition scrimmages in Greenfield and

Haverhill, Massachusetts. In Greenfield, a rancher named Cowboy Jim Crawford from Greybull, Wyoming, booted a 52-yard field goal. At the latter venue, the local police escorted the team across the border into the local stadium, a rare perk as the players usually had to dress before they got on the team bus for these events. It got better; by the end of that July the team enjoyed a twilight parade attended by perhaps as many as 100,000 people before its first exhibition against the Bills.

The team's early preparations did bear some fruit because the club had hired a good coach in Lou Saban, ably assisted by such men as Mike Holovak. In their talent evaluation, they made some very good moves by signing such future stars as Gino Cappelletti, back Larry Garron, and end Jim Colclough. They also signed up Butch Songin at quarterback, a Boston College product of such an advanced age that he had served during the invasion of Normandy in WWII.

Unfortunately, they simply did not have enough good players to compete even in the new league and they only slightly outpaced Denver that year, finishing with a 5–9 record. Early the next year, the club sacked Saban, installing Holovak at head coach as the team nearly reversed its record at 9–4–1. Cappelletti shifted from cornerback to receiver and Babe Parilli came over from Oakland to guide the offense, and with some key additions at defense, the Patriots became very competitive.

Still, for many New Englanders, the club lost its innocence after that first camp, a time when almost anyone could rightly claim he could make a professional football team, and on occasion, that candidate proved correct in his self-assessment.

14 Ben Coates

Russ Francis won All-World accolades from commentator Howard Cosell, but as great a tight end as Francis was, future Patriots tight end Ben Coates proved even better. Like many Pats stars, Coates was chosen relatively late in the NFL draft—a fifth-round selection in 1991 out of a small North Carolina college named Livingstone—and his first two years seemed to bear out his pecking order in that draft as he caught only 30 total passes.

Then came Drew Bledsoe, the first draft pick chosen in 1993, and while he certainly had the ability to throw far downfield, whipping the ball in the flats to Ben Coates became his favorite and most lethal option. That ensuing year, Coates pulled in 53 passes, becoming a huge offensive weapon on a surging franchise. Patriots offensive coordinator Larry Kennan perceived the magical nature of their relationship, positing, "What [Drew] shares with Ben is a special kind of chemistry." When it once took five opposing defenders to wrest Coates out of bounds, an appreciative tackle, Pat Harlow, yelled over to Bledsoe, "That guy's a man!"

It only got better as Coates set what was then the all-time single-season receptions record for a tight end in 1994 with 96 snares, en route to his first of five straight Pro Bowl selections.

He starred again the next season with 84 receptions, and even though his production dropped somewhat in 1996, he led his team on January 26, 1997, in the Super Bowl against the Green Bay Packers with six receptions, also good for most receiving yards for his club. In the first quarter, he caught a four-yard pass from Bledsoe for a touchdown, giving New England its first and only lead in the game.

Despite his team's loss in the Super Bowl, Coates continued to lead the Pats in regular season receptions the next two years, but change had come to New England as head coach Bill Parcells had walked away from the team in a huff after the Super Bowl (some would say before the title game), replaced by a kinder and gentler coach, Pete Carroll. A somewhat exasperated Coates saw his own production fall, once stating, "It has been kind of frustrating watching this offense because I am capable of making so many more plays. I have always been there for Drew, helping him get to where he is today. Sometimes it doesn't seem that way when I go through a whole game only seeing two balls. But when he's in trouble, Drew reverts to me." Of course, by this time most other NFL teams knew this, and they tied up Coates with double coverage or by jamming him at the line.

Although Carroll had a better record than Bill Parcells in New England, most perceived that the club had begun an irreversible decline, and by Carroll's last year at the helm, no one personified this trend more than Coates, who at age 30 only caught 32 passes. Coates had posted his third-highest yards-per-reception average of his career, but he failed to make the Pro Bowl. Quite suddenly, the gridiron gods had transformed the great tight end into an old man.

The Patriots released Coates before the 2000 season, but fortuitously he hooked up with the Baltimore Ravens for one last season, a Super Bowl–winning campaign. He retired with 499 receptions and has been enshrined in the Patriots Hall of Fame. At the time of his retirement, only Ozzie Newsome, Shannon Sharpe, and Kellen Winslow had caught more passes from the tight end position. One last tribute to this most talented receiver and blocker: when asked once what play he would call with his team near the opposing goal on fourth down, needing to score, Bledsoe unhesitatingly responded, "Do I have Ben Coates on my team?"

15 Finally, a Super Bowl

For starters, 1985 was the year that the Patriots finally defeated the Miami Dolphins in a road game (okay, technically it occurred in 1986 in the AFC Championship Game), a feat that the team had not accomplished since the old AFL days. It also marked the first time that the Pats participated in a Super Bowl, and briefly football captured the attention of even casual local fans, a luxury for a team consigned to a seemingly intractable fourth place in the hearts and minds of New Englanders.

It provided a long deferred reward for some of the players who had starred in the 1970s on some very good teams and remained with the club, including John Hannah, who was in his final professional season. New mixed with old, with Tony Eason starting at quarterback, then being replaced by Steve Grogan for a 6–0 run until Grogan suffered a broken bone in his left knee and ligament damage. Other stars such as Tony Collins and Craig James in the backfield and Stanley Morgan at wide receiver propelled the offense while the linebackers and defensive backs steeled the defense. In all, eight Patriots earned selection to the Pro Bowl that year.

To understand how they got to this pinnacle, it helps to go back to the middle of the 1984 season, when talented head coach Ron Meyer began to clash with owner Billy Sullivan and some of the players themselves. An innovative coach, Meyer is best known today for calling out a snow plow during a scoreless game against the Dolphins in 1982 in order to give kicker John Smith a clearer surface, a tactic that worked and drove opposing coach Don Shula crazy. Meyer took his team to 5–4 and won AFC Coach of the Year honors that season.

The problem was Meyer seemed intent on bringing the team back down again after orchestrating its ascent. His criticism of players did not motivate them; in fact, it angered many, and GM Pat Sullivan had to conduct at least one meeting with players to calm the situation. Undaunted, according to Sullivan, Meyer then tried to trade many of the stars of the club, including but not limited to Mosi Tatupu, Hannah, Robert Weathers, Rick Sanford, and Tony Collins. Correctly sensing that the Patriots were much closer to excellence than to a rebuilding project, none of the players departed.

Having failed to dump a number of players, Meyer cast about and decided to terminate defensive coordinator Rod Rust. In a loss against the Dolphins, Meyer disapproved of Rust's defensive schemes, supposedly in large part because it isolated a linebacker on a Miami wide receiver. True or not, Meyer had enough of Rust and fired him, even though he apparently did not have the ability to do so. During Sullivan's ownership of the franchise, it was accepted wisdom that no one cross the owner, and Meyer had just laid down the gauntlet. Predictably, Sullivan fired Meyer on October 25, 1984, even though the team had a 5–3 record at that time, and named assistant coach Raymond Berry the new leader.

Raymond Berry guided the Patriots to a 31–14 victory over the Miami Dolphins in the 1985 AFC Championship Game.

Berry, an even-tempered man, immediately rehired Rust and squired his men to a final record of 9–7. Importantly, he stabilized the team and recognized the talent at his disposal and began to utilize his players in a manner designed to allow them to succeed. Eschewing Meyer's desire to dump players, Berry largely kept a pat hand in his personnel decisions, with the late-1984 version of the Patriots closely resembling the starting roster of the club at the beginning of the next campaign.

Unfortunately, the club stumbled at the dawn of the 1985 season, losing badly to the Bears and Raiders en route to an early 2–3 record. From that point on, however, the Pats only lost two more games during the regular season, a three-point loss to the Jets and a three-point loss to Miami. Much of the credit was due to Grogan's leadership, and even after his injury, the team did not fold. Eason finally began to play within himself, and having a steady hand in Berry at the rudder staved off any tendency to panic or underperform. The Pats made the playoffs.

In the wild-card game, the team squared off against the Jets for the third time, having split their regular season rivalry. Long forgotten, the most telling blow in this contest occurred in the third quarter when Andre Tippett hammered Jets starting quarterback Ken O'Brien on a sack. O'Brien, who to that point had completed 13 of 17 passes, never returned that day and his replacement (Pat Ryan) determined that the hit on O'Brien "might have been the worst I've seen." The Patriots won in East Rutherford that day by a 26–14 margin.

Continuing to travel, the Pats visited the Raiders. Though the Raiders had previously blown out New England in Foxboro that year, mistakes by Raiders quarterback Marc Wilson negated a fine running performance by Marcus Allen (who had a slightly better performance than New England's Craig James) as the Pats won 27–20. Today the game is remembered more for what happened after the final gun sounded, when GM Pat Sullivan started hollering at the Raiders' Howie Long. Long's teammate, Matt Millen, stepped in and hammered Sullivan in the noggin with his helmet, and Sullivan spent some time in the trainer's room afterward having his wounds nursed.

Another road win. For the first time ever, the Patriots owned the air waves, with radio stations coming up with topical jingles such as "Squish the Fish" before the final Miami game, a take-off on Pete Townshend's anthemic song "Face the Face." In current New England sports consciousness, the Pats own the region, but until January 1986, they commanded a rather small core of committed fans before millions of casual observers jumped onto the bandwagon.

On January 12, 1986, in the Orange Bowl, the Patriots not only reversed their road-game curse of futility against the Dolphins— they blew them out (31–14) behind the punishing running of James, Tony Collins, and Robert Weathers. Tony Eason threw for three touchdowns, one to tight end Derrick Ramsey, while Tatupu plowed a one-yard run in for another score. Dan Marino played well in spots but threw key interceptions to Fred Marion and Raymond Clayborn, ensuring the Patriots would play their next game in the Super Bowl.

The Super Bowl itself was not anticlimactic; it was simply ugly. The Chicago Bears had assembled one of the greatest defenses in NFL history, led by Mike Singletary and Wilber Marshall at linebacker, Dan Hampton and Steve McMichael on the line (with some help from William "the Refrigerator" Perry), and a defensive backfield solidified by Gary Fencik and Dave Duerson. The focus of the offense was cocky quarterback Jim McMahon, but running back Walter Payton provided the class and all the talent the team needed. Chicago rolled 46–10.

If you were Patriots fan, there was no joy in Mudville, and within a few years, the Patriots had drilled themselves solidly back into fourth place in the hearts of local sports fans.

16 Visit Fred and Steve's Steakhouse and Wicked Good Bar and Grill

Nestled in the Twin Rivers Casino Complex in Lincoln, Rhode Island, Fred and Steve's Steakhouse is a must for diners in this bastion of Patriots Nation as well as other states in New England. Its owners, of course, are Fred Smerlas, originally from Waltham, Massachusetts, and Steve DeOssie from the Roslindale district of Boston. Although Fred and Steve only played briefly (two years apiece) for the Patriots, they have remained in New England as popular radio and television analysts, and their restaurant stands as another reminder that they never really left, even when starring for opposing teams.

As you might gather, great steak and fresh seafood abound, enhancing the Twin Rivers entertainment experience. The autographed game jerseys of the owners (and Zak DeOssie), the autographed game balls, and Steve DeOssie's Super Bowl trophy do not engulf the decor, and the owners themselves quite often stop by their restaurant to talk to diners and fans alike.

Right next door is the Wicked Good Bar and Grill, an immensely fun new sports bar for fans of all New England teams. One room is dominated by a 60-foot bar, while another spacious room contains many of the establishment's 25 large televisions sets. Not your normal generic sports bar, Wicked Good makes its own delicious ice cream, rotates 65 different brands of beers, and serves such local specialties as stuffies (quahogs to Bostonians, stuffed hard shell clams to those who live far from the coast).

Danny Woodhead from the Pats has stopped by this promising new pub, and part of a wall is dedicated to a montage of the team's many successes. To top off the experience, Wicked Good has opened up a memorabilia store for fans.

17 Fire!

Curiously, few fans recall one of the most sensational events in club history: a fire that consumed a section of the stands in the team's temporary digs at Boston College's Alumni Stadium. The inferno ignited on August 16, 1970, during an exhibition game against the Washington Redskins.

Before a sellout crowd of 25,584 patrons, the Redskins had already rung up a 7–0 lead en route to a 45–21 win when fans started bolting from the seats and jumping onto the playing field. Naturally, most in attendance just assumed that the throng had collectively lost confidence in the Pats' awful defense and had taken matters into their own hands, figuring only they had a chance of impeding Sonny Jurgensen and company.

Not so. As events transpired, a large amount of Styrofoam lay underneath a canvas below the stands, combusting once someone errantly threw a cigarette or cigar on top of the pile. Since it was tied down and because no fire extinguishers were in evidence, it took the Newton Fire Department, backed up by the Boston F.D., to bring their trucks in to control the potential disaster.

The Blazing Braves

Patriots fans escaped the fate of the 19th century fans of the old Boston Beaneaters, the lineal predecessors of the Boston Braves and thus the Atlanta Braves. On May 15, 1894, a match landed in a pile of dry wood beneath the seats, causing the majestic South End Grounds to burn completely along with 20 acres of residences in the surrounding Roxbury neighborhood. Of course, Billy Sullivan had once worked for the Braves, so the cynic might be excused in perceiving a link between the two fires.

Miraculously no one was killed, and play resumed after only about a 30-minute delay.

In the interim, pandemonium mixed with the mundane. A youngster handed Pats safety Don Webb a program for an autograph but was stopped when teammate John Charles called out, "Hey Webb, you can't sign that. You can't sign an autograph during a game." What game? Technically all the players and patrons were participating in simply the latest of notable Patriots mishaps, with nobody tossing around the pigskin or a Redskin.

Many of the displaced fans were permitted to stand along the sidelines when play continued, their seats (20 rows' worth) having burned during the conflagration. It was a time when fans of professional football smoked at games and sat on wooden seats. Surveying the smoldering ruins and perhaps viewing the fire as a metaphor for his own snake-bit franchise, owner Billy Sullivan mused, "What else can happen to us?"

18 How Victor Kiam Almost Ruined the Patriots

Before he became the Patriots' owner in 1988, Victor Kiam had endeared himself to millions of American consumers as the CEO of Remington Products. In a particularly well-crafted television advertisement, Kiam related the story about how his wife bought him a Remington shaver and "I liked it so much, I bought the company!" The spot conveyed warmth, and with the possible exception of Lee Iacocca, Kiam exemplified in a most positive manner the products he endorsed.

Unfortunately he liked the New England Patriots so much that he bought them in 1988, and whatever Midas touch he possessed at Remington deserted him once he gained control of the team. In a classic blunder, he purchased the club but not its stadium, permitting Bob Kraft to buy what was then called Schaefer Stadium. Although the team had played in Super Bowl XX, he bought it during a sharp period of decline, a factor that further exacerbated his misfortunes. Little did poor Victor know it at the time, but much darker days were ahead.

Perhaps Kiam's worst wounds were self-inflicted, a fact that became evident in the days that followed the sexual harassment of *Boston Herald* sportswriter Lisa Olson in the team's locker room on Monday, September 17, 1990. Having just won an exciting early season game against the Colts (ultimately the club's only win that season), some of the team members decided to harass Olson as she interviewed defensive back Maurice Hurst. Opinions differ concerning what occurred exactly, but the NFL later concluded that something very objectionable indeed transpired.

Initially, Olson kept the incident quiet, but she did speak to a writer from the competing *Boston Globe* about the incident, and a very small article ran in that paper. Quickly the firestorm spread, with Kiam completely swept away by events, spasmodically careening from either trying to apologize quickly, blame Olson, or take on the whole issue of female reporters being allowed access to the locker room. Whatever keen instincts he possessed to buy Remington completely deserted him in the following days.

Kiam's behavior reached its nadir after the team's next game, a blowout loss to the Cincinnati Bengals, when he entered the team's dressing room after the game and acted obnoxiously around Olson. One of the players allegedly taunted her too, but Kiam's boorish behavior is most remembered, as he proclaimed (and later almost as forcefully denied) in front of a room full of reporters that he considered Olson "a classic bitch." He also joked at an event around this time that Saddam Hussein's Iraq and Lisa Olson had something in common, to wit, "they've both seen the Patriot Missiles

The Victor Kiam era was marred by embarrassing episodes on and off the field.

up close." A classic male chauvinist, Kiam had just sealed his fate in New England, a fact that soon became apparent even to him once he learned of a potential boycott of Lady Remington products.

Some class acts emerged, as cornerback Ronnie Lippett loudly and publicly supported Olson, and receiver Cedric Jones echoed this backing for the beleaguered reporter. Soon thereafter Olson began receiving death threats and was taunted mercilessly by some Pats fans after at least one home game, a fate shared by Kiam, too.

The NFL stepped in and ordered an investigation by Philip Heymann. The league concluded that Pats players Zeke Mowatt, Robert Perryman, and Michael Timpson had "degraded and humiliated" Olson, fining Mowatt $12,500 and his two teammates $5,000 apiece. The Patriots organization was fined $55,000 due to its failure to act promptly and properly, and GM Pat Sullivan ultimately walked the plank over the fallout, severing the team's last link to its founding family.

The wrong guy got fired, as Kiam had the ability to quash the matter quickly instead of serving as an active accelerant, his problem laying in obstinately standing by his man, the useless Zeke Mowatt. He should have immediately released Mowatt and Perryman, and tried to trade Timpson, a player who at least possessed some trade value. He needed to contact his public relations people and follow a script of public apologies, instead of uttering crass and stupid statements of his own.

Olson, who loved sports, took an overseas assignment for several years to avoid the threats to her life and other harassment, eventually suing the Patriots and settling for a considerable sum of money. Mowatt, Timpson, and Perryman eventually became ex-Patriots and Kiam, having completely embarrassed the franchise, sold the team in 1992 to James Busch Orthwein.

Although he acted like a buffoon, Kiam actually sported a pedigree and a life's work that suggested quite the opposite, with an education that included matriculation at Yale, the Sorbonne, and Harvard. He had wielded a Midas touch everywhere he went, transforming struggling businesses into robust success stories. When he died, the *Independent* ran an obituary in which it related Kiam's meteoric turnaround of Remington: "When Kiam bought it from Sperry Corporation, Remington was a loss-making company which employed 428 people. Less than a decade later, its workforce had expanded to 2,500 and, with 43 percent of the market, it was America's dominant electric razor manufacturer; and sweetest irony

Kiam the Clown

Victor Kiam may have lost his team but he never lost his sense of humor, a trait he did possess when not venturing into the objectionable. After winning a libel verdict in an English court shortly before his death, he observed, "I liked the verdict so much I wish I could have bought the jury." If only he could have bought some class.

of all—until he bought it in one of the first leveraged buyouts in U.S. business history, Kiam had been a wet-shave man."

A bright and innovative man, Kiam stubbed his toe after he purchased the Pats because, to quote Lennon and McCartney, "he didn't notice that the lights had changed." He came from a poor upbringing, but once at the summit he failed to notice that his world had already begun to change; the days of three-martini lunches, trips on Eastern Airlines, and smoke-filled rooms of men telling bawdy jokes were over. He virtually invented political incorrectness.

Worst of all, he got outsmarted by someone more intelligent than he (and infinitely more dedicated to football in New England), Bob Kraft. Unlike some past Patriots owners, Kiam's tenure is irredeemable, one completely resistant of even partial rehabilitation with the perspective that the past can often provide.

19 Touchdown Ron

Estimable Ron Burton, one of New England's finest men, first gained positive recognition as a speedy back on coach Ara Parseghian's Northwestern Wildcats, leading an upstart program to upset victories over Michigan and Ohio State. Against the Buckeyes in November 1958, the star player scored the key touchdown after "Dick Thornton found halfback Ron Burton running free as the breeze behind the Ohio State secondary and laid a perfect lead pass into his arms for a 67-yard touchdown play," according to *Sports Illustrated.*

Proving the play no fluke, Burton led the Wildcats in all-purpose yards for three seasons, earning All-American recognition in 1959 and eventual induction into the College Football Hall of Fame.

At the advent of their inaugural American Football League season, the Boston Patriots shrewdly chose Burton as their first draft choice (or at least their first back, with some confusion surrounding exactly how picks were made). Problem was, the Philadelphia Eagles of the then-competing NFL also tabbed Burton with their first-round pick. Fortunately for the Pats, Burton chose them and immediately rewarded the team in his rookie season with a phenomenal 40.3 yards-per-kickoff-return average, together with 21 pass receptions and a 4.2 yards-per-carry average out of the backfield.

In his sophomore campaign, Burton's numbers as a halfback dipped a bit but he continued to excel on special teams, averaging 16 yards gained per punt return and 26.7 yards gained on each kickoff return, with one failed extra-point attempt returned for a touchdown. By his third professional season, he excelled in all aspects, earning top-10 recognition in the AFL's 1962 league leaders in rushing yards, rushing average, receptions, yards from scrimmage, all-purpose yards, and punt return yards.

"With the First Pick…"

Traditionally ascribed as the Patriots' first selection, lingering confusion concerning how the AFL pioneers actually conducted their college draft has clouded the issue of when Boston chose Ron Burton. While it has been long assumed that the AFL let each team pick players they wanted in a predetermined order, an opposing viewpoint holds that they actually drafted by position first; for instance, if they started with quarterbacks, each team chose a quarterback and then they all moved on to another position. No matter; Ron Burton remains first in the heart of fans no matter how the AFL operated before the 1960 season.

Unfortunately, he underwent a spinal disc operation, which prevented him from playing a single down during the 1963 regular season, although he gamely returned for the playoffs that year. Much less widely known, he had also injured both his ankles, as the club had to account for its deficiencies in its power running game by calling upon Burton to alter his style. He returned for two final seasons after that layoff, and while he ranked in the top 10 for yards per touch as a back in 1964 and yards per punt return in his final season in 1965, his role increasingly was taken up by other backs such as Jim Nance. By then injuries had deprived Burton of his full ability to utilize his natural talents, a sad development because a healthy Burton would be recognized by consensus as one of the greatest players in American Football League history.

Burton continued to distinguish himself after he retired from the Patriots, serving as an executive at John Hancock Insurance Company and founding the Ron Burton Training Village for Disadvantaged Children, an effort by Burton to assist disadvantaged young people, a tribute to the people who raised him from a childhood of poverty to one of promise and eminent achievement. He also tirelessly provided his service to other charitable organizations and causes.

Like many Boston Patriots, "Touchdown Ron" Burton died too young, a victim of bone cancer, but his legacy continues to be honored by the National Football Foundation, which annually graces one deserving sportsman with the Ron Burton Distinguished American Award. And the Ron Burton Training Village endures, carrying on the work that graced his life.

20 Visit Patriot Place

For too long, the area in Foxboro surrounding the Patriots' stadia felt largely abandoned, except on game day or during New England Revolution soccer games. Thanks to the phased introduction of a giant mall in 2007, the environs never stop being lively.

Besides Gillette Stadium itself, the crown jewel is the Hall at Patriot Place, a fitting tribute to the team and its fans from the club's inception to the present. The Hall is actually attached to the stadium, spawned by the generosity of Bob Kraft, Raytheon, and the Waters Corp. Built in 2008, it now welcomes Pats fans on most days, major holidays excluded.

You have to stop by. While no rules exist to tell a visitor where to start or what to see, a fun first venue is the on-site theater that shows a 17-minute team history a few times an hour. Intimate and cozy with its 150 seats, the sound system is terrific and the action is barely contained on a 45-foot screen, permitting theatergoers unique and intense access to some powerful sideline moments and vivid physical contact on the field. The film itself does not hide the team history beneath a haze of rosy-eyed 3D glasses, but starts with some of the mishaps of the early years in blooper fashion and does not shy away from some of the near-miss heartbreaks as the franchise developed. Still, the experience is largely an ascendant one with plenty of championship moments in the storyline.

Like any museum, the Hall rotates exhibits, one moment honoring Patriots cheerleaders and then on another date tastefully placing a Tedy Bruschi throwback jersey on display. While the costumes and routines of the cheerleaders have changed, due note is given to the first team cheerleader, Dino DiCarlo, who dressed like Paul Revere and rode a horse along the sideline in the club's infancy. Bruschi, of course, needs no long introduction.

The Hall does not restrict its focus to the franchise alone, providing exhibits dedicated to local high school football and to the history of the game itself. While some relics are on loan from other archives and institutions, if you arrive at the right time you can see a Providence Steamrollers uniform, circa 1931; a 1920 Harvard Rose Bowl football; and an 1876 Harvard-Yale football.

But if you go to see just the Patriots, you will be richly rewarded in your quest. The Patriots Wall of Fame contains the glass-like plaques of the club's Hall of Famers ascending toward the sky, while on a more sublunary level you may view a Patriots Super Bowl ring.

You can join a simulated huddle of Patriots players or reasonable facsimiles of them, or sidle up to four stations where you can press a menu in ATM fashion to learn about the members of the

Patriot Place is a wonderful place to spend a few hours either before or after a Patriots home game.

Patriots Hall of Fame. Exhibits chart the history of the Patriots, with important documents and other items of memorabilia providing effective visual accompaniments to the written narratives provided. You can compare your hands to Troy Brown's, match grips with Steve Grogan's, or step into some very big footprints of some of the more formidable former team members. You can also see for yourself the reproductions of lockers of Tom Brady, Kevin Faulk, and Jerod Mayo, or view the four championship rings.

One of the three floors is dedicated to a very large and comprehensive gift shop, containing small and large helmet reproductions, uniforms with the numbers of favorite players, color photos, and even some footballs. The Pro Shop is worth the trip alone, particularly when birthdays and holidays approach.

The Hall at Patriot Place is itself but a small constituent part of Patriot Place, where multitudinous dining experiences await, from burger emporiums to very upscale dining. Retail clothing and (naturally) sports-themed businesses abound, and a state-of-the-art movie theatre, the Cinema de Lux, has 14 screens. Bands, comedians, actors, and other acts have a live stage at Showcase Live. Stroll along the modern mall and you are walking down the main street of Patriots Nation.

One of the most attractive venues in the complex is the CBS Scene Restaurant, a restaurant and sports bar for certain, but what it offers permits it to transcend these limitations. The food exceeds usual sports pub fare, crafted by chefs and not by cooks. The atmosphere is quite cutting edge, with a number of flights connected by grand circular stairways in the middle. At each table, the diner has a television set, cued off-season to any number of vintage CBS network television programs from *Everybody Loves Raymond* to *The Twilight Zone*. On game day, you can watch the live action on a 360-square-foot projection, and many of the postgame television productions take place at the CBS Scene.

Patriot Place awaits fans and shoppers, and as time passes, hopefully its plethora of attractions will entice more patrons on days when the home team does not play.

21 Saddle Up at the Eagle Brook Saloon

Open since 1981, the Eagle Brook Saloon is a favorite gathering place for fans who want to eat and drink well before heading a bit north to see their Patriots. Although it is not officially sanctioned, some fans leave their car on the premises or in the area and walk to the game, although it's a bit of a hike.

Once co-owned by tight end Russ Francis, the Eagle Brook combines many of the elements of a western saloon (long bar, second-floor mezzanine eating) with a singularly New England touch: wooden fixtures, railing, and molding supposedly removed from a nearby religious school that was being razed.

The pub fare is quite good, especially the chili before a cold afternoon outside. The proprietors pride themselves on their own beers, with the Dog's Breath and Brady Beer as excellent as any pint you will ever order from the heart of England itself. The Eagle Brook does not have a plethora of televisions on the walls, but they do exist for those not fortunate enough to get tickets for the game. Occasionally a Patriot will stop in, and after the team returned from its first Super Bowl victory, Bill Belichick feasted there with all of his coaches. Though the days of seeing huddles of players there passed with Francis himself, it is still a great place to eat and meet and drive out of your way for.

22 Mike Haynes

Like Nick Buoniconti, Mike Haynes split his Hall of Fame career with the Patriots and another team, an inexcusable loss of such a vastly talented man and a class act. Selected to six Pro Bowls during his seven years in New England, the club lost him to the Raiders in 1983, after Haynes played out his option in a period of labor relations more favorable to management. In the ensuing settlement, he left along with a seventh-round draft choice for first- and second-round draft choices from Los Angeles (they were on a self-imposed exile from Oakland back then). The "trade" stunk, redeemed only partially by the Pats later packaging the rights to that future first rounder and three other picks to obtain Irving Fryar.

Haynes departed during a particularly toxic time in the franchise's labor history, marked most starkly by the holdouts of John Hannah and Leon Gray, and the trading away of Gray after a "decent interval" had passed. In an interview about a year after Haynes moved to the West Coast, he made at least an oblique reference to these types of issues, opining, "What I learned during my career was that some teams don't *want* to go to the Super Bowl. Winning costs them money, in salaries and that. So if winning isn't the wisest thing to do, you've got to have an ego that has to win. And Al Davis has that ego. He's a contrarian. Maybe that's why I like him." Thankfully, that era has long since passed, and fans can now appreciate Haynes for his contributions to the club both as a cornerback and a special teams star. He has been named to the mythical Team of the Decade for the 1970s, the 50th Anniversary Team, and the Patriots Hall of Fame.

This rookie from Arizona State certainly commenced his professional career in grand fashion, intercepting eight passes and garnering NFL Defensive Rookie of the Year honors and a nod to his first Pro Bowl, his first of five straight. On special teams, he finished second in the NFL that year in total punt return yards, an often overlooked element of his contribution to his team. As a Pat, he played a very physical and intelligent game, traits that remained with him even after he departed New England.

Haynes subsequently punished the Pats for years, with three Pro Bowl appearances in his last seven years, and like Carlton Fisk in baseball, he often played his finest games against his old team. In 1984, he intercepted six passes, pacing the NFL with 220 return yards from interceptions. In 1984 and 1985, he produced his only first-team All-Pro seasons, well after he departed New England.

His departure haunted New England immediately and for years after. In 1984, Dr. Z of *Sports Illustrated* named the ex-Patriot to his mythical All-Pro team, commenting, "Mike Haynes of the Raiders is the consummate cornerback. The Shadow. It's hard to separate him from the receiver he's covering." Haynes got the nod from Dr. Z after the next season also, though by then he was 32 years old, a ripe age for a corner even for a specialist of "bump and run" tactics. Haynes swiped a total of 46 passes in his career, which barely keeps him in the all-time top 50, but the statistic does not

Beware the Midnight Hour

Want to blame someone other than the Sullivans for Mike Haynes leaving the Patriots? Try Kenny Anderson. The Pats had completed the deal with the L.A. Raiders, but the settlement fell outside of the perceived trading deadline, i.e. by 5:00 PM the day after the last game ended in the league's sixth week. The alert son of Haynes' agent, Howard Slusher, pointed out that he believed that the last of the sixth week's games might have gone past midnight on Tuesday morning. A quick check by Slusher confirmed this: due to the delay caused by the injury to Kenny Anderson of the Bengals, the game went past midnight, so the deal shipping Haynes to L.A. was still within the trading deadline period.

reveal the number of times he neutralized the opponent's finest receiver or kept the opposing quarterback from tossing the ball to his area of the field.

Lester Hayes, his teammate and fellow cornerback with the Raiders, might have assessed Haynes the best, "The most fantastic thing about Mike Haynes is that here is a gentleman who has been to six Pro Bowls, who's a devout family man, a man who's so intelligent, who has it all—but he's not so great that I can't share things with him…Believe me, beneath that clean-shaven, boyish face lurks a man who would tear out your heart on Sunday and eat it raw."

That is why it is never a good idea to lose a player like Mike Haynes.

23 Reverend Fryar

Irving Fryar could have gone down in Patriots history as an all-time screwup, a chilling example of how too much fame and fortune achieved too early can ruin the life of an enormously talented athlete. That his story did not end badly and continues to inspire honors Irving as a man who saw his life leading into an abyss and reversed his course.

A massive star at the University of Nebraska, Fryar was the first player chosen overall in the 1984 draft, and by his second year with the Patriots had played in a Super Bowl and earned a Pro Bowl selection. Although mainly honored as a special teams player, he did catch 39 passes in his sophomore season, not a bad total for that era. However, shortly after New England lost Super Bowl XX to Chicago, Fryar was named by the *Boston Globe* as one of a number

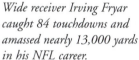

Wide receiver Irving Fryar caught 84 touchdowns and amassed nearly 13,000 yards in his NFL career.

of Pats who had used drugs that year, one of the first and certainly not the last faux pas committed by Irving Fryar in New England.

Soon, he seemed more in competition with the Red Sox's Wade Boggs for local sports star gone amok than he appeared focused on defeating opposing teams. Indeed, Boggs once mused that people might be considering him the "white Irving Fryar," a prescient observation as the Sox third baseman willed himself invisible to avoid scrapes. As events unfolded, Fryar's two cut fingers sustained during the 1985 playoffs apparently sprung from a domestic incident, and his nagging irresponsibility behind the wheel of his car seemed fated to end his life or the lives of innocent people. He either lucked out or was saved by some amazing grace.

Although he continued to field punts and kickoffs and his receptions gradually increased, he never again played in a Pro Bowl during his remaining seven seasons in New England, and frankly he never threatened to enter the top 10 for receptions during his nine years with the club. When Bill Parcells took over the Patriots, one of his first acts involved shipping Fryar to the Miami Dolphins.

In Miami, Fryar staged a personal and professional Renaissance, and although he cared little for Dolphins quarterback Dan Marino, he started participating in Pro Bowls again, earning four selections in the final eight years of his career. Splitting his time roughly between Miami, Philadelphia, and Washington, D.C., Fryar finally realized his vast potential in the twilight of his career, rising in league-wide categories including receptions and receiving yards.

Somewhere in his path less chosen, he also either found or rediscovered religion and became an ordained minister. Shifting away from selfishness and immature behavior, his family life blossomed and he became an inspiration to those around him. He had lost too many years in New England, and while he still stands in the all-time NFL top 25 in lifetime receptions, had he performed up to expectations in the first half of his career, today he might be spoken of in the same breath as Jerry Rice or Tim Brown.

Fryar found God before God lost him, and recently he has been honored during the Sports Museum Legends evening event with such other luminaries as John Havlicek. Irving Fryar arrived too late, but he arrived just in time.

24 Giants Fans

Every Patriots fan should know that a fifth column of New England football enthusiasts secretly root for the New York Giants as their favorite club. It is suspected that a number of these misplaced souls even materially aided the Giants' defeat of the Pats in the Super

On Enemy Soil

A NY Football Giants Fan Club of New England has existed for more than 20 years, and in addition to publishing a newsletter and having a website, the club sponsors annual banquets with speakers ranging from Steve DeOssie to Zak DeOssie.

Bowl after the 2007 season, marring an otherwise perfect season for Bill Belichick's men.

This peculiar phenomenon has less to do with anyone's feelings about the Patriots than it does with the past paucity of professional football options in the region, as the Boston Redskins and the Boston Yanks folded soon after their founding. Bereft of any viable options in New England, many fans shifted their allegiance to the closest option: the Giants, those powerhouse title-winning teams behind Y.A. Tittle, Charlie Conerly, Del Shofner, Joe Morrison, Frank Gifford, Jim Katcavage, and Dick Lynch. For several years the club held its preseason training camp at St. Michael's College in Winooski, Vermont, further cementing the allegiance to the New York Giants in New England.

Founded before the 1960 season, the Patriots played their first decade in the AFL, thereby never directly challenging the NFL's Giants or causing any division in loyalties. A Giants fan could ignore the upstart Pats or root for both Boston and the Giants with no apparent conflict of interest so long as that same fan vigorously hated the Jets. Once the AFL and NFL merged, the Pats and Giants began to clash occasionally, though they have never developed a rivalry. Young local fans have mainly grown up liking only the Pats, and after more than 50 years, many of the old Giants fans have passed to that great gridiron in the sky or have shifted their loyalties to the Patriots somewhere along the way. After all, why drive to New Jersey to see a home game with Foxboro and Gillette Stadium just down the road on Route 1?

Except for congenital contrarians, few fans native to the greater Boston area still root for the New York Giants, their very existence spoken of in almost hushed, semi-mythical tones usually reserved for alleged sightings of Bigfoot or the Melungeons of the Appalachian region. Yet like the farmers of Boston's north shore who still say "thee" and "thou," they are still there as surely as leprechauns exist. It is hoped that when the Giants did defeat New England twice in the Super Bowl, these scattered remnants at least felt a bit of a twinge in their hearts for the Patriots.

25 The Greatest Running Back You Have Never Heard Of

Although you will not find his name among the honorees on the Patriots' 50th Anniversary Team, Curtis Martin is the greatest running back in New England's history. His sin lay in playing most of his career with the New York Jets, but that does not excuse his consignment to the dustbin of local sports history.

The Pats originally got him cheap, a value pick if there ever was one, in the third round of the 1995 draft out of the University of Pittsburgh. His first coach, Bill Parcells, never gushed over a player, but in Martin's rookie camp, the coach admitted, "He seems to have taken to pro football fairly well and I like his athletic ability. But I think we're a little presumptuous about how he's going to do here." Parcells exercised unwarranted cautious optimism; not only did Martin attack the defense with 4.4 speed, but he also quickly grasped the less glamorous aspects of a good back's assignments, namely blitz pickups and blocking.

In his rookie season he not only did the little things well. He ran the ball for 1,487 yards and bailed out Drew Bledsoe with 30 timely receptions. He earned his first Pro Bowl nod and Offensive Rookie of the Year honors. He did everything but attend local kids' birthday parties…no, wait, he did that, too.

Martin gained more than 1,000 yards on the ground in 1996 and improved his receptions to 46, as he made another Pro Bowl and played in the Super Bowl, scoring a touchdown as the Pats lost to Green Bay. Parcells had acted up all week leading up to the Super Bowl, but it seemed as if he had at least one disciple in Curtis Martin. After the Big Tuna left, Martin gained another 1,000-plus yards and caught 41 passes but bolted to New York after 1997 to rejoin Parcells.

After departing New England, Martin played eight more years, perhaps the worst loss to New York in Boston sports history since Babe Ruth cursed the Red Sox on his way to the Bronx. Martin compiled career totals of 14,101 yards rushing and 484 pass receptions. At age 31, in the next-to-last year of his career, he gained an incredible league-leading 1,697 yards on the ground. Heading into the 2011 season, only Emmitt Smith, Walter Payton, and Barry Sanders had gained more career yards rushing in NFL history.

Curtis Martin always carried himself with dignity and class, and it is past time for him to receive the appreciation of Patriots fans for his accomplishments in New England.

26 Happy to Be Alive

Perhaps the saddest tragedy in Patriots history occurred on August 12, 1978, during an exhibition game against the Oakland Raiders when wide receiver Darryl Stingley went up for a Steve Grogan pass only to sustain a savage hit from defensive back Jack Tatum.

Stingley hit the field hard, and he spent the rest of his life as a quadriplegic as a result of his injuries.

Many of the side stories are fairly well known, such as the fact that heartbroken Raiders coach John Madden visited Stingley daily or that Stingley and Tatum never reconciled (an attempt to bring the men together did occur, but it was canceled because Stingley felt it only served to helped promote Tatum's upcoming book). Less known is that Stingley had ceased breathing after the hit, and survived for the next year due in equal parts to his indomitable will and state-of-the-art medical technology. That's how hard Tatum hit him.

The tragedy transcended much of what has been written about Stingley's life, so insufficient attention has been paid to the fine career he did have in football. A star receiver at Purdue, the Patriots selected Stingley with their first pick in the 1973 draft. He snared 23 passes as a rookie, and even though he only played in five games in his sophomore campaign, he caught another 10 passes that year.

A promising football career was tragically cut short when wide receiver Darryl Stingley was paralyzed after a hit by Oakland's Jack Tatum. Stingley passed away in 2007.

The Dangers of Flag Football

Although nowhere nearly as devastating or tragic as the injury sustained by Darryl Stingley, another serious hit was meted out to Patriots running back Robert Edwards after the 1998 season. Drafted to replace Curtis Martin, Edwards posted a very strong rookie season, rushing for 1,115 yards and rolling up another 331 yards receiving the ball. As part of that year's Pro Bowl festivities, Edwards participated in a rookie flag football game, a seemingly innocuous event. Sadly, he sustained an injury to his knee so severe that he skirted amputation by a narrow margin. He missed the next three seasons before signing with the Dolphins for one year, after which he took another hiatus from the game, this time for two years. Reemerging with the Canadian Football League in 2005, Edwards rushed for 1,199 yards.

The Pats did not restrict Stingley to catching Steve Grogan's offerings, and during his five-year career he was utilized as a running option from scrimmage, with his 28 career rushes culminating in a stunning 244 yards, an average of almost nine yards per run. His great friend, tight end Russ Francis, also appreciated other aspects of Stingley's game, once stating, "Darryl wasn't just a good receiver, he was a classic receiver, and a tough receiver. He was the first guy looking to hit somebody, looking for somebody to block, if somebody else caught the ball."

He enjoyed his finest professional season in 1977, his fifth year, when he caught 39 passes for an average of 46.9 yards per game. By 1978, Stingley stood poised for certain NFL stardom.

Adversity ended his career in that 1978 preseason, but it did not define Darryl Stingley as a man because he dedicated the remainder of his life to good works, setting up a foundation to aid at-risk youths in his hometown of Chicago, a humanitarian as revered as Ron Burton. He served as the Pats' player personnel director and earned his college degree in 1992, and with Mark Mulvoy wrote a book titled *Happy to be Alive*. Though Darryl struggled mightily with his situation, he ultimately concluded that "I have relived that moment over and over again. It was only after I stopped asking why that I was able to regroup and go on with my life." Darryl Stingley died on April 5, 2007, as Patriots Nation mourned its fine receiver, the finest of men.

27 Get a Burger and a Bucket at Lewis'

It is hard to get to and difficult to find even if you have stopped by before, but Lewis' Restaurant and Grill deserves a visit; it is a true Massachusetts historic treasure, no less cherished than the Freedom Trail or Plymouth Rock. Nestled on a side street in the center of Norwood—92 Central Street to be precise—it started out as a classic New England diner in the 1940s and remains a very popular spot for sports fans and for aficionados of good old-fashioned bar-and-grill fare.

Although Lewis' expanded and added modern dining and function facilities in the 1990s, it has not strayed far from its roots as a sports bar before there was such a thing. The older section, containing a long bar and stools along the side with some tables, doles out the fare for the longer-term customers. A tasteless painting or two adorn the walls but they are largely ignored, and someday hopefully they will vanish.

The signature dish is the Lewis Burger, about which a Brockton native once noted, "Don't worry about what's inside, just eat it, it's great." The mystery of the Lewis Burger is not so vexing since they now tell patrons in the menu what constitutes one; aside from the burger and bun, it reportedly contains egg salad, ham, onion, lettuce, tomato, and mayonnaise. It works.

Also, when ordering a beer, ask for a "bucket" and you will receive an ice-cold 16-ounce beer.

A number of burger variations and steak tip orders dot the menu, but Lewis' also serves some serious seafood, such as swordfish, scallops, salmon, haddock, shrimp scampi, baked stuffed shrimp, and lobster roll. Seafood is baked, boiled, or fried, and a large part of the menu contains Italian food dishes. A heretical group insists that the pizza even tastes better than the Lewis Burger itself.

A bit hard to get to, even more difficult to forget, Lewis', like Worcester's Wonder Bar, still stands several decades after its founding as a jewel of friendly New England dining, a great place to meet people and talk football.

28 Steve Grogan

If you grew up in New England in the 1970s or early 1980s, your father loved Steve Grogan, and long after you ceased even trying to listen to the old man about going to church or going to bed early or turning down the damned stereo, you still knew that somehow he knew what he was talking about when he spoke of the quarterback's greatness.

My father was a veteran of World War II, and he worked for the same company and hated his job for more than 30 years until even that security disappeared. Despite his difficulties he always posted for work, figuring that if Steve could suit up for a game with a sundry of serious and chronic injuries, the least he could do was get in the car and work a full day himself.

Statistically, Grogan will not overpower fantasy purists. For instance, during a career that began in 1975 and ended in 1990, he completed 182 touchdown passes at the expense of throwing 208 interceptions. He never played in a single Pro Bowl, and yet with the exception of Tom Brady and Drew Bledsoe, most Pats players and fans consider him the finest quarterback in team history.

Reality meets fantasy when factoring in his prodigious leadership skills, as he praised his teammates and urged them to improve their games, and he took hits and blamed no one else. Irving Fryar once stated that he considered Grogan the top quarterback he ever played for—even better than Dan Marino—due to Grog's ability to get along with teammates and bring out their best efforts. High praise, but also a realistic assessment.

Indeed, one of the serious misconceptions is that because Grogan hails from Kansas, he somehow possesses a taciturn and humorless demeanor, the kind of fellow who peppers his conversation with phrases like "where I come from we shoot first and talk later." A man for whom every waking moment is a series of tests, like Gary Cooper in *High Noon*. The Steve Grogan of reality is an intelligent guy and a seasoned conversationalist, someone who loves a good story and loves to laugh, another reason why his teammates fought for him.

Chosen in the fifth round of the 1975 draft (simply hoping at the time to "stay around long enough to make a strong enough impression so that when I got cut I might be able to catch on with somebody else"), he replaced starting quarterback Jim Plunkett about midway through that rookie season, a testament equally to Grogan's leadership skills even at that stage in his professional career and the need for Plunkett to reinvent himself on the West Coast where he felt most comfortable. As New England converted into a more run-oriented offense and Grogan continued to mature, the club traded Plunkett to the 49ers, one of their finest transactions ever as the club scored on the draft picks they obtained in return. For the next decade, the Patriots became Grogan's team while coaches came and went.

Grogan flat-out ran the ball well, as demonstrated by his 4.9 yards-per-carry career average and his 35 career rushing touchdowns. And no NFL quarterback approached the 12 rushing touchdowns he accumulated in 1976 until Cam Newton broke it with 14 in 2011. That final stat bears out another strong fact about Grogan. The guy was tough. He once played through a season with a broken vertebrae in his neck.

In 1976 and 1978, he helped lead his team to the playoffs, running often but also exerting leadership by example, as he absorbed hit after hit from opposing defenders. Although the Patriots drafted Tony Eason out of Illinois in 1983 as Grogan's heir apparent, after a balky start in 1985 (with the team at 2–3) head coach Raymond Berry reinserted Grogan as his starter, a move that provided dividends. Grogan reinvigorated his offense and the Pats became a contender. Subsequently Grogan broke his leg, though the club made its first Super Bowl that year.

Facing the Bears in Super Bowl XX, Eason started poorly, failing to connect once to a receiver, so Grogan was again called into the breach. Although the strong Bears defense mauled the Patriots that game, Grogan at least provided stability, completing 17 of his 30 passes.

Although the Patriots enjoyed a decent 1986 regular season, the team struggled during the final years of the decade, a period that became professionally taxing for Grogan. During the brief tragicomedy that constituted the Victor Kiam era, Grogan was told that he had to sign a waiver to play due to his precarious physical state. Grogan refused.

In 1990, the Pats' 1–15 record was a dismal epitaph to their star quarterback's career, as he retired after having played 16 injury-wracked and pain-filled seasons, a franchise record. He also owned most of the club's all-time quarterback records, and although Bledsoe and Brady have broken many of them, neither one of these later QBs could approach Grogan's prowess on the field as a running back, and probably no one ever will. A member of the Patriots' All-Decade teams for the 1970s and 1980s, he is also a member of the Patriots Hall of Fame.

Appreciating Steve Grogan does not require blind faith but it does require faith, something his teammates always had in him. So when your father or grandfather tells you how great Steve Grogan was as a player, know this: the old man is not lying to you.

Gronk

Even a demure Aaron Hernandez remarked about the relative wildness of Rob Gronkowski's 2013 summer. While Hernandez allegedly chilled, Gronk had already burnished an impressive off the field resume of unrestrained fun. And just released, there was a book written about him and his family titled *Growing Up Gronk*.

Gronk has been photographed wearing nothing but a strategically placed football, thankfully full of air and not deflated. He danced shirtless in Vegas at club named XS and wrestled a friend, proving that whatever happens in Vegas does not necessarily stay in Vegas. And don't forget that he spent some quality time during a bye week with an adult film star, tore up the Espys one year, and danced shirtless after a Super Bowl loss on a bum ankle.

He also has played with back injuries and a forearm that naggingly requires surgery, works out when other teammates are at home, and drives a defender like Sergio Brown out of the club. And won a Comeback Player of the Year Award. Traditionally, Belichick and free spirits clash, but Gronkowski possesses too much talent and works too hard to spend any time in a dog house. Plus he connects with Tom Brady.

Rob Gronkowski holds the Lombardi Trophy aloft after defeating the Seattle Seahawks 28–24 to win Super Bowl XLIX. (Photo courtesy of AP Images/Tom DiPace)

And he is compiling a body of work on the field that, if he can stay relatively healthy, may make him a consensus choice as the greatest tight end in NFL history.

Even when covered well, he gets free, he reads Tom Brady better than receivers brought onto the team with Pro Bowl credentials elsewhere and he gains yard after he catches. No man his size should moves so fluidly and quickly.

But then watch some videos of Rob Gronkowski blocking, and while the analysis of his talent in this area is necessarily more subjective, he is without peer in this area, a throwback to the Mike Ditka era. The Pats won their most recent Super Bowl with a renewed dedication to the running game and much credit must be given to their superstar tight end. You won't see this in a Gronk highlight film, which all rightly focus on this athletic and sure-handed receiver, punctuating his excellence with spikes in the end zone. To appreciate his blocking prowess, rewatch a Pats' game and focus on Gronk during a running play.

And he scores touchdowns—96th all-time in receiving TDs in the NFL after only five, sometimes injury-marred seasons. Again, the Patriots won their most recent Super Bowl because they scored touchdowns and did not settle for field goals. And because they had a healthy Rob Gronkowski.

30 Steals

Unlike most other sports, football clubs make very few stinker trades because relatively rarely do two teams swap established players for one another. Veterans are more likely to be swapped for draft picks, and those trades go only as well or as ghastly as the careers of the future considerations.

In the spring of 2007, the Pats made two of their most lop-sided deals. In March, they picked up the Dolphins' Wes Welker for draft choices and continued the fleecing a month later, this time duping Oakland into trading them Randy Moss for a fourth rounder. These coups came a few years after the club had obtained Corey Dillon from Cincinnati for a second-round choice.

Of course, beauty—or the lack thereof—does lie in the eye of the beholder. After three-plus seasons of superlative statistics, the team dumped Moss in midseason to the Minnesota Vikings for a third-round draft choice.

The new millennium constitutes the most fruitful decades for trades. In addition to the aforementioned deals, the club obtained Ted Washington for a fourth-round pick in 2003 and also obtained the rights to picks used to draft Asante Samuel and Vince Wilfork.

Historically, the Pats do not have batches of great trades, generally receiving equivalent value for their swaps. In the 1960s, the club fleeced lineman Houston Antwine from the Oilers for what we would now term a second-day draft pick, and certainly obtaining Babe Parilli saved the team during its formative years.

This changed with the team's finest blockbuster trade, which occurred in April 1976 when they unloaded disgruntled quarterback Jim Plunkett on San Francisco for Tom Owen and a number of draft choices, later used to select offensive lineman Pete Brock, safety Tim Fox, cornerback Raymond Clayborn, and running back Horace Ivory. Plunkett did not play that well for the 49ers and though he redeemed himself with the Raiders, the Pats still traded well.

The 1980s did not produce a truly lopsided trade, but in 1996 Tedy Bruschi came aboard through a shrewd draft-day deal with the Lions, as did Kevin Faulk a few years later via the Titans. While some frustrated fans express exasperation with Bill Belichick's endless finagling and dropping down for value during drafts, fact is, the new millennium is the golden age for profitable trades.

31 Allegedly Aaron Hernandez

On July 16, 2012, Daniel Jorge Correia de Abreu and Safiro Texeira Furtado were murdered, shot to death in the South End of Boston. On June 17, 2013, in another section of the city, Odin Lloyd was picked up in a car and later murdered, his body left in a suburban industrial park.

Seemingly unconnected, all these crimes were attributed to Patriots' star tight end Aaron Hernandez, with indictments against him issued in all instances.

In disgust, the Patriots promptly released Hernandez after his first arrest. Briefly a fad called Hernandezing erupted on the net, common people posting selfies of themselves in imitation of Hernandez holding a gun or being perp-walked out of his house with his handcuffed hands covered by his undershirt.

But most people simply wondered why, why three young innocent people had their lives ended, particularly at the alleged hands of one of the wealthiest athletes in the world.

Unlike the O.J. Simpson case, where the former Bills back had allegedly murdered his ex-wife and a man who happened to be at the wrong place, Hernandez was alleged to have murdered two strangers and a casual friend. And allegedly shot out the eye of another friend in a separate incident. Crimes committed seemingly with no motive.

There will be no requiem for this tough guy, other than rounds of trials and appeals with occasional appearances in expensive suits and impeccable hair styling. Abandoned by most of his fans, he sustains an odd cult of loyalists consisting of internet weirdos, thugs, goblins, women who have been jilted at the altar by Charles Manson, macabre jock wannabes, folks who never leave their basements, and autograph hounds. In other words, pretty much the same types of friends he surrounded himself with before he started eating for free.

32 Bill Goes for It on 4th and 2

Since Bill Belichick began his tenure in New England—a period graced by three championships in his first five years—most fans subscribe to the slogan "In Bill We Trust" with few exceptions. Restlessness has arisen in Patriots Nation since the last Super Bowl

Kevin Faulk was stopped short on a controversial 4th-and-2 play against the Indianapolis Colts in Week 10 of the 2009 NFL season.

victory, however, and a new period of questioning has emerged, one where the infallibility of the coach is at issue.

Most notably, the second-guessing of Belichick formally began after his decision on November 16, 2009, to have his offense attempt a play against the Indianapolis Colts on 4th and 2 from their own 28-yard line. The game was played at Lucas Oil Stadium, and the Pats were nursing a six-point lead with 2:08 remaining. For those of you who do not want the surprise spoiled or have subsisted in an unceasing state of denial since, skip ahead. Virtually no one would have challenged the call if it had worked, which of course it did not, as Peyton Manning proceeded to march his Colts the short distance down the field for the win.

Promisingly, the Patriots had played quite well in the dome during the first three quarters, leading by 17 points early in the fourth and having thoroughly outplayed the Colts on offense.

During the first five years of the millennium, the Patriots always seemed to have just enough talent or savvy to narrowly defeat the Colts, but New England's defense no longer possessed the type of smart, veteran players who always had the ability to stifle Manning when necessary. To win, the Pats had to stage a shootout, scoring more than their young and porous defense inevitably allowed. In idyllic times, Belichick's veterans seemingly always held a lead.

Problem was, Belichick had traded Richard Seymour to the Raiders before the season and also disposed of linebacker Mike Vrabel. Without these types of players, the club simply did not possess enough defense to match Tom Brady's prolific offense. That is the way that many fans saw the situation, and perhaps the head coach had begun to feel the same way.

To Err Is Human...

One reason it is rarely advisable to play Monday morning quarterback against Bill Belichick is that some fans and analysts contend that the infamous 4th-and-2 play actually worked. View the play on the Internet and you can see why adherents of the local Flat Earth Society, Bill is God Chapter, see what they want to see: that the refs blew the call. Kevin Faulk had the ball in first-down territory, but he did not have firm possession of it until he was tackled and came up short. Unchastened by criticism, Bill did it again on October 24, 2010; on 4th and 1 from his own 49-yard line, he went for it with the Patriots ahead of the San Diego Chargers 23–20 and just two minutes remaining in regulation. Brady handed off to BenJarvus Green-Ellis who was hit behind the line of scrimmage for a loss. The Chargers took over possession on downs, and advanced the ball deeper into Patriots territory. With time running out, the Chargers elected to kick a game-tying field goal to send the game into overtime. Unfortunately for San Diego, they were penalized five yards, meaning their kicker, Kris Brown, had to now make a 50-yard field goal. Brown kicked the ball long enough but it hit the goalpost off to his right and clanged off harmlessly. The Patriots won, and Belichick's judgment was affirmed. Sort of. In Bill we trust.

In the game with the Colts, logic dictated that Belichick should have called out his punter and forced the Colts to score a touchdown from a safe distance, perhaps as far as 60 or 70 yards. He did not, and to compound the confusion, the punter had already trotted onto the field before Belichick called a timeout.

The Patriots were going for it. Brady took the snap in the shotgun formation and whipped a bullet to Kevin Faulk on his right. Faulk had the yardage but Colts safety Melvin Bullitt smacked him, and by the time Faulk had stopped juggling the ball, he was tackled short of the first-down marker. It took just four plays for Manning to engineer the winning touchdown for Indianapolis.

The call by Belichick did not bring out every Monday morning (or evening) quarterback in New England so much as it permitted fans to take the bolder step of becoming amateur psychologists. Or for the literarily inspired, it encouraged fans to analyze Belichick as some flawed Shakespearean protagonist. To go for it on 4th and 2 from the 28, that is the question.

Ignoring the point that if the play had worked, those same analysts would have lauded Belichick's genius, the fact that the play failed exposed Belichick as a very human figure. He did not know all, and he could make a very bad mistake. Particularly in the confused state of affairs that preceded the play, he should have punted. Was he arrogant, out of it, deluded? Had the spirit of onetime Red Sox coach Grady Little possessed him?

Even Belichick did not seem to know why he did it.

Colts defensive end Dwight Freeney might have had the sagest perspective on the debacle: "It even happens in video games. You go for it on fourth down when you're not supposed to and something bad happens." In Patriots Nation, Bill Belichick had lost his invincibility.

33 Bam

Nicknamed "Bam," Sam Cunningham's moniker only partially defined him. Yes, he could plow through a line and had the weight and power to do so, but he did so much more. If you did not have the privilege of seeing him play during his college or pro career, watch some film of him, particularly how he utilized his legs. To gain yardage he leaped over people, propelled himself to great speeds, and even if he knew he was being tackled, his legs often shot up into a defender's chops to make certain he gave better than he got. He more closely resembled his brother Randall, the elusive star quarterback for Philadelphia, than he did an uncreative battering ram fullback.

A Rose Bowl Hall of Famer—having scored four touchdowns in a Rose Bowl game as a back for USC—Cunningham earned All-American honors in 1972. One story has it that Alabama speeded up its integration efforts after Cunningham embarrassed a team that Tide detergent could not have made any whiter in 1970. Unfortunately, the story lacks the essential element of truth; Bear Bryant had already recruited his first African American player, Wilbur Jackson, who did not suit up in that contest due to freshman ineligibility. However, if skeptical Alabama fans needed any evidence integration had come and was a very good thing, Cunningham alleviated them of any misconceptions that day.

He also excelled during a particularly prominent era in Trojans history for running backs from the mid-1960s to the early 1980s, which featured fleet stars such as Mike Garrett, O.J. Simpson, Anthony Davis, Charles White, and Marcus Allen. Although he specialized more as a blocking fullback in college, Cunningham distinguished himself enough as a runner that in their magnificent

1973 draft, the Pats chose Sam along with John Hannah and Darryl Stingley in the first round (and picked up Ray Hamilton in the 14th), laying a strong foundation for some of the very good teams of the 1970s and '80s. As a professional, he outplayed many of the more heralded products out of Southern Cal.

Cunningham got to work right away, rushing for more than 500 yards in his rookie season and then followed that effort up with 811 yards on the ground for a 4.9 yards-per-attempt average in his second year. As he matured, Sam became a threat at receiver as well, pulling down 210 receptions in his career. In 1974, Cunningham did not even lead the team in rushing despite his terrific efforts, as diminutive Mack Herron slightly outgained him. It was all to the general good though, as the Pats that year finished 7–7, not bad for a club that posted losing records for the previous seven seasons.

The Pats stunk in 1975, but in the Bicentennial Year, coach Chuck Fairbanks had molded quite a powerful club as evidenced by an 11–3 record. Paired this time with back Andy Johnson, Cunningham gained 824 yards for a 4.8 yards-per-attempt average, and only a controversial loss to Oakland in the playoffs kept this edition from perhaps contending for their first Super Bowl title. Sam also finished second on the team for pass receptions with 27.

Need further proof of Cunningham's versatile elegance and excellence? In 1977, he led the Pats in receptions with 42 (accounting for more than 25 percent of the entire team's production) while rushing for more than 1,000 yards. Inexplicably, he did not earn Pro Bowl recognition that year, although he did the next season, with less production. Of course, in the 1970s New England famously did not handle success well, with Chuck Fairbanks ruining their playoff run that year with the announcement he intended to take on the role of head coach at the University of Colorado.

The Pats and Cunningham both produced in 1979, but by the next year their fortunes had plunged and Bam did not play a down. He returned in 1981 and 1982, but by then the club had begun to rely on younger backs such as Vagas Ferguson, Don Calhoun, and Tony Collins. Despite this phase-out, he still overran defenders, a point clearly made with his then-rookie teammate, future Hall of Famer Andre Tippett, who recalled his first meeting with Sam in training camp, "The offense called a run play, so John Hannah came pulling around and my head started shifting back and forth. Then I looked straight and here came Sam. And he hit me. Everybody on the sideline got quiet and all you heard was, 'Ooh.' That's all I heard when I was on the ground."

Sam's career ended before the 1983 season, but New England had not said good-bye to him. At their first preseason game in 2010 against the defending Super Bowl champion New Orleans Saints, the Pats honored Sam Cunningham as their most recent inductee in the Patriots Hall of Fame.

34 The Undefeated Season

Despite narrowly losing to Indianapolis in the AFC Championship Game, the New England Patriots' 2006 season went down as a massive disappointment for virtually everyone who cared about the team. With each succeeding year, that 2006 campaign feels more and more like a fiasco, this for a fan base that grew accustomed to Lombardi Trophies, not 12–4 seasons with two playoff wins.

With every action a counter-reaction invariably occurs, none more so than the club that Bill Belichick assembled for the 2007 season. Dissatisfied with the low productivity of receivers such as Reche Caldwell, Jabar Gaffney, and second-round draft choice Chad Jackson, the coach embarked on a shopping spree for gifted receivers, netting Randy Moss, Wes Welker, and Donte Stallworth.

Running back Corey Dillon's three-year tenure with the club—and his NFL career—ended, but Sammy Morris came aboard to join Kevin Faulk and a still-promising Laurence Maroney in the backfield. Once again, Tom Brady had weapons and options.

Defensively, Belichick added linebacker Adalius Thomas to stiffen an already staunch defense, and while that move backfired, the club still had very effective backers in Mike Vrabel, Roosevelt Colvin, and the inspirational Tedy Bruschi. Richard Seymour, Vince Wilfork, and Ty Warren formed the finest defensive line in the league, while Rodney Harrison and Asante Samuel anchored the defensive secondary. Barring injuries, the team had every expectation of returning to the Super Bowl.

David Tyree's miraculous "helmet catch" in Super Bowl XLII prevented the Patriots from posting the second undefeated championship season in NFL history.

No one seriously predicted an undefeated regular season, given the relative perceived decline in the team due to the previous season's finale and a shaky performance in the preseason. But as former Red Sox reliever Sammy Stewart once said, the preseason games "don't mean dog," a point punctuated by the Patriots winning their first game of the regular season, a 38–14 pasting of the Jets in the Meadowlands.

Yet as the denizens of Patriots Nation soon learned, the win over New York and former Pats assistant Eric Mangini came with swift consequences: the emergence of the notorious Spygate scandal, whereby the league confiscated a camera on the Pats' sideline used to tape the Jets during the game, an act prohibited by the league. The issue engulfed the team and eventually cost both the club and Belichick a lot of money in fines and the loss of a future first-round draft choice.

Counterintuitively, the club responded in its next game with a blowout win over the Chargers, a challenger that would eventually win the AFC West. The explosive wins kept coming in the next six games, with the Pats ripping apart the Bills (38–7), Bengals (34–13), Browns (34–17), Cowboys (48–27), Dolphins (49–28), and finally the Redskins (52–7). By the time the club had humiliated Washington, Belichick's men had become the neighborhood bullies, seemingly delighting in rolling up a huge score against their adversaries with embarrassing ease. The Patriots did narrowly defeat the Colts in their ninth game, but went into their bye week comfortably poised to continue to overrun their adversaries.

Relaxed and refitted, the Patriots continued to dominate, defeating Buffalo 56–10, but by this time a pinch of hubris may have seeped into the team's successful recipe, as Brady and Moss went about pursuing passing and receiving touchdown records. Thereafter, the competition stiffened, and while the Pats won their next six games to complete an undefeated perfect season, in three of their last six games they only bested their foe by three points.

A Little Perspective, Please
Sudden and senseless tragedies spare no one, professional athletes included. On May 27, 2007, popular defensive lineman Marquise Hill died accidentally while riding a jet ski with a friend in Lake Pontchartrain in New Orleans. He had saved his friend, Ashley Blazio, before succumbing. His teammates wore his number 91 on their uniforms all that ensuing season.

Perhaps the other franchises had begun to catch up to the Patriots' offensive schemes, or maybe New England had forgotten what had made it great in the early half of the decade. No matter, when they narrowly defeated the Giants in their last regular season game, the undefeated had begun to look vincible.

Prototypically, the club had skated through the playoffs when they won their past titles, with a three-point victory reserved for their triumphant Super Bowl victories. In their division championship game against Jacksonville (a 31–20 win) and their conference championship victory (by a mere 21–12 margin, with the Chargers intercepting Brady three times), Wes Welker and Kevin Faulk constituted receiving threats, though ominously, Randy Moss had disappeared. They won, but they did not humiliate their opponents as they so often had in the past.

Moss rebounded in the Super Bowl a bit and the indomitable Welker and Faulk continued to excel under pressure, but running back Maroney had a dismal day as the Giants' strong defensive line harassed Brady all day. Dumb luck came into play as well, with Eli Manning completing a key heave to David Tyree late in the game, while Samuel dropped a certain game-ending interception. The Pats lost 17–14.

The Patriots had finally fallen despite their gallant efforts throughout the year, spearheaded by eight Pro Bowl invitees. Oh, the humanity!

35 Hail the Chef at the Eire Pub

In the very early 1960s, two institutions came to Boston: the Patriots and the Eire Pub. While the ownership of the local football club has shifted around since then, the Eire Pub remains in the Stenson family. Thomas Stenson founded the pub, and although he has since "gone to glory," as many of his Irish patrons say, his son John continues to operate one of Boston's enduring treasures.

Don't have tickets to Sunday's game? Just drive over to Adams Village in the Dorchester district of Boston and stop by the Eire Pub. You cannot miss it as it sits next to an American Legion Post with either a howitzer or naval gun out front. "Eire" is pronounced "eerie," though a less sinister place does not exist. It more closely resembles another renowned Boston gathering place from the turn of an earlier century, Nuf Ced McGreevy's Third Base Saloon in Roxbury.

On any given day, the Eire stands out as a friendly pub, with the bartenders making everyone from lawyers to bricklayers feel welcome. No one gets out of hand and no one remembers a fight even taking place there. Troublemakers are not allowed back in, ever.

There is no bad time to visit the Eire, advertised as Boston's Original Gentleman's Prestige Bar, and what makes it an appealing sports bar is that it does not try to be one, it has set the standard for too long. Yes, you have access to five televisions along the long horseshoe bar together with six sets along the walls, but instead of serving generic sports bar glop, the Eire still plates ham and cheese sandwiches, BLTs, and club sandwiches. And although they do not overcharge for their fare, the staff is serious about the food it sells,

Famous Faces at the Eire

Since the Patriots moved from Boston to suburban Foxboro, few team members hang out in neighborhood bars any longer, but team owner Bob Kraft has stopped by at the Eire occasionally, once commenting on the need to have more Patriots memorabilia on the premises.

Still, you might have a better chance of seeing a president there, as Ronald Reagan and Bill Clinton have both visited, in addition to Bertie Ahern, the former Prime Minister of Ireland. Photos of Clinton (with Boston mayor Ray Flynn) dot a wall at the Eire, albeit with no bronzed remembrance of his appearance, perhaps because by the time he came by, a drop-in by a president was no longer that unusual an event.

with a giant "Play Like a Champion Today" plaque over the kitchen door, the motto of the football team of the owner's alma mater.

On Sundays when the Patriots play, the staff wheels out a huge buffet during halftime, consisting of about a dozen boxes of pizza and buckets of Chinese food, all free of charge to its patrons. Not a scrap of food remains by the time of the second half kickoff, but if you choose to experience the game-day atmosphere do come early, as the seating capacity restrictions impose limits for latecomers and casual fans. No one leaves the Eire unhappy.

36 Raymond, Meet Will

Dozens of local reporters from both the print and electronic media have covered the Patriots, perhaps none so prominently as the late Will McDonough. When it came to owners or coaches or players, Will never seemed to have a neutral thought about any of them. Some of his worst brushes came with baseball players, with Will verbally jousting with Mo Vaughn and Roger Clemens, the advantage always lying with McDonough.

What separated McDonough from so many of his colleagues was his ability to accumulate reliable sources, particularly in league suites or front offices of sports franchises. He parlayed this knack to a stint on national television, not bad for a tough kid from South Boston.

As it relates to Patriots history, McDonough got caught up in the lingering tensions between team owner Bob Kraft and head coach Bill Parcells in what ultimately culminated in the Big Tuna's last year in New England. At first, McDonough tried to mediate, but when that did not work, he reported Parcells' discontent at the particularly sensitive point just before the club's second trip to the Super Bowl. McDonough always cornered his story and had an entertaining and sharp way of conveying it to his readers.

Yet in all of his pointed and professional years of reporting, his best moment may have occurred after the Patriots' 56–3 victory over the Jets in the second week of the 1979 campaign. Taking exception at what he perceived as the surly behavior of star defensive back Raymond Clayborn, he called him on it. Clayborn got into McDonough's face, allegedly poking the reporter in the eye with a finger.

Although accounts vary widely on what next occurred, most agree that McDonough drew on his ingrained street smarts and proceeded to take a swing at Clayborn and lay him out. McDonough had just taken the step that hundreds of sportswriters had dreamed of taking since the day that rugby turned into football.

A couple of last thoughts on McDonough and this brief altercation. Reportedly with his eye discolored and in pain, Will prepared his report for his employer, the *Boston Globe*, for the next morning's edition. He also supposedly later became friends with his former sparring mate. As for Clayborn, he forever more walked with a merry step and a sweet tune in his ear, saving his greatest hits for opponents on the gridiron.

37 Spygate

Spygate was an embarrassing and wholly avoidable chapter in club history, centering around the taping of the opponent's sideline during a game in a supposed effort to steal their signals. The NFL had implemented a clear written policy concerning what it prohibited, but the Patriots ignored it and did so at their considerable peril at a September 9, 2007, game against the New York Jets. The Jets had hired former Bill Belichick assistant Eric Mangini as their head coach, and not coincidentally NFL officials confiscated the recording device during that game.

The Original Spygate?

The Pats, back in their Boston Patriots days, were also the alleged victim of some espionage directed against them by the San Diego Chargers. The late Will McDonough of the *Boston Globe* oft related a story about Chargers head coach Sid Gillman telling Pats head coach Mike Holovak that he should practice his men at a naval installation just prior to the 1963 AFL title game. Supposedly the Chargers dressed up some spies as sailors and thus knew what the Pats meant to do on every play during the championship contest, a game won by the Chargers 51–10. Of course, it had nothing to do with the Chargers playing at home after posting an 11–3 regular season record against a Boston team that finished 7–6–1.

Don't feel too bad for the Patriots; a non-sanctioned form of cheating took place in the early 1960s during a game against the Dallas Texans, nee the Chiefs. The Texans had the ball deep inside Patriots territory, and as the teams set up for the play, a fan raced through the end zone and lined up at linebacker, just out of the peripheral view of the referee in the center of the field. The Texans' Cotton Davidson dropped back to pass and threw the ball not to the intended receiver but rather to the fan, who promptly knocked it down. That was the AFL.

The league ultimately found against the Patriots, fining the club $250,000 and Belichick $500,000. In addition, the club lost its first-round draft pick for 2008. It is unclear what value, if any, the Patriots ever received from these tapes. Certainly if someone could hastily review them during halftime, they might be able to match a call to a play, but this assumes the other team did not know it was being spied on and would not change some signals during halftime.

In addition to the penalties inflicted by the NFL, the harm extended to sullying the achievements of the team both that year and in previous campaigns. It permitted every Patriots critic to claim that the team only won because it cheated, and Belichick himself soon earned the moniker "Belicheat."

Such criticism misses the wider issue of why the club so brazenly departed from the spirit and clear letter of the league policy, particularly when considering the fact that the risks of getting caught clearly outweighed the paltry and dubious benefits obtained. It also introduced a win-at-all-costs element to the team's success, an unnecessary credo since the club had first-rate management and players.

In response to the league's edict and criticism from the media, the club spent the remainder of the 2007 season running up the score mercilessly against weaker opponents, punctuating the point that they did not need to cheat to win.

38 Good Things Come in Small Packages

Collect bubble gum cards long enough and one sees that linemen went from a respectable if not staunch 235 pounds per man to behemoths easily exceeding 300 pounds, with concurrent increases in height and bone mass. Iconoclastically, Bill Belichick has often pursued the course less traveled, judiciously choosing ballplayers over body sizes to the considerable advantage of his team.

As a secondary coach for the New York Jets from 1997 through 1999, he undoubtedly saw diminutive receiver Wayne Chrebet chew up his teammates in practices and opponents in games, despite measuring just 5'10". But Chrebet had already starred for the Jets before Belichick got there, parlaying a genie's wish granted to him after departing from a lightly regarded Hofstra squad to snare 84 receptions in 1996.

Belichick merely eschewed a dogmatic approach to what an NFL football player had to look like once the Patriots hired him, a considerable risk since now Belichick had to defend all of his decisions. This considered impulse caused him to hire Doug Flutie as a 43-year-old backup quarterback in 2005, and after watching Flutie drop-kick the ball in practice, Belichick decided to test this technique out during a live game on an extra-point attempt. Flutie took the snap, dropped the ball on the turf, and then booted it through the uprights for the first score on a drop-kick in an NFL game since December 21, 1941, when "Scooter" McLean performed the feat in a title game. "Flutie might have been there the last time it happened," joked Adam Vinatieri of his seasoned teammate.

Four years later, when an early season injury to back Kevin Faulk terminated his season abruptly, former Jet Danny Woodhead netted considerable attention when he came to New England and played well immediately despite his 5'9" size and a college career spent at Chadron State. Tom Brady playfully joked about his tiny new back, but Woodhead is actually listed as an inch taller than Faulk, the man he replaced. Belichick had relied on Faulk for so long and so justifiably that many Pats fans could be excused for overlooking Faulk's actual height, given the stature at which he always played.

And what about 5'9" receiver Wes Welker, catching more than 100 passes, many in traffic in the middle of the field?

Obviously the days of the 235-pound guard, with his hands crooked and staring over into a faux television screen on a Topps football card, have long since ended, but Belichick has found very valuable and fearless players in the backfield and in the defensive secondary more than equal to the task of calling themselves Patriots.

39 Harpo

One of the most enduring and popular characters in Patriots history is Bob Gladieux, also known as Harpo, because he looked a lot like Harpo Marx. Even before he turned professional, his reputation as a frequent libation partner of Notre Dame quarterback Terry Hanratty and fellow back Ron Dushney preceded him. He never denied attending his share of parties, but in the 1966 NCAA national championship game, he caught a pass from Coley O'Brien for the Irish's only touchdown in their 10–10 tie at Michigan State. Although the 1966 cast of Hanratty, Gladieux, Larry Conjar, and Rocky Bleier is not as renowned as other Notre Dame backfields such as the Four Horsemen and the Forgotten Four, all four had NFL careers.

Gladieux's was by far the most interesting. Picked in the eighth round of the 1969 draft, he played most of the next four years with the Patriots, suiting up for two games with the Bills along the way. He only gained 239 yards from scrimmage in his entire career, but his rookie season coincided with the first year of head coach Clive Rush's tenure, another free spirit if there ever was one.

Rush had cut him, and Gladieux manfully attended the next Pats game at Harvard Stadium with a friend. When the friend left his seat to buy some refreshments, the PA announcer called Gladieux to the dressing room, where he immediately became a member of the club. While the whole crowd watched the game in astonishment from the stands, Harpo made the first tackle of the game on the opening kickoff.

After Rush left the team, John Mazur became head coach and Harpo played a role in one of the more interesting episodes of local sports annals. Running back Duane Thomas had just come to Boston via a trade with Dallas, and Mazur called on Gladieux to show Thomas some formations and some stances he was expected to use on the field. It did not get far, as Thomas resolutely refused to get into the stance, soon finding the next flight back to Dallas. Not even Bob Gladieux was that independent.

The Patriots once had whole rosters of Harpos, characters who experienced good times off the field but always prepared to answer the call on the gridiron. Before God called him to the mountain, receiver Irving Fryar got into more trouble more often than Eddie Haskell, sometimes involving fellow end Hart Lee Dykes. In Fryar's case, however, his antics did not resemble thrill-seeking so much as the acts of a fundamentally decent man seeking something better in life. And Harpo? He is a successful businessman and family man in South Bend, Indiana.

40 The Second Super Bowl Victory

The defending champion New England Patriots embarrassed themselves in 2002, posting a mediocre 9–7 record, "good" for a three-way tie in a weak division. The offense played well enough, hovering around 10th in the league in scoring, with Tom Brady directing an offense fueled by a still-effective Antowain Smith and very good receivers and tight ends, including Troy Brown (97 catches), Deion Branch, David Patten, Christian Fauria, and rookie Daniel Graham. It was the defense that began springing leaks, a deficiency that Bill Belichick partially filled in before the 2003 season by importing massive nose tackle Ted Washington, who fit in right away in the club's gap-closing schemes. With Washington, he did not close gaps in the line so much as ensure that they never existed at all.

Exasperatingly, safety Lawyer Milloy had gone from star to someone who took up space without filling it, so Belichick dumped him and replaced him with Rodney Harrison, a hitter who quickly personified the toughness that the team wished to project on defense. Although he seemed to get worse each year he played in the NFL, draft pick Eugene Wilson also helped Harrison and Ty Law establish a shut-down secondary. In one year, the club went from having a porous defense to the one that surrendered the least amount of points in 2003.

The season did not start off well, as ESPN's Tom Jackson claimed that the players hated Belichick, and on opening day, expatriate Patriots Drew Bledsoe and Lawyer Milloy helped contribute to a 31–0 waxing of New England. The game seemed to presage a team collapse, but outside of a narrow loss to the Redskins, New England won all of its remaining games. Fittingly, the Pats faced Buffalo in the final game of the regular season and this time they turned the tables on the Bills by a 31–0 score. The club had finished with a 14–2 record and would face the Tennessee Titans in its playoff opener.

These two teams had squared off earlier in the fall, with New England barely eking out a victory. The Titans had exhausted back Eddie George (3.3 yards-per-carry average) and tight end Frank Wycheck (only 17 receptions), yet quarterback Steve McNair and receiver Derrick Mason still starred. On defense, Jevon Kearse surprised everyone who viewed football players only through the prism of size, as he thrived on the line with a young Albert Haynesworth.

Even by New England's wintry standards, the game conditions were abysmal; the wind chill made the temperature 10 degrees below zero before game time, an atmosphere so Antarctic that the club handed out free hand warmers and coffee to its fans. Very early in the game, Brady hooked up with rookie receiver Bethel Johnson for a 41-yard touchdown pass, but after that auspicious start the game devolved into a war of attrition, with McNair and the Titans bearing down late in the game in New England territory with the score knotted 14–14.

The Titans went into reverse with clumsy penalties and never threatened again. As they had so often, the Patriots relied on Adam Vinatieri to kick them to victory, a feat he accomplished with a 46-yard field goal for the 17–14 win and a berth in the AFC Championship Game. The attempt was not automatic; Vinatieri had atypically experienced difficulty all season converting from more than 30 yards out, and the frigid temperatures caused the game ball to almost literally become a rock. Still, when a team has the greatest clutch kicker in NFL history, the team is going to win, a point punctuated by admiring teammate Troy Brown who exclaimed, "He's money, man. That's why he makes all that money. That's why he's selling furniture on TV, and Fords, and all that other stuff."

Super Bowl Snafu

Only a beautiful woman can upstage Tom Brady, and during the halftime extravaganza of Super Bowl XXXVIII, Janet Jackson succeeded in doing so when she experienced her notorious "wardrobe malfunction" while performing with Justin Timberlake. Things got crazier later when a naked fan tried to line up for the play during a Panthers kickoff, but he had far less luck than Ms. Jackson. A Carolina player popped him and he was promptly apprehended.

The next week his team had to face a much more prominent television pitchman in the form of Peyton Manning, who in the Colts' two playoff wins had posted a combined quarterback rating of 156.9 (out of a perfect score of 158.3), briefly earning the sobriquet "Mr. Inhuman." The nickname never stuck because in the AFC Championship Game, Manning lofted four interceptions, three into the loving arms of Ty Law, a cornerback who bedeviled him for years.

Law deflected attention from himself and credited his quarterback, opining that "Tom Brady is the greatest winning quarterback in the league right now. What good are stats when you are sitting at home?" Brady distributed passes generously all afternoon to receivers Brown, Givens, and Branch, while Smith rolled up 100 yards rushing. Kudos also went out to Pats linemen Richard Seymour and Jarvis Green, who constantly executed incursions into the Colts' backfield throughout the game, causing turnovers and making Manning feel high anxiety. That left only the Carolina Panthers between the Patriots and a Super Bowl title.

While Manning has achieved sustained excellence throughout his tenure, it is difficult to recall now how effective Panthers quarterback Jake Delhomme was when he led his team that year. He had fine receivers in Steve Smith and Muhsin Muhammad, not to mention Ricky Proehl, while back Stephen Davis gained 1,444 yards that year. During the season the Panthers had racked up a deceiving 11–5 record, illusory because their offense during the course of that campaign barely outscored their opponents.

Their luck held out almost the entire game against the Pats as neither team scored until the second quarter. Before the half, Brady found Branch for a touchdown and later notched a second TD with David Givens on the receiving end for a 14–10 advantage. Boredom returned in the third quarter as neither team scored, but during the fourth quarter, each team lit up the scoreboard for one of the most thrilling finishes ever.

In the last minutes of the third quarter, Brady had directed a drive from his own 29-yard line that culminated in an Antowain Smith scoot for the touchdown and a 21–10 Patriots lead early in the fourth quarter. But then Delhomme and his best receiver, Steve Smith, started connecting on long passes, and the Panthers' DeShaun Foster ran for a 33-yard touchdown off the left side of his line. The only break New England caught was when the two-point conversion failed.

Leading 21–16, Brady led his teammates down to the Panthers' 9-yard line before disaster struck. The Panthers' Reggie Howard picked off a Brady pass near the end zone, and three plays later, Delhomme completed an 85-yard touchdown pass to Muhsin Muhammad. For the first time in 10 games, the Patriots trailed an opponent, 22–21.

After the Carolina kickoff, Brady did what he does best: leading drives down the field late in the contest. Starting from his own 32, Brady passed to seemingly every eligible receiver on his roster, with only three short running plays altering the plan of keeping the ball in the quarterback's hands. The drive culminated in a one-yard TD pass to "tight end" Mike Vrabel, and when Kevin Faulk ran the ball for the two points, New England led 29–21.

But then Delhomme took *his* team down the field, culminating the effort with a 12-yard scoring pass to Ricky Proehl, the same Proehl who had so bedeviled New England when he played for the Rams in the Super Bowl two years prior. The score was 29–29 with 1:13 left to play in regulation.

The Carolina Panthers had played over their heads all afternoon, but the Patriots still had Tom Brady and Adam Vinatieri to answer them. On the last great drive of the day, Brady completed three straight passes to Troy Brown, then found Daniel Graham for four yards and Deion Branch for 17 yards, to take his team to the Panthers' 23-yard line with nine seconds remaining.

Naturally, Vinatieri kicked the game winner, and the Patriots had a second Lombardi Trophy to display for their fans.

41 Tedy Bruschi

For Pats fans, February 16, 2005, threatened to augur the worst news regarding a popular player since Darryl Stingley's paralysis, for on that date beloved linebacker Tedy Bruschi suffered a stroke. Certainly he would never play again, and many despaired that he might not survive the ordeal. Not only did he survive, but he vowed to return to the playing field, a promise he kept for another four seasons after his stroke, earning the NFL's Comeback Player of the Year Award the next season.

Drafted by Bill Parcells with the team's third-round pick in 1996, Bruschi had excelled as a pass rusher/QB nemesis at Arizona, tying an NCAA career sack record with 52. But the brain trust in less visionary organizations passed on him because he seemed too small to play on the line of scrimmage and shake off 300-pound opposing linemen. Parcells placed him at linebacker, where the newcomer's keen sense of where the opponent meant to run or pass the ball usually led him to a fruitful target. Before too long, about half of Patriots Nation seemingly donned Bruschi jerseys at the team's home games.

As a signature, Bruschi became quite adept at intercepting passes and running them in for defensive touchdowns. He had developed such a sixth sense after repeated practice and review of opponents' keys that he could catch bare-handed a pass zipped by the quarterback in midair like he was catching a bullet. In 2002 and 2003, he returned two interceptions for touchdowns each

One of the most beloved players in franchise history, linebacker Tedy Bruschi spent his entire 13-year career with the Patriots.

campaign, and by 2004 he had finally been selected to his first Pro Bowl, an honor that he frankly had earned several seasons earlier.

Seemingly Tedy Bruschi had arrived, a player appreciated by NFL fans worldwide, no longer simply a local treasure. Then shockingly, Bruschi was admitted into Massachusetts General Hospital with the stroke diagnosis, felled not on the gridiron but in regenerating peacefully at home for the next training camp. Some years earlier the Red Sox lost the future services of promising pitcher Jeff Gray for the same reason, and most fans assumed that their beloved Patriots linebacker had also played his last game at the Pro Bowl.

Not so. He returned and played not only during that next year, but he also kept coming back, playing for three more years after that 2005 miraculous season, recording another 156 tackles. Finally, having played 13 seasons, he retired during the 2009 camp, a development that even choked up seemingly stoic head coach Bill Belichick.

The Bruschi story has a happy ending, as Tedy seamlessly left his linebacker spot to become a very insightful and fearless television commentator, at one point challenging the heart of some of his recent teammates on the Patriots defense. That's fine; he ticked off a bunch of them in the locker room when he still suited up, a small price to exact for urging everyone to commit one's whole self to the team. Fearless. That is who Tedy Bruschi was, is, and will forever be.

42 Attend a Victory Parade

In the event you have not formed part of the madding throngs at the previous three championship parades, it is more than past time for you to attend a victory parade along its route through the hopelessly mislaid Boston lanes. Unfortunately this is not something you can just pack up the station wagon with the family and do on a whim, the team has to win another title. That's not entirely true, if you go to a game, you can cheer louder for the home team.

Clustered around a four year period during which the team captured three titles,, the parades did not markedly differ from each other, centered around the players, coaches, owners and other lucky people cramming themselves on the tourist friendly amphibious Duck Boats. The players wave and the Lombardi trophy is held high, although earlier on Tom Brady and Bob Kraft danced badly in public.

By early 2005, it seemed that the victory parade had become ensconced into local tradition, along with such perennials as clams chowder, brick-laid sidewalks and the Boston Marathon, but then they abruptly stopped. Children who attended the rallies with their parents grew up and left home and worried about more weighty things like booze and hooking up and in rare sober moments, their futures. Once the sidewalks of Boston emptied after the last Rolling Rally, the workers cleaned up the debris and parents stopped hoisting children on their shoulders to espy Tom Brady and Troy Brown.

It is beyond time for rallies to continue, meandering slowly through the ancient street of Boston, where such original patriots such as Sam Adams, John Hancock and Paul Revere once cavorted. The children who once accompanied their parents to the parades will be starting their own families soon and need to indoctrinate their offspring to the winning tradition of the Patriots.

It will happen again…and again, but a caveat on the Parade, the next time it rolls around. Wear two pairs of socks and warm mittens because you must get onto the streets early and stay a long time, and contrary to popular myth, the Puritan forefathers did not install heating elements underneath the brick sidewalks all those centuries ago.

And don't be surprised if one of Tom Brady's children steals the show again.

43 Troy Brown

Drafted in the eighth round of the 1993 NFL Draft by New England, Troy Brown was lucky the drafting went that late back then; in today's seven-round selection process, he would not even qualify for "Mr. Irrelevant." His first coach, Bill Parcells, did not shower him with encouragement during his first training camp either, and after Brown muffed an attempt at returning a punt that led to an opponent's touchdown in the final preseason game, Parcells cut him. Parcells smartly re-signed the errant rookie well into the 1993 season, and Brown hung on for his first two seasons as a punt and kickoff return specialist, only catching two balls as a receiver during his infancy in the league.

Gradually his receptions increased until he became a reliable outlet for Drew Bledsoe, yet still he did not approximate the proficiency of Ben Coates, Terry Glenn, Shawn Jefferson, or arguably even Vincent Brisby during much of his early career. He quietly continued to return punts and kickoffs and performed every task assigned to him with professionalism and dedication.

It is tempting to surmise that Brown's career only truly ascended with the advent of Tom Brady as the starting quarterback, but actually he experienced his breakout season as a receiver with 83 catches in Bill Belichick's first year as head coach in 2000. In that season, he became Bledsoe's favorite target, surpassing the achievements of Glenn and Kevin Faulk. When Bledsoe got hurt in early 2001, Brady took over and Brown's statistics went through the stratosphere with 101 catches and top-10 season-ending statistics in catches made and receiving yards.

It bears noting that Brown's star ascended as quickly as Glenn's fortunes declined, fundamentally due to self-immolation. Glenn was faster, more talented, and a higher draft choice than Brown, but Glenn turned into a loser while Brown persistently found more ways to help his team win. Admitted a young Tom Brady, "He's a source of safety for me. Every time I look to him, he's open. That's a nice security blanket to have."

In a 2001 playoff game against the Steelers, Bledsoe drew raves for his "Last Hurrah" performance in place of the injured Brady, but it was the dependable Troy Brown who scored the most telling blow in the contest, a 55-yard punt return for a touchdown to place his team in the lead (he also caught eight passes). In the Super Bowl against the Rams, Brown kept his club in the fray the entire time with six receptions. That year was also notable because Brown made his last kickoff return, though he continued to field punts, and earned his first and only selection to the Pro Bowl. Incidentally he also rushed for 91 yards on 11 carries and led the NFL with 14.2 yards per punt return. Surveying his success, Brown once stated, "I've said all along, it all depends on what your teammates think about you. If guys in your locker room trust you, you don't have to worry about too much else."

A bright spot in an otherwise disappointing 2002 season, Brown caught 97 passes and continued to perform brilliantly on special teams, yet it was during the next two seasons that he perhaps performed his most selfless service for the team. While his production dropped, he became one of the key team leaders in the campaigns that ultimately led to the team's second and third championships. For example, he played a mean defensive back in 2004, intercepting three passes for a depleted secondary, all the while continuing to field punts. In 2005 and 2006, by then in his mid-thirties, his production hovered around 40 receptions a year as the team sought to find new targets for Brady. His teammates succeeded magnificently with the 2007 acquisition of Randy Moss (like Brown, a product of the Marshall football program), by which time Brown's tenure in the league came to an end.

Brown now analyzes football with the same precision and dedication with which he ran routes for coaches Parcells, Carroll, and Belichick, not bad for a onetime eighth-round pick. He has earned selection to the 50th Anniversary Team and no Patriots receiver has ever made more receptions (557) than he did. Only Steve Grogan played longer than Troy Brown in New England. Hopefully he will not be overlooked by the Pro Football Hall of Fame, though he was inducted into the Patriots Hall of Fame in 2012.

44 Andre Tippett

Having just endured a 2–14 season under Ron Erhardt in 1981, the Pats named Ron Meyer their new head coach and expended almost all of their picks on defensive players in the 1982 draft. It constitutes one of the least appreciated and difficult to fathom quirks in club annals, particularly since the team already fielded a number of stars such as Steve Nelson, Tony McGee, Julius Adams, Raymond Clayborn, Roland James, Mike Haynes, and Tim Fox. They did need a defensive tackle, but they had one and did not know it in Bob Golic, miscast as a linebacker and then cast off after the 1981 season to start playing in Pro Bowls as a member of the Browns thereafter.

The strategy backfired in that first-round choices Kenneth Sims and Lester Williams never approximated their collegiate successes, but even with a misguided scheme and poor talent evaluation, the brain trust did score with a fifth rounder, Fred Marion, and succeeded brilliantly with their second-round selection of Andre Tippett out of the University of Iowa.

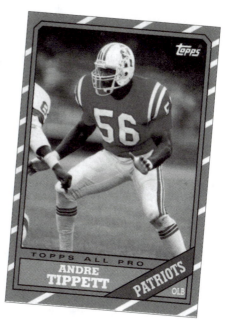

A five-time All-Pro selection, linebacker Andre Tippett was enshrined in the Pro Football Hall of Fame in 2008.

Tippett played little in 1982, but by the following season he had become a massive threat at outside linebacker, a man often mentioned in the same sentence as the Giants' Lawrence Taylor, an imposing foe who dared opposing offenses to single-cover him. In 1984 Tippett earned a Pro Bowl nod, his first of five consecutive appearances. Injuries kept him from at least one more appearance as he lost the entire 1989 season while on injured reserve.

During a memorable four-year stretch from 1984 through 1987, he placed second each season in the NFL in sacks, with the exception of 1986 when he played in only 11 games. During this period, his coaches and teammates generally penciled him in for about 10 sacks a year and approximately 100 tackles. In 1984, he generated 18.5 sacks, then nearly replicated that feat the next year with 16.5. To this day, he holds the franchise record for sacks at an even 100.

The risk of focusing too much on Tippett's sacks is to ignore or even negate the total game he provided his team's defense. Andre

A Man of Many Skills

Andre Tippett is a member of the NFL's Hall of Fame, the Patriots Hall of Fame, and the National Jewish Hall of Fame, but his accomplishments do not stop there. He is also a black belt in karate.

Tippett's signature moment as a pro occurred when he drove a Jets back who dared tried to block him backward as he made the tackle. If you have not seen a clip of this bit of roughhousing, indulge yourself and catch one of the niftiest plays in NFL history on YouTube.

In the unlikely event you believe that Tippett concentrated too much on one phase of his game, treat yourself to spools of footage of Patriots games in which he participated. He did not simply devour quarterbacks, he also shed off blocks and moved laterally quite well to respond to opponents' runs. And although he only intercepted one pass in his career, he prevented many receptions with his quick reads and coverage of backs and tight ends.

Yet, satisfying as career vignettes might be, they do not capture Andre Tippett the man, a gentleman still associated with the New England Patriots years after his playing career terminated. He grew up in Newark, New Jersey, a city that destroyed itself during the 1967 riots, having since philosophically concluded, "I am proof you should do everything you can to live your dream, whatever that may be. I did not have the material advantages, but through commitment to achieving my goals, using the advantages that I did have, and listening to the wise men and women who offered their support, I was able to live my dream. This was my dream!"

45 The Jets

Every fervent New England Patriots fan loathes the New York Jets, and a plethora of reasons suggest why. Originally called the Titans, today's Jets were, like the Pats, one of the eight founding franchises in the AFL, so their rivalry stretches back a half century. While the merger of the AFL and NFL in 1970 helped dissipate many of the strong feelings longtime fans had about most of the other AFL clubs (the Pats play the Chiefs, Raiders, Chargers, Broncos, and Tennessee (nee Houston Oilers) infrequently), the Pats and Jets still tee off against each other twice each year. True, the Pats and Bills also face off twice a year, but Buffalo as a city does not project the same negative visceral reaction that New York elicits for Bostonians. Once the Patriots discovered how to win away games in Miami, their series dimmed a bit, too.

The Jets/Patriots rivalry remained a dormant one until the mid-1990s, when the Jets hired Bill Parcells away after the Pats' second appearance in the Super Bowl; the Big Tuna craftily grabbed star running back Curtis Martin from New England, which only exacerbated matters. The Patriots returned the favor by wooing Bill Belichick away from New York a few years later, and then the feud gained more steam when former New England assistant coach Eric Mangini headed south on Route I-84 to coach the Jets. It was Mangini or his minions who alerted the NFL to Belichick's use of prohibited videotape during a game between the teams, a move that cost the Pats a first-round draft choice and Belichick $500,000. It cost Mangini a hug or two from his old mentor Belichick.

The Enemy of My Enemy is...Indianapolis?

Hated though the Jets may be by the New England faithful, the Patriots might play with an even higher level of vengeance against the Indianapolis Colts. Initially because of the comparisons between Tom Brady and Peyton Manning and the fact that their teams set the standard in the NFL (along with the Steelers) for the first decade of the new millennium, a natural disdain has developed. So much so that most Pats fans become ill when viewing Manning's commercials on television. The teams did not play each other in the 1960s due to the AFL/NFL wars, but they did play in the same division from 1970 through 2001, and due to parity and strength of schedule they are almost always pitted against each other.

Unwittingly, the Jets might have done their rivals a bigger favor when their linebacker Mo Lewis delivered a devastating hit to Pats quarterback Drew Bledsoe in 2001. Bledsoe sat for several weeks with the ghost of Wally Pipp while backup Tom Brady took over the team, never to relinquish control of his position.

While the Jets and Pats often split their series each year—the teams had a dead-even record against each other going into the Pats' surprising playoff loss to the Jets after the 2010 regular season—the Jets/Pats rivalry better resembles the old J.R. Ewing/Cliff Barnes feud from the TV show *Dallas*. The Pats almost always win the big prize in the end, and since Joe Namath's 1969 Super Bowl effort, the Pats are the only team in the rivalry that wins Super Bowls. The Jets remain the Cliff to the Pats' J.R. Don't tell Jets fans that, though, because the Patriots remain their most-hated foe, and the feeling is reciprocated.

46 Stanley Morgan

Selected to the Patriots' All-Decade teams for the 1970s and 1980s and its all-time team as a wide receiver, Stanley Morgan did not pass through Foxboro unappreciated. Unfortunately, outside and beyond Route 95 this gifted receiver has not received his proper due as one of the finest receivers of his generation.

He certainly played his collegiate ball at a program prominent for producing wideouts, drafted in the first round out of Tennessee in 1977. Parenthetically, that first round not only netted New England a future star in Morgan, but also allowed them to draft Raymond Clayborn, an all-time cornerback. Morgan had a good rookie year and sophomore season under head coach Chuck Fairbanks, but he hit his stride professionally in 1979 under new coach Ron Erhardt, leading the NFL in yards per reception and receiving touchdowns, and earning his first Pro Bowl nod.

He again led the entire league in yards per reception the next year and warranted selection again for the Pro Bowl, yet because he played for some very good teams which sputtered either through coaching upheavals or personnel shortcomings, he never played in the final game. The trend continued in his fifth year in the league—and his last as a teammate of the estimable Harold Jackson—as Morgan paced the NFL in yards per reception for the third year in a row on a team that fell apart with a final 2–14 record.

Thereafter, Morgan excelled in anonymity while the team struggled for three more years until 1985, the magical season when the team came out of nowhere to play in its first Super Bowl. The reporters swarmed around the oft-frustrated team veterans after they defeated the Miami Dolphins on January 12, 1986, in the AFC Championship Game, including the estimable Morgan, who

Patience Is a Virtue

Stanley Morgan can take solace that some day he will receive his overdue recognition by following the experience of a wide receiver he played against in high school in South Carolina named Jim Rice. Of course, Rice's induction into the Hall of Fame occurred in Cooperstown, New York, for his production with the Boston Red Sox.

relished this rare triumphant moment. "It never bothered us what people thought," he said. "We just came out and did our job and let the scoreboard say the rest. We knew what we could do and we know we got better each and every game."

That victory against Miami proved the high-water mark for Morgan and his teammates, as the Bears dismantled them in the Super Bowl. Shortly thereafter, ugly drug rumors circulated in the press concerning several players, and while the 1986 Patriots made the playoffs, they lost in the first round to Denver.

The calm in the eye of the storm, Morgan caught 84 passes in 1986, dwarfed his previous best in that category, and earned some long-deserved recognition and his third Pro Bowl selection. His 1,491 receiving yards placed him second that year in the NFL, behind only Jerry Rice of the 49ers, reestablishing his reputation in the league as a deep threat. No complainer, Morgan did reflect long after his career ended, "I think if there was one thing I would do different is that I would have thrown the ball a lot more. Back when I was playing we basically relied on our running game and threw when we had to. It wasn't uncommon to go a couple of games and not have a pass thrown to me if our running game was doing well. I just wish we threw the ball a bit more, but I am sure you will hear that from every receiver."

In the odd strike year of 1987, Morgan's receptions had diminished, and although he received his fourth invitation to the Pro Bowl, deep team rot had set in and he compiled the second-lowest yards-per-reception average of his career. The next two years in

New England continued this downward trend for player and team, and Morgan actually spent his last season in 1990 reunited with old coach Ron Meyer in Indianapolis.

Morgan has enjoyed a prosperous post-playing career in business and in devoting himself selflessly to charity in Memphis, Tennessee, a well-led life marred only by the incomprehensible fact that this fine man and player has not received enough votes for induction into the Pro Football Hall of Fame. Tied for 10th in NFL history for career yards per reception, Morgan waits for admission while far less team-oriented and statistically deserving players have gone to Canton and will continue to do so unless some day his accomplishments and his devotion to team goals receive their true due.

47 The Good Old Days

Certain adherents of the Flat Earth Society find value only in the old days, a simpler time when everything and everyone was so much better. Unfortunately, time travel does not exist to return these folks to a different time in space or at least to cure them of their ambivalence toward the improvements in how we live. One trip to a Pats home game a few decades ago would shock even the most cruelly afflicted straight.

It was not just the awful old stadium in Foxboro, given a bunch of names because no one truly wanted to claim it as their own.

It was the fans.

Early in Boston Patriots history, when the mostly male audience often showed up for home games in suits and fedoras at Fenway Park or wherever else, there may have been a hint of gentility along the 50-yard line and the bleachers alike. Since the Patriots were visitors in their many home stadiums until the franchise shifted to Foxboro, people tended to be on their better behavior, lest they and their team not receive an invite back.

Safely ensconced in Foxboro, the Patriots players enjoyed improved facilities and played before larger crowds (or more empty seats as the seasons unfolded), but the stands themselves became a largely lawless collection of man's inhumanity to man. Drunks and potheads fought each other and the members of their own tribes, everyone smoked cigarettes when they did not light up something else, and feelings were hurt all over the place. In the event that the bathrooms had filled up or more likely the toilets backed up, many sports fans resorted to urinating in public. Louts screamed profanities, creating a rich Dickensian brew of what it must have been like to reside in the East End of London in the 19th century. And to many of the fans and players, it seemed as if Ebenezer Scrooge himself ran the team.

If you took your children to a game, neighbors reacted as if you were a bad parent: "Are you crazy, you're taking (fill in names) to a Patriots home game? Good luck! I would never do that." Foxboro was Dodge, and most families kept their Dodges in the garage and watched the game at home.

Ah, the bygone days of yore. A whole generation has grown up and gone to college, never exposed to the horror that once passed as a Pats home game. No one smokes in a public gathering like a sporting event any more, and the local constabulary and the Staties have become quite adept at nailing drunks the minute they get in the car and drive off. People want to share their lives with their children and do so in a safe and sane environment, an impossibility under conditions where immaturity was condoned or even fostered.

Weep not helpless romantics, there is still a place for you in the new stadium. At the end of each end zone, there are 10 men in tricornered hats prepared to fire off muskets every time the team does something truly remarkable.

48 Nadir

Annus horribilis, 1990. That was the year that the often star-crossed Patriots put up their worst record ever, this from a club that had participated in a Super Bowl at the conclusion of the 1985 season.

Even that Super Bowl team contained too many players content on receiving paychecks and not recognizing their potential, but in fairness the 1990 edition fielded a batch of truly awful ball-players. Head coach Raymond Berry saw the handwriting on the wall, wisely walking away after the 1989 season when incompetent owner Victor Kiam demanded Berry make some major changes. No one told Raymond Berry what to do, particularly a know-nothing like Kiam, so the reins of the team passed to longtime coordinator Rod Rust, the same Rust who years ago prompted the firing of head coach Ron Meyer when the Sullivans refused to let Meyer fire Rust. Confusing? You bet, but nowhere near as clueless as many of the Pats of that vintage 1990 season.

The fish rotted from the head down with Kiam, the club's all-time worst owner, at the helm. A male chauvinist if there ever was one, Kiam did not really know how to lead men, at least not a host of professional football coaches and players, a fact that became even more apparent as this tragic year unfolded. The whole support system set up by the Sullivans since the team's founding largely disappeared, and into this abrupt lack of continuity fell Rust, a man as unprepared to shift from coordinator to head coach as Clive Rush was years earlier.

The club lacked a quarterback, with 37-year-old Steve Grogan in awful shape after absorbing shots for 16 professional seasons. Through most of the year, ineffectual Marc Wilson and Tommy Hodson fought for the leadership of this particular *Titanic*. They

Gathering Rust

If you have never won a bar bet, change your fortune by asking a card-carrying member of Patriots Nation what happened to Rod Rust after 1990. Like most coordinators who did not trip the light fantastic as head coaches, he went back to becoming a reliable if not prized coordinator in the NFL. Except for the 2001 season, while New England was winning its first Lombardi Trophy, Rust took over the helm of the Canadian Football League's Montreal Alouettes and guided them to a winning record up until the time he received his pink slip before season's end, the victim of a nasty losing streak.

had few viable targets to throw to with Irving Fryar catching the most, but former punt-pass-and-kick champ Hart Lee Dykes and onetime Red Sox draftee Greg McMurtry contributed little. They had been running John Stephens ragged the past two seasons, and even though he still had a decent 808 yards rushing in 1990, he gained less than four yards per carry in his last good year as a back. Bruce Armstrong anchored a thin offensive line, with Danny Villa shifting from center to right tackle as needed.

The defense still had a number of very good players; they simply did not have enough of them. The club had two first-round draft choices that year, but squandered them on defensive lineman Ray Agnew and linebacker Chris Singleton, two rookies who never did much for the Patriots or anyone else for that matter. The star defenders continued to age and too many gaps existed where youth should have gradually filled them.

With these imbalances, the club surrendered 446 points and scored only 181, good for second-to-last and dead-last, respectively, in the NFL.

Oddly enough, the season did not begin that badly. The Pats lost by three points in the opening game to the Miami Dolphins, a team that just missed playing in the Super Bowl that year. In the second game, they defeated a mediocre Colts team, and it appeared the team could play with anyone. Then the dam broke, with successive losses to the Bengals (41–7) and the Jets (37–13). Not only did they not win again, but they only came within three points of tying a game twice for the remainder of the season.

The year just kept getting uglier, with some slugs intimidating *Boston Herald* reporter Lisa Olson in the locker room, followed by Kiam accelerating the mayhem caused by this incident with his own outwardly boorish and insensitive behavior. This was the same year Kiam tried to foist a waiver onto Grogan to exonerate and hold harmless the Patriots in the event the estimable quarterback got seriously hurt, another thoughtless faux pas from a man who never should have owned a professional sports team at any period after the Visigoths sacked Rome.

Meanwhile, as losses mounted, head coach Rust declined to place any of the blame on the players as the ugly season meandered to its conclusion.

Rust lasted just that last year, replaced by Syracuse University coach Dick MacPherson, who improved the team somewhat in 1991 with six wins, then succumbed himself to poor health in 1992 as the team slipped up again. But by 1993 New England had a new coach named Bill Parcells, a man who exhibited no use for an underperforming player and had no compunction in criticizing such a player or even cutting him off at the quick. The nadir was 1990, but by 1993 Patriots Nation rose from those ashes.

Gino

Like many early players in the old American Football League, Gino Cappelletti played college ball in the 1950's, then seemingly had forsaken football forever until representatives from the new league came calling. As a running back and quarterback with the University of Minnesota anchored by 1953 Heisman runner-up Paul Giel (who lost to Johnny Lattner of Notre Dame and Forgotten Four fame), the modest Gino did not garner the spot light and after his college career ended, he did not catch on with the Detroit Lions. Cappelletti continued to play football when the opportunity arose at a semi-pro or local level, but by 1960, he tended bar while any aspirations he still had to play professional football faded.

Fortuitously, Lou Saban, the head coach of the newly minted Boston Patriots began to search in Minnesota for old Golden Gopher players and though Cappelletti did not initially show up on the radar, Gino contacted Saban and secured a try-out. Having booted a 43 yard field goal once for Minnesota, back when an extra point often did not split the uprights, Gino demonstrated his skills in that area and his versatility earned him a roster spot for the Patriots.

Though most often considered a wide receiver or kicker, he spent most of his on-field time in his rookie season as a cornerback,

Gino Cappelletti was the AFL's Most Valuable Player in 1964 and was elected to the Patriots Hall of Fame in 1992.

The Boot
How did Gino become such a great kicker? As a lad, he had to stomp on grapes for the wine his father bottled, which in part may explain how he achieved his later feats.

intercepting four passes. He did get his leg on the ball, scoring eight field goals and thirty extra points. His rustiness with kicking showed up statistically, as he only converted on only 38.1% of his field goals and missed all nine of his attempts over 40 yards.

In 1961, he improved dramatically, as he shifted him from defensive back to receiver, and he became a favorite target of new quarterback Babe Parilli, with that tandem responsible for 45 receptions and a very productive 768 yards. His kicking also came together, as he made over 53% of his field goal attempts, second highest in the league. In 1962 and 1963, he showed similar consistency.

Training camp in the summer of 1964 apparently presaged the diminution of Cappelletti's role as kicker and receiver. Then coach Mike Holovak might have denied it later, but more likely he had already decided to gradually lessens Gino's time on offense in favor of a more restrictive role on the team. Injuries to other, younger players, ended this type of speculation, culminating in Cappelletti's selection at the end of the 1964 season not only to his third Pro Bowl appearance but his earning the MVP award for the American Football League.

He continued to kick well, leading the league in field goals made, third in field goal percentage and fourth in total extra points. His 155 points paced the league, with 7 touchdowns and even a two point conversion contributing to the tally. On the receiving end of Babe Parilli's tosses, he placed in the top ten league wide in catches made, receiving yards, receiving yards per game and receiving yards per reception. Explained Cappelletti, "When I signed my contract last June, I told Mike [Holovak] that I wasn't ready to be a swing man just yet and I wanted the chance to play regular." He got his wish, and all he missed that season was a part of a championship, after helping to lead his team to a fine 10-3-1 record.

He played six more seasons for the Patriots, one of the few people who participated in every club the team fielded in the AFL. Although Adam Vinatieri scored more points than Cappelletti, Gino is still on the Patriots' top ten list all-time for receptions and is a member of their Hall of Fame. Gino retired from broadcasting in 2012, having broadcasted 585 games with Gil Santos.

50 Weird Sam Jankovich

During the "anything goes" days of the Victor Kiam era, Sam Jankovich became the CEO of the Patriots. Jankovich had found success in transforming the University of Miami from a backwater to the strongest program in intercollegiate football. Around this time, the Boston Celtics had elevated David Gavitt, the man most responsible for the creation of the Big East Conference, to a similar position of power.

As an early Christmas present, Kiam appointed Jankovich on December 20, 1990, a gift that Jankovich should have kept unwrapped. The club had declined magnificently since its 1985 Super Bowl campaign, eventually concluding the 1990 season at 1–15, and the club had barely weathered the recent sexual harassment of reporter Lisa Olson. Soon thereafter, Jankovich or Kiam or some other person in the disorganization fired the head coach, Rod Rust, and in retrospect they probably should not have hired beloved coach Dick MacPherson out of Syracuse. MacPherson was very enthusiastic, often hugging players who just completed a big play, and he did pull six wins out of the club in 1991. But in 1992 the team went on a prolonged losing streak and finished 2–14 as MacPherson missed the last half of the season due to illness.

It was not all Jankovich's fault, of course. It is always difficult to succeed under weak ownership, and Kiam was the worst owner in franchise history by a number of furlongs. But Jankovich did not account for the difference between running a college program and a professional one, and while "The U" in that era cultivated an outlaw image, the last thing the Pats needed at that juncture was to retain their considerable cache of underperforming knuckleheads. Most vexingly, he did not have the power to fire the owner.

Coach MacPherson lost his job on January 8, 1993, and one day later Jankovich walked the plank. A relatively colorless soul, Jankovich either did not understand or did not appreciate why a member of the media dubbed him "Weird Sam," in honor of Weird Al Yankovic. Unfortunately, Sam Jankovich was a victim of sorts, a capable guy caught in the franchise's last full-body heave before it took its first serious steps to become one of the world's premier professional sports teams.

51 Best Drafts

The annual NFL has become a virtual holiday, three days in April where a family can get together on the couch, wear their favorite player's replica jersey, eat chips, drink beer and leave household chores for another day. The Boston Patriots' first draft experience, over a half century ago is shrouded by confusion and lapsed memories, although the club did pick up Ron Burton, a man for whom the term IR meant "I'm ready," not injured reserve. Since Billy

Sullivan and his partners did not have a lot of money, they generally did not have the wherewithal to compete with NFL teams for players, so they lost out on talented prospects like Fran Tarkenton. Their best draft in that first decade was probably in 1965 when they signed Jim Nance, Jim Whalen and Tom Neville.

Once the NFL and AFL merged, the strapped Pats no longer had to woo players and they drafted quite well that decade, none better than in 1973 when they incredibly brought John Hannah, Sam Cunningham, Darryl Stingley and Ray Hamilton aboard. These were the Bucko Kilroy years, with this remarkable talent evaluator serving as either Director of Player Personnel or General Manager from 1971 to 1982. One useful and overlooked draft haul occurred in 1983 under Kilroy's successor as GM, Pat Sullivan, when the team obtained a number of very good players in Ronnie Lippett, Johnny Rembert, Craig James, Stephen Starring and Tony Eason.

From 1993 through 1996, Bill Parcells oversaw some productive drafts, although his final one, in which Terry Glenn was chosen over his objection supposedly helped paint his way out of town (ego and restlessness had much more to do with the decision) Still, the Tuna hauled in some pretty good groceries in Drew Bledsoe, Troy Brown, Corwin Brown, Chris Slade, Willie McGinest, Ty Law, Ted Johnson, Curtis Martin, Tedy Bruschi and Lawyer Milloy. Preceding Parcells, the club scored one of its biggest successes in the dark days (and nights) of 1991 when they chose tight end Ben Coates, tackle Pat Harlow, quarterback Scott Zolak, running back Leonard Russell and cornerback Jerome Henderson.

With the new century, the club prospered with very good drafts in 2001 (Richard Seymour and Matt Light) and 2003 (Ty Warren, Asante Samuel and and Dan Koppen) before tailing off a bit and then a lot. They rebounded nicely in 2010, with Devin McCourty, Rob Gronkowski and Aaron Hernandez contributing mightily, with other rookies from that class demonstrating promise.

And their drafts since then have contributed to another Super Bowl ring, netting Nate Solder, Shane Vereen, Chandler Jones, Dont'a Hightower, Jamie Collins, and Bryan Stork. Not forgetting that they did not fare poorly with a free agent named Malcolm Butler.

Best draft ever? It may have been 2000 when the team bombed out with most of its picks before Tom Brady was chosen in the sixth round, but at the risk of heresy, give the slight edge to the 1995 draft, with Ty Law, Ted Johnson and Curtis Johnson as the first three choices. Had the club kept Brad Dusek instead of trading him to the Redskins for little in return, the 1973 draft would have been the greatest one.

52 Coliseums, Past and Present

Before the Pats' current home, Gillette Stadium, was built, the team played in Foxboro in a stadium that had all the charm of Boston's City Hall. They could not even keep the name straight, with the venue known at various times in its little more than 30 years of existence as either Schaefer Stadium, Sullivan Stadium, or the more generic Foxboro Stadium. Nice it was not, but at least it had enough seats and had been built with the express purpose of housing a professional football team.

Until 1971 the team did not even have that, as professional football had almost no toehold in New England until Billy Sullivan spawned the Boston Patriots. The couple of teams that did try to make it foundered before their ownership attempted to build their own home. Boston College, Harvard, and Boston University had some luck at various times and did have places to play, but high school football had much more of a hold on the region, with local gridiron stars becoming household names in the Commonwealth of Massachusetts.

Since Sullivan had barely enough money (with others) to secure an AFL franchise for his Patriots, he hardly had enough capital to break ground in 1960 for a permanent home. Banks did not cotton to the new club, so he had to find a local college or university where his new team could stage its home games. For their first three years, the Patriots played at Boston University's field, the location of so many exciting games with collegian and later Red Sox star Harry Agganis.

In 1963, the Patriots shifted to Chestnut Hill to play at Boston College, an arrangement that lasted a year. In 1964, Sullivan and the Pats hit the big time, leasing space from Tom Yawkey and the Boston Red Sox at Fenway Park, a bandbox oddly configured for baseball, not to mention football. They somehow squeezed the gridiron in between the first-base line and the Green Monster in left field and made do, in a matter of speaking. Another issue arose since the Sox played in September, so if the baseball team had home games that month on a Sunday, the Patriots had to play on the road. When the Red Sox finally made the World Series in 1967 after more than two decades of futility, the Patriots did not play in Friendly Fenway until the seventh game of the season.

Backed Up

The City of Foxboro once threatened to shut down Gillette's predecessor due to improper and insufficient plumbing. The Pats brought in emergency plumbers and 320 volunteers were assembled to flush all 640 toilets in what probably would have gone down as the largest mass flushing in world history had Guinness kept such a record at that time. The flushing worked and the game went ahead as scheduled. And say what you wish, but the old venue went out in style, with the Pats defeating the Raiders in the notorious "Tuck Rule Game" in 2001. For the truly nostalgic, you can revisit the old stadium site by visiting Patriot Place, which sits over much of the old field.

With that in mind, the Patriots started their 1968 home season at Alabama's Legion Field against the Jets, whose starting quarterback, Joe Namath, played his college ball there. Some home opener. By the end of 1968, the Patriots were fed up and moved back to Boston College for another year. The Pats actually played some preseason ball at B.C. in the summer of 1970, until a fire broke out in the stands during an exhibition against the Redskins. The Patriots ended up playing in Harvard Stadium in 1970, after which they moved to the green pastures of Foxboro, where they remain today.

The old Schaefer/Foxboro/Sullivan Stadium excited few sports fans and even fewer architects, but when juxtaposed to their previous nomadicism, the Pats felt there was no place like home.

Many Boston Celtics and Bruins fans lamented the razing of the old Boston Garden, and to suggest that the Red Sox's Fenway Park might someday face the wrecking ball incites charges of blasphemy, but when the Patriots' first permanent home in Foxboro came down after 2001, no one seemed to mind. In 2002, the club ushered in Gillette Stadium in class, with a Monday night football game against the Pittsburgh Steelers.

Easing the transition, the team constructed a state-of-the-art facility next door, eschewing the old reliance on drabness, an overuse of concrete, and poor public restrooms. The old stadium looked like a facility from Chernobyl, some cold Eastern Europe Warsaw Pact venue; the "new one" is a public work of art, a Coliseum in comparison. That aside, the old venue itself oozed a decidedly non-family atmosphere, more of a giant ugly open-air gin joint than a field of dreams. While much of the rowdiness and plug-ugly drunkenness ebbed considerably after Victor Kiam left town, the stadium looked even worse to a more sober crowd.

Okay, some of the motives for Gillette did not spring wholly from concerns for aesthetic beauty. The old barn only seated about 60,000 patrons, not a bad capacity when the team stunk, but totally insufficient for a world-class team. Plus, it did not have luxury boxes, the bane of most fans who bravely fight the elements with their heroes outside, but a massive revenue source nonetheless.

Yet even the most dedicated spectators had a rough time with the antiquated high school–quality seats, and the lines for food and drink were ridiculous. There were not enough facilities for folks who had to go to the bathroom, and let's mercifully leave it at that.

Wisely, in Gillette the amenities improved, but so did the physical plant. The seating is modern and comfortable, and the rows of seating are set out like tectonic plates. Aesthetically, a giant bridge was built so fans could walk across and enjoy a unique view, while a massive lighthouse-like structure adds not just beauty but a tip of the helmet to the region's navigational heritage.

One thing has not changed concerning the experience of watching a game at Foxboro: they put a train line in and rerouted traffic and have tried everything in creation, but it still takes about an hour to begin to get appreciably away from the stadium after a game. Foxboro is still a small town with insufficient egresses to major highways, so when you go, grab something to eat at Patriot Place after the game and avoid the traffic jam.

53 Hatin' Peyton

Hating Denver Broncos' quarterback Peyton Manning is not something a Patriots' fan should do before they die, because they already hate him. It is more important to dig deep from within to determine why we hate him. After all, he seems like a nice enough chap and doesn't do drugs, get into suspicious car accidents or hang around Paris Hilton.

Early in his career, his Colts played the Pats twice during the regular season as a then-divisional foe, but familiarity did not breed contempt so much because from 1998-2001, Peyton and his teammates only won two out of eight games. Wisely, their team hired Tony Dungy as head coach before the 2002 season, but the Pats and Colts did not play each other at all that season.

In 2003 and 2004 Manning scared us a bit at times, but again, in each year New England won the regular season game and the playoff game. How many times can Superman let Lex Luthor frighten him or even annoy him?

The trend changed in 2005 when Peyton's Colts won the regular season game and then in 2006 won the rivalry in the ninth week of the season and the playoffs. The Colts won the Super Bowl and Manning went on to even more exposure on television as an ad pitchman than before, of so it seems. One can understand that a company might want a clean-cut superstar to act as a spokesman for its product, but who really thought it was a good idea to run Peyton Manning's spots in the northeast after he had guided them past New England in the AFC playoff game?

From 2007 through 2010, the teams split their regular season games, but by then Manning had seemingly gotten into the head of Bill Belichick, who in 2009 called a play for his offense on 4th and 2 deep in his own territory against the Colts, rather than provide his depleted defense an opportunity to try to stop Manning.

Yet Tom Brady wears four Super Bowl rings while Manning only has one, which suggests that Tom Brady is a better quarterback than Peyton Manning—perhaps the greatest ever. Rather than hate Peyton, perhaps we should empathize for him, because while he compiled dazzling numbers throwing the ball to Marvin Harrison and Reggie Wayne, Brady made do with less and performed much better in the postseason.

This great quarterback rivalry soon will end, with Patriots fans hopefully able someday to appreciate Peyton Manning as one of the top 10 at his position at the time of his retirement.

54 Thriller

The late pop star Michael Jackson may have had as little to do with football than any of the millions of Americans born after the Baby Boom began, and other than a halftime appearance at a Super Bowl it is quite possible he had no exposure to the sport at all. Revered by millions as one of the greatest entertainers of his generation, he is reviled by many who believe he committed awful crimes, and yet he played a huge role in Patriots history.

If Jackson knew little about football, arguably Billy Sullivan's son Chuck did not know enough about modern music concert promotion before he signed on to promote the Jackson Brothers Victory Tour in 1984. To underwrite this venture, Chuck Sullivan collateralized it with the Patriots' stadium and then signed on for a $41 million guarantee to the Jacksons for the tour, which ran from July of that year through the beginning of December.

One recurring myth that surrounds the extravaganza is that it was a huge failure, when in fact it set all-time records for the time with a gross of more than $75 million. Problems did arise with ticket sales and the like; Don King came in as a co-promoter early in the proceedings, and dates had to be added to ensure greater gates. Huge amounts of money went out to staging and venues and staff and crews, culminating in a financial disaster for Chuck Sullivan, who endured a heart attack and a bankruptcy before he righted his ship.

Michael Jackson reportedly gave all his money away to charity, while the Pats' stadium went up for sale in bankruptcy. The buyers? None other than current owner Bob Kraft and a partner.

55 The Big Tuna

It takes little effort to disparage former Patriots head coach Bill Parcells years after he left that post. Although he had brought the club to only its second Super Bowl appearance, he behaved in a petulant manner leading up to that penultimate game, particularly in his relations with owner Bob Kraft. Basically he was insubordinate and he became the show instead of the team, as Brett Favre, Desmond Howard, and the Green Bay Packers won the Lombardi Trophy at the Patriots' expense. Parcells never coached another game for New England and shortly thereafter became truly hated when he ascended to the head coaching position with the archrival New York Jets.

Having buried Parcells, it is now time to praise him, because his exit marred an otherwise largely successful tenure for the coach, nicknamed somewhat affectionately, "the Big Tuna." Few people know this but Parcells first came to New England in 1980 as a linebackers coach under Ron Erhardt. When he finally got his first head coaching job with the New York Giants, he took full advantage of the opportunity, and with such stars as Lawrence Taylor, Phil Simms, Harry Carson, and Mark Bavaro, he led that team to two Super Bowl titles.

Squirrelly Patriots owner James Busch Orthwein performed one lasting service to New England by hiring Parcells, by then a retired coach and a network analyst, to lead the team in 1993.

Certainly during his introductory press conference on January 21, the new head coach charmed most fans and even members of the cynical local media, who had seen one bomb after another detonate in Foxboro. Gushed Parcells, "This is my last deal, no doubt about that. After that, I'm John Wayne." In the end, he would turn out to be more like the perennially retiring Favre, but we're getting ahead of ourselves.

One of Parcells' first decisions as head coach was to decide who the Patriots would draft in 1993: the choice came down to either Notre Dame's Rick Mirer or Washington State's Drew Bledsoe, both quarterbacks. He chose Bledsoe, a wise choice because although Mirer earned Rookie of the Year honors that year, his star soon faded while Bledsoe became a central element to the foundation for the Patriots' reversal of fortune.

Seemingly Parcells thrived on building a franchise from the ashes, and he astutely picked up valuable draft choices and free agents. He might go wrong with a Scott Secules or Scott Sisson here or there, but he deserves credit for helping to transform New England from a long-standing joke to a professional and competent organization. Besides Bledsoe, the Patriots picked up Todd Rucci, Troy Brown, Chris Slade, Vincent Brisby, and Corwin Brown in Parcells' first draft, a very solid congregation of rookie players. Symbolically, he parted ways with Irving Fryar, a player who had

Numbers Don't Lie

An intelligent and often thoughtful man, Bill Parcells uttered what has come closest to Sacred Gospel in football. In his famous utterance on the deeper meaning of a team's final record, Parcells said, "Whatever you finish, that's what you are. If you're 1–15, you're a 1–15 team. If you're 2–14, you're 2–14. No better, no worse. You can look in the brochure and see that the team is 5–9, but it only lost six games by a total of nine points. You follow me? The reason the team is 5–9 is because it wasn't any good in close games."

never really fulfilled his promise in New England, as he consolidated control over his men.

He quickly became a regional favorite, fueled primarily by his entertaining press conferences. Parcells has a fierce and biting wit and he employed it on these occasions, relishing his interaction with the media. Sometimes he might snarl at a question or denigrate a player, but mostly he just enjoyed the give and take with the press corps, and he endeared himself to the public immensely with his observations and the manner in which he delivered them.

In his first season with the team, Parcells guided his charges to a 5–11 record, an improvement over the previous year's 2–14 mark, and except for early blowout losses to Buffalo and the Jets, he kept his team competitive in almost every game. While he did not take full advantage of receiver Troy Brown, rookie Drew Bledsoe got off to a promising start and Ben Coates became a force at tight end. Unfortunately, the coach did not possess enough skilled guards and centers to complement fine tackles in Bruce Armstrong and Pat Harlow or enough defensive ends and defensive backs to seriously mount a run at the playoffs.

In 1994, the Pats again started poorly but rattled off wins in their final seven games, earning them a playoff spot in the wild-card game against Bill Belichick and the Cleveland Browns (Belichick won that head-to-head matchup). Still, in the regular season Bledsoe continued to mature on offense, finding not only Coates but also wide receivers Vincent Brisby and Michael Timpson with increasing frequency. Veteran Vincent Brown anchored an improved defense around young players such as Willie McGinest, Chris Slade, Todd Collins, and Corwin Brown.

Inexplicably, the club tanked in 1995, compiling a 6–10 record and finishing fourth in its division. The team had solved its rushing game problems by stealing Pitt's Curtis Martin in the third round, and Bledsoe continued to find Coates and Brisby (and now occasionally Brown). But the defense reeked, giving up 83 more points during the course of the season than the offense scored, though the team did draft well, picking up rookies Ted Johnson and Ty Law. Still, the defensive line stunk and safety Myron Guyton served season long as a destructive sieve.

Critical mass for Parcells occurred during the 1996 draft; the coach craved a defensive lineman with the first-round selection, but team owner Bob Kraft overruled him and the Patriots selected gifted wide receiver Terry Glenn out of Ohio State. Glenn only went out that season and caught 90 passes, then an all-time record for rookie receivers in the NFL, but for Parcells it was the principle of the matter. He had drafted extremely well in his first three seasons with the Patriots, and Parcells thought that he had earned the faith of his owner. Bob Kraft correctly pointed out to Parcells that the owner had the final say. It did not help matters later in that same draft when Parcells got his lineman, Christian Peter, only to

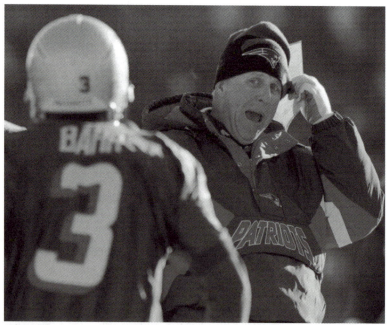

Though his exit may have lacked grace, there is no denying the positive impact head coach Bill Parcells had on the Patriots during the mid-1990s.

have the club release the rookie due to some very serious allegations made concerning Peter during his undergrad days.

The bad feeling seeped into the season as the Pats lost their first two games, but then they won 11 out of their final 14 behind a strong offense led by Bledsoe and Martin and a developing defense. They handled their first playoff foes easily and on paper looked good enough to beat their Super Bowl opponent Green Bay. Unlike the club's first foray into the Super Bowl against a very strong Chicago Bears congregation, the Pats seemed well-matched against the Packers.

Then everything seemed to cave in between the AFC Championship Game and the Super Bowl, a disgraceful period covered in more detail elsewhere.

Suffice it to say, Parcells left New England to coach the New York Jets, fully expecting to see the team fold without him, which it began to do the next three years under new coach Pete Carroll. Unfortunately for Parcells, Bill Belichick did not wish to coach the Jets after Parcells had had enough, and with owner Bob Kraft, Belichick turned New England into a perennial winner and rendered Parcells a bit of a whiner.

While his term was tumultuous, Parcells must have won a lot of games in his four seasons in New England, right? Not really, his four-year regular season record with the club was a very mediocre 32–32. What the statistics do not reveal is that even though he did not get to choose all of his "groceries," he did not, like Old Mother Hubbard, leave the cupboard bare; he drafted and developed some terrific players. Want another stubborn fact? Without Belichick on his staff, Parcells has won zero Super Bowls.

His odd personality aside, Parcells helped build the New England Patriots from a laughingstock into one of the premier franchises in the NFL. He drafted well and developed his young players, casting aside malcontents or poor performers. He inherited the least interesting and followed of all the Boston area professional teams and took it to the summit. After Parcells came to town, no one would ever again be content with the Patriots as a group of genial losers.

Meanwhile Parcells soldiers on in quixotic fashion. After departing New England, he curtain-called with the Jets, Cowboys, and has come and gone from Miami, a talented and amusing guy, but no John Wayne.

56 Patronize Grogan-Marciano Sporting Goods

Talk about the coupling of two New England sports dynasties. This independent sporting goods retailer and wholesaler combines the toughness and smarts of Patriots Hall of Fame quarterback Steve Grogan with the legacy of the family of Brockton boxing great Rocky Marciano. The Brockton Bomber's brother founded the store in 1973, but by 1994 Steve Grogan perceived the keen business opportunities in taking over ownership from Peter Marciano's successor and took advantage of them, successfully expanding the business to the present.

Not only does Grogan-Marciano maintain its traditional site in Mansfield, across from the old train depot, but it also now conducts most of its business on the wholesale end, with three agents in the field, primarily in southern Massachusetts and Rhode Island. The sporting equipment, chosen from among almost four dozen quality suppliers, is all handpicked for being high-end quality, reflecting the motto of the store, "sporting goods for the serious athlete."

For the historian, there are jerseys from Steve's high school, college, and the Pats, and while most Patriots replica hats and the like are left to others, you can buy a Grogan replica jersey and

Steve will sign it for you. A native of Kansas, Steve has made New England his permanent home, one of many former Patriots players who have come to love the region. You cannot go wrong patronizing the store of one of the most admired Patriots of all time.

57 Moss Sets Touchdown Record

Like Corey Dillon before him, Randy Moss came to New England at an embarrassingly discounted price with a checkered reputation, a gift to a team that knew how to take advantage of the generosity of others. Unlike Dillon, whose reputation was fostered from a dissatisfaction with losing, Moss brought much of the scorn onto himself, with classless displays during games and a tendency to give less than 100 percent.

The change of scenery agreed with Moss though, as he clicked with Tom Brady, and statistically Brady achieved heights normally reserved for Peyton Manning. In his first year in New England, Moss rewarded his new employers with 23 touchdown receptions, an NFL record, as Brady helped set a team touchdown reception record with such other skilled players as Wes Welker and Kevin Faulk contributing to the haul.

While Brady missed nearly the entire 2008 season with an injury sustained in the opening game against the Chiefs, Moss helped substitute Matt Cassel have a good year as the team went 11–5. With Brady's return in 2009, Moss had another productive season, and yet the team had begun to decline. Moss got blamed by many fans and commentators on the basis that he demanded too much of Brady's attention and the team dynamic had changed to one that catered to Moss' demands.

Enigmatic wide receiver Randy Moss set an NFL record with 23 touchdown catches in his first season as a Patriot in 2007.

By 2010, Randy Moss still possessed exceptional ability, but he had begun to shoot his way out of town beginning with a rambling press conference after the team's Week 1 victory against the Cincinnati Bengals. By the fourth game, the club pulled the trigger on a trade with the Minnesota Vikings, trading their star receiver for a third-round draft choice. Moss returned to face off against the Patriots soon after, fittingly enough on Halloween Night, and after a lackluster game with his new team, he walked into another press conference and profusely praised his old organization. Promptly thereafter, Vikings coach Brad Childress waived Moss.

Final verdict on Moss: he was the most talented receiver in Patriots history, but he was not the greatest.

58 Speed the Snow Plow

From 1967 until 1985, the Patriots did not win a single away game against the Miami Dolphins, and frankly they did not fare that well against their old AFL rivals back home in Foxboro either. That futility abated a bit on December 12, 1982, when Patriots coach Ron Meyer gave the phrase "home-field advantage" a unique and quaint application late in a scoreless and quite snowy game against the Dolphins.

All day the field conditions had impeded each team from moving the ball effectively, and with the teams scoreless with 4:45 remaining in regulation, the Pats attempted a field goal on possibly their final possession. Out trotted kicker John Smith, a native of Leafield, England, to win the game for New England. Parenthetically, Smith's own job stood a bit in the balance at this juncture, having just cleared waivers to remain with the club.

Wherefore Art Thou, Plow?

For fans of John Deere 314 model snow plows, the Pats' infamous plow now hangs from the ceiling at Patriot Place. It belonged to GM Bucko Kilroy, a product of the budget limitations during the Sullivan years. As a partial gauge of the depth of the snow that fell before the game, the referees lost the coin they used to determine who kicked off in the white drifts at Schaefer Stadium. One final note: Patriots back Mark van Eeghen (a native of Cambridge) gained 100 yards on the ground under those tundraic conditions that day, while Mosi Tatupu rushed for another 81 yards.

Although he had played in New England for nine years, he had never booted a game-winning kick.

To ensure that his kicker had the optimal conditions to boot the game winner, Coach Meyer ordered Mark Henderson and his snow plow onto the field to clear a spot for Smith and his holder. Reasoned Meyer, "That timeout gave me time to think. I looked out on the field and I saw John chipping away at the ground and I saw [holder Matt Cavanaugh] chipping away and I thought, *Let's get the sweeper out here.*"

Dolphins coach Don Shula admitted that initially he "didn't see it happening," although he went apoplectic on his sideline once he figured it out. Unable to run out on the field to physically block the plow, he watched helplessly while Henderson completed his task and Smith drilled home the game-winning field goal.

The Dolphins protested, but no rule then existed to prevent this type of escapade from occurring. The referees later maintained that if Miami had a last-second chance at a field goal, they would have ordered the plow onto the field, but few believed them. Even if they tried, Ron Meyer probably had only gassed the snow plow to make one—and only one—foray onto the frozen tundra.

59 Prepare Ye the Way

Not normally an indecisive person by nature, Patriots head coach Bill Parcells spent dozens of hours dissecting tape, seeking out advice, and perusing scouting reports throughout the winter and early spring of 1993, all to decide whom to draft with the club's first pick in that year's college draft: Washington State's Drew Bledsoe or Notre Dame's Rick Mirer. Having just inherited Dick MacPherson's woeful 2–14 congregation, Parcells focused on a franchise quarterback as the most certain and speediest way to reverse the course of the Patriots.

To his credit, Parcells made the right pick, for while Mirer proceeded to win Rookie of the Year, his production precipitously and irreversibly declined thereafter, while Bledsoe became the finest quarterback in the franchise's first 40 years.

By their fourth and final year together, Bledsoe and Parcells brought their team to its second Super Bowl ever, as young Drew drew on a plethora of offensive weapons: running back Curtis Martin, tight end Ben Coates, and receivers Troy Brown, Shawn Jefferson, and Terry Glenn. Bledsoe led the NFL in passing attempts and completions en route to the second of his four Pro Bowl selections, and was seemingly on his way toward eventual enshrinement in the Pro Football Hall of Fame in Canton.

In that penultimate Super Bowl, Bledsoe passed poorly, completing only 25 of 48 attempts, tallying two touchdowns but surrendering four interceptions. Historians have mostly absolved him from blame for the ultimate loss to Green Bay, however, because the Packers' Desmond Howard had a career day on special teams and Parcells allowed the team to become distracted by his plans to leave New England for the Jets' head coaching job after the game.

While Bledsoe placed fifth in the NFL in completion percentage in 1997 and earned a third Pro Bowl nod, the more relaxed coaching manner of Pete Carroll ultimately did not work well with the then-veteran Patriots quarterback. Additionally, certain traits that Bledsoe had displayed (a tendency to only see the primary receiver, a propensity to take a sack, and a knack for fumbling) as a younger player had not disappeared with experience and seemingly had calcified. Without an All-Pro cast surrounding him, Bledsoe appeared lost too often, and in the salary cap era, the club did not have the luxury to continually supply him with that type and quantity of talent as players like Martin departed for other clubs.

In an otherwise exemplary public and charitable off-the-field image, Bledsoe committed one notable indiscretion during the

Drew Bledsoe was unquestionably the greatest quarterback in Patriots history before ceding his position to Tom Brady in 2001.

middle stage of his career, jumping in a mosh pit in a Boston bar during an Everclear concert. Some of his teammates joined in, and allegedly in the midst of the revelry, a young woman was hurt. Pictures of Bledsoe at that concert appeared in the papers, eyes firmly at half-mast, conveying a cluelessness for a bright and tough team leader. Perception became reality, and this lone indiscretion perpetuated a growing sense that the team's highest player resided in the *Land of the Lost.*

After Carroll left the team, new coach Bill Belichick could have cared less about the mosh pit incident, other than the fact that Belichick liked Bon Jovi more than Everclear. Unfortunately, it became ever more clear that Belichick only tolerated Bledsoe at quarterback in 2000, and once the Jets' Mo Lewis popped poor Drew out of the second game of the 2001 season, the head coach not only inserted Tom Brady as the team's starter, but he also kept him there even after Bledsoe recovered from his injuries.

Bledsoe enjoyed one final glorious moment in New England, when he guided his team to the AFC Championship Game against Pittsburgh on January 27, 2002, spelling the injured Brady. But Bledsoe did not return for an encore in the Super Bowl and was traded for a No. 1 pick (Ty Warren) before the 2002 season.

With the Bills in 2002, Bledsoe passed for the highest completion percentage in his career and made his fourth Pro Bowl team, but he continued to take an ungodly amount of sacks (54) that year and the next season (49, for an NFL-leading 371 yards lost due to sacks). His production tailed in his final two years in Buffalo. He had a productive season in 2005, reuniting with Parcells in Dallas, but by the next season, Bledsoe gave way to an emerging Tony Romo. Then it was over.

By then, the better looking, more engaging, and more talented Tom Brady had led the Patriots to three Super Bowl victories and a place in the New England sports pantheon up there with Bill Russell, Larry Bird, Ted Williams, Carl Yastrzemski, and Bobby

Orr. Bledsoe had compiled NFL all-time top 10 totals in passes completed and passing yards, yet his totals clanged hollow in juxtaposition with most of the other Hall of Fame–caliber quarterbacks around him (with the exception of another former Pat, Vinny Testaverde), the stats not revealing poor judgments, plays improperly read, fumbles, bumbles, and sacks needlessly taken.

That said, the time for burying Bledsoe and not properly praising him needs to cease. To compile the type of career passing stats he did cannot wholly obscure the fact that he did many things well, and perhaps if Parcells did not go a-bawling before the Super Bowl against Green Bay, Bledsoe might have led the Pats to their first title. To this day he is the second-finest quarterback in New England Patriots history and he should be appreciated for what he accomplished for his team, not condemned because he was not and never could be Tom Brady.

60 Gil Santos

Producers of Broadway plays once opened in Boston to let their actors and actresses hone their characters before going to New York City and allowing the newspaper reviewers to see the shows. Similarly, many sports commentators passed through Boston before going national, with Curt Gowdy, Sean McDonough, and Jon Miller following that path. Fortunately, Boston has kept a number of terrific television and radio voices like Johnny Most, Jerry Remy, and Fred Cusick for decades.

Patriots listeners have been similarly blessed with Gil Santos, literally a throwback to the AFL years, having started calling games as a color man in 1966 and shifting to play by play in the 1970s.

Most people forget that he did not call the games from 1980 through 1990, but since then he has been paired with Patriots legend Gino Cappelletti.

Off the air, Santos is well versed in choosing the finest restaurant in town when the Patriots have an away game. Knowledgeable Patriots staffers and management types, knights of the keyboard, and sundry other members of the media alike will wait in the lobby of hotels and wait for Gil to come down from his room and tell everyone the best place in town to dine. Santos retired after the 2012 season.

61 The Redskins and the Yanks

The Red Sox owned Boston virtually from the team's turn-of-the-century inception, a sad fact for Braves fans like a young Bob Kraft who witnessed their team move after the 1952 season. Similarly, the Bruins monopolized the public's attention during the winter, at least until the Celtics came to town, and arguably until Larry Bird left Indiana State, the Bruins still constituted the most popular polar sport.

Professional football did not rivet New Englanders either until late in the 20th century. The Boston Bulldogs in 1926 played one game at Fenway Park and one at Braves field and folded after one season in the original American Football League. When the NFL's Pottsville Maroons folded, that franchise moved to Boston for a year, appropriating the name of the Bulldogs with somewhat similar results. Had Maroons star back Johnny Blood played in Boston, perhaps he might have generated some fan excitement, but sadly, the new Bulldogs pulled up stakes after one year, never to return.

Years later, George Preston Marshall tried mightily to ensure that football flourished, installing his new Boston Braves franchise in baseball's Braves home field in 1932. It was a dull team in a boring league with six of the 10 games involving either the Braves or their opponents not scoring a single point. The team went 4–4–2 under Lud Wray, frustrated by a back who could not pass (less than 20 percent completion rate) named Honolulu Hughes, although the club fielded one star, future Hall of Famer Cliff Battles.

In 1933, Marshall renamed his team the Redskins and shifted their home to the Sox's Fenway Park, replacing Wray with a Native American coach named Lone Star Dietz. Although Battles continued to excel, Dietz proved incapable of motivating his mostly mediocre other group to anything but mediocre records: 5–5–2 in '33 and 6–6 in '34. Turk Edwards provided a lone bright spot as a particularly mean tackle.

The team dumped Dietz as its coach, replacing him with Eddie Casey, who drove his team to a 2–8–1 record in 1935. Marshall hired a terrific coach, Ray Flaherty, who helped lead the team to its finest record yet (7–5), aided considerably by exciting rookie and

Those Were the Breaks

Professional football in Massachusetts seemingly has had a happy ending…sort of. In 1983, the USFL fielded a local franchise, the Boston Breakers, for exactly one year in its inaugural season. The Breakers did not embarrass themselves on the gridiron, sporting an 11–7 record, but simply did not inspire fans to come out to see them in their home at Boston University's Nickerson Field, hemorrhaging attendance figures even by USFL standards. Banned in Boston, the Breakers moved to New Orleans the next year and eventually died in Portland as the league folded. The spirit of the club lives on with the current Boston Breakers holding down a women's professional soccer franchise. And do not ignore Boston's other championship football team, the Boston Militia, which won the Women's Football League world title in 2010, 2011, and 2014.

future Hall of Famer Wayne Millner from Roxbury. This mundane record permitted the club to play the Green Bay Packers for the NFL championship on December 13 at the Polo Grounds in New York. The locale was a peculiar choice, as Marshall had home-field advantage for the title game, but infuriated by the lack of fan support (fewer than 5,000 showed up for the final regular season game), the club owner decided to downgrade his men to a neutral site. Unfortunately, the Packers defeated the Redskins 21–6.

The Redskins continue to this day as one of the NFL's marquee franchises, beginning with two championships under Flaherty in 1937 and 1942, but Boston missed out on the glory as Marshall relocated the team to Washington after the 1936 season.

One of the factors chasing Marshall out of town was a competing football franchise, the Shamrocks, who outdrew the Redskins and lasted a few years, from 1936 to 1938. The Shamrocks alternated between Braves Field and Fenway Park and won a championship in 1936 in one of the early "American Football Leagues."

Ted Collins, most famous as the manager of singer Kate Smith, founded the Boston Yanks in 1944. The Yanks faced similar hurdles as their predecessors (lack of fan interest, no venue fit for football, and poor personnel), and it is perhaps with this team that Bostonians first chanted "Yankees suck!" Because they did.

In their premiere season, the club amassed a staunch 2–8 record. Wisely, the team hired Ted Williams to play left halfback; unfortunately they signed the wrong one, because this unsplendid splinter gained only 13 yards on 52 carries. Williams' mates in the backfield stunk mightily, with fullback George Cafego toting the rock for 31 yards on 61 carries and right halfback Johnny Martin losing a total of seven yards on 19 carries. Both of the club's only victories came against the Brooklyn Tigers (those Tigers must have been one hell of a team).

Oddly, in 1945, Kopf coached a pseudo combination of the Boston/Brooklyn Yanks/Tigers to a 3–6–1 record. (Must have had something to do with wartime rationing.) Cafego shifted to quarterback, and Martin actually gained some yards, handsomely grinding out 4.9 yards per carry.

The team slipped in 1946, not winning until the ninth game of the season despite the efforts of Chelsea native and Holy Cross back John Grigas and his 5.1 yards per carry on the ground. The club installed Clipper Smith as its new coach before the 1947 season and slightly improved to a 4–7–1 record, featuring Lynn native and Notre Dame star Boley Dancewicz at quarterback. The collective last gasp of the club occurred in the 1948 season, a dismal 3–9 affair, punctuated with the Yanks' trademarks of no team stars, too many points allowed, and too few touchdowns made.

And that was it, the team defeated the Philadelphia Eagles on December 5, 1948, and then moved to New York rechristened first as the Bulldogs, then as the New York Yanks. The nomadic existence of the team continued as they resettled in Dallas as the Texans in 1952. They lasted one year in the Big D, then moved to Baltimore and became the Colts. So if you ever run into an elderly fan who cheers for Peyton Manning and the Colts against the Pats, claiming he or she is only rooting for their old team, they are right. The Boston Yanks, like the Milwaukee Braves and union organizer Joe Hill, never died.

62 The Hartford Patriots

Connecticut's capital city of Hartford fielded two minor league football teams in the 20th century, the Charter Oaks and the Knights, but after 1973, big-time football abandoned the Insurance Capital of the World. With the possible exception of jai alai, nothing seemed to stick in Connecticut, as the NHL's Whalers finally relocated to traditionally hockey-mad North Carolina, of all places, in 1997.

The most densely populated and wealthiest state in America should have a plethora of professional major league clubs within its borders, but poor Connecticut does not. For a brief midwinter beginning on November 20, 1998, though, the citizens had hope, the realistic expectation that Patriots owner Robert Kraft might move the club there in the midst of local reluctance in eastern Massachusetts to permit him to build a new stadium. Connecticut governor John Rowland led a campaign to entice the Patriots away from Foxboro, reportedly offering the club $350 million (later reported at almost $25 million higher) in public funds to construct a 68,000-seat stadium along the banks of the Connecticut River.

Early efforts to move the franchise back to Boston failed due to local opposition, and it appeared that the state might lose its football team. The proposed relocation of the team to Boston, more specifically along the South Boston waterfront, seemingly knit together many loose ends. It appealed to those nostalgic romantics who pined for a return to the old Boston Patriots moniker, and more concretely promised to solve many of the logistical issues surrounding getting to and from a Patriots home game. Foxboro provided a surfeit of buildable land back in the day, but it never acted as an efficient spur for moving traffic in and out of the stadium area, particularly troublesome after the conclusion of a game when most folks wanted to get home and prepare for their real lives back at work for the next week.

Dreams aside, the locals hated the proposal, and only one local city councilor even suggested that the offer be at least listened to. More significantly, a backlash had begun against publicly funded windfalls to rich franchise owners, and few in Massachusetts wanted to pony up a fortune to assist a team it had put up with for nearly four decades. The planned move to Boston stalled and the situation threatened to devolve into a free fall. If there was to be no

Boston Patriots, then all of New England beckoned as a potential suitor for the Pats.

In early 1999, Kraft had reached a tentative agreement to relocate the team to Hartford, but by then, the momentum had shifted away from Connecticut. The NFL did not want to lose its sixth-largest market and Massachusetts politicians became more malleable, agreeing to at least $70 million for local infrastructure improvements. Kraft exercised his out clause just before the deal with Connecticut would have become binding, and financed the new stadium privately.

As a boy, Kraft bemoaned the relocation of his beloved Boston Braves to Milwaukee, and he did not have to move his Patriots away when furnished the opportunity. The Patriots would stay in Foxboro and start winning titles, as fans continued to endure traffic jams on their way out of the newly constructed stadium.

63 The Butler Saved It

It started in the Patriots' training camp, summer of 2014, the opportunistic ball-hawking propensities of undrafted rookie free agent Malcolm Butler. He picked off fellow rookie Jimmy Garoppolo, but also Tom Brady during practices. In a skeleton drill, Brady completed a pass to Gronkowski, who promptly had the ball knocked loose by Butler. In an exhibition game against the Eagles, Butler started in place of an injured Brandon Browner and forced a fumble.

Malcolm Butler made the final cut that fall, the only undrafted free agent that made the team, but by then even veterans like Vince Wilfork had taken notice, commenting later: "We call him 'Scrap'

Another Big Pick

Malcolm Butler would never have made his interception to ice the Lombardi Trophy had another previously unheralded Pats defensive back not made a great play. In the first playoff game in January 2015, with 1:46 left in the game, Joe Flacco threw to Torrey Smith, only to see a cheating safety named Duron Harmon intercept the pass. While Flacco later had one late last chance to win the game with a Hail Mary pass, Harmon's interception likely saved the game and the season for New England.

because the first time we saw him he was just so scrappy and he found himself around the ball all the time. I think that was one of the main reasons he was in the game. Throughout the course of the year, he shows up at practice and he makes plays."

In the second half of the blow-out loss to the Chiefs in game four, Malcolm Butler came off the bench to play the second half; in another game he was inserted in the first half to defend against Peyton Manning and the Broncos, steadily gaining experience. As the season progressed, his cornerbacks coach Josh Boyer observed, "He's got a good burst, he's got good speed, he's very competitive on the ball, he's got good instincts with ball skills,"

Very competitive on the ball. Good instincts with ball skills.

He needed all of those skills late in the Super Bowl after the Seahawks' Jermaine Kearse made a miraculous catch on the Pats' 5-yard line, after which Butler alertly tackled him. These types of late-game heroics in Super Bowl losses have dogged the Patriots, and with ample time left, the Seahawks seemed destine to polish off the day with an easy touchdown score.

You've seen the play dozens of times by now. Russell Wilson jams the ball into the center of the field and Butler jumps the route and intercepts the ball. Game over.

And that might not be the only surprising thing about Malcolm Butler.

His JUCO coach at Hinds had kicked him off the team, after which Butler went to work at Popeye's. Allowed back on the team, Butler played well enough only to receive an offer to play at Division II West Alabama. His coach at West Alabama noted, "He turned his life around. Malcolm's not just a quality football player. He's a quality person."

Tom Brady won the Super Bowl MVP Award but gave the truck to Butler. He went to Disney World and the Grammy Awards with Julian Edelman. And the best news, his Patriots career has just begun.

64 Come to Roost at the Red Wing Diner

Either you enjoy diners or you do not, and if you are one of those fortunate people who patronize them, you will savor the Red Wing Diner on Route 1, a short drive north up the road from Gillette Stadium. Not too long ago, this stretch along Walpole and Foxboro contained a number of joints like the Red Wing, but they have long since shut down, most likely victims of Patriot Place's numerous restaurants and pubs.

Open for nearly 60 years, the diner still hosts fans every day, filling up on Patriots game days and attracting fans of the New England Revolution soccer club, which also plays its home games at Gillette. If you cannot get a seat on Sunday, stop by any weekday to find a chair.

By way of a caveat, if you base your impressions of the Red Wing on a drive-by or a scan of an Internet article, you have not done justice to it, as it more closely resembles the clam shacks that once dotted the shores of New England, which have nearly vanished along with outdoor movie theatres. The Red Wing survives by generating hearty and heaping plates of food served well. Many online articles incorrectly squawk about how the Red Wing has not undergone a renovation since Nixon sat in the Oval Office, an observation belied by the new sign outside and by extensive improvements in the booths and tables in the main dining area. The walls have been brightened, crowded with a nice group of people.

If you want to replicate an experience from your youth, you should enter the side door where you can sit in a stool by the bar or in one of the four tables off to its side. This area has not changed much at all since the dawn of time, so for nostalgia buffs, the bar area is indistinguishable from a working man's diner from the World War II era (save for the smoking ban).

Longtime fans rave about the Red Wing's buffalo wings, which excel particularly when hot, but if you are tired of monitoring your cholesterol and want to walk on the wild side, order the fried clams served on a mound of tasty french fries. Load up at the diner and you and your party will save plenty on concessions. For lighter fare, there is pasta and salads, so do not feel compelled to restrict yourself to fried foods unless under doctor's orders.

In these latter days where the gulf between a sports fan and a star athlete remains virtually unbridgeable, it is no surprise that you will most likely never encounter a Pats player at the premises, but in the event you wonder about what they eat, quite often large takeout orders are routed to the players after a practice. Need another recommendation? Former Boston Bruins defenseman (and current television analyst) Mike Milbury drops by frequently.

That the Red Wing survives and continues to thrive serves as a testament to the wonderful food and friendly atmosphere inside. This is not a sports bar, there are no big-screen TVs, and you might not even see a photo of a star on the wall, but Boston's Phantom Gourmet likes the place. If your family has resided in New England for at least a few generations, you might have stopped by with your grandfather or your father, and if you have converted into a lapsed Red Winger, you might want to revisit this veritable shrine.

 **Ty Law**

Generally, I enjoy sitting down all weekend with my newspapers and magazines sorting through draft weekend every April, but one year I visited friend during the first round, so I can distinctly remember where I was and what I was doing when I heard that the Patriots had chosen Ty Law with their first draft choice out of Michigan in 1995. And did then head coach Bill Parcells ever choose his "groceries" well that year, also adding to the club's roster Ted Johnson and Curtis Martin in the next two rounds.

Law split time his rookie season at right cornerback with veteran Maurice Hurst, and then as Hurst's career ended, Law deftly made the transition to the starting cornerback role during the club's 1996 campaign toward a Super Bowl appearance. During that season, he intercepted his first pass for a touchdown, something of a future specialty, eventually intercepting 7 passes for touchdowns, eighth all-time in the NFL when he retired.

After Parcells left, Law thrived under Pete Carroll, earning his first of five career Pro Bowl selections in 1998, leading the NFL with nine interceptions. Chimbed Carroll, "It was as dominant a season at cornerback as I have ever seen in this league—and I have seen some great ones." In ensuing seasons, his interception totals dropped off for the elemental reason that opposing coaches avoided calling passing plays to Law's territory. Despite this and because of this, Law merited selections to Pro Bowls at the conclusion of each season from 2001 through 2003, as he held down his corner

Patriot First
Before Ty Law paced all defenders with nine interceptions in 1998, no Patriot had ever led either the AFL or the NFL in interceptions in a season

position during three Super Bowl seasons for the Pats early in the millennium. In 2001, he sparked his team with an opportune interception off of the Rams' Kurt Warner for a 47 yard touchdown return for the Pats' first points in their first NFL title-winning game.

Famously, he also picked Peyton Manning three times during the 2003 NFC championship game. Marvelled the Boston Globe' Ron Borges after that game, "[Law] is fast, quick, athletic, confident, brave, and tough-minded, yet he is more than that. He is smart relentless and one of those rare players who can hit you in the mouth if that's what it takes...." Echoed Law after mugging the Colts' star receiver Marvin Harrison all day, "Peyton has confidence in Marvin and he should, but I felt I was up to the challenge. I'm a pretty confident guy also."

Sentiment never a prevailing emotion for the modern Patriots, the club released Law after an injury plagued 2004 season, a casualty due more to his formidable salary cap number than a loss of effectiveness, a point Ty himself made during the 2005 season with the Jets as Law again led the NFL with picks, this time with ten. Now in his early thirties, he became more of a gypsy than a fixture, starting for the Chiefs from 2006-2007 and serving part-time with the Jets in 2008 and the Broncos in 2009, at which time his career ended amidst rumors that he might return to New England for a Last Hurrah that never materialized.

Like many former Pats players who left the team just before their careers began to irreversibly reverse, Ty Law has become a bit of a non-person around Foxboro an unfortunate trend that merits an immediate termination. This star player intercepted 53 passes during his career, just outside of the top twenty all-time in the NFL, rising to an even higher level in the playoffs, a clutch anchor to the excellent Patriot defenses in their first three title years. And unlike Deion Sanders, another exceptional cornerback of the era, Ty Law did not eschew initiating contact with opposing receivers. The man flat out loved to hit. Law himself did not shy from the comparison, once stating, "I want to be known as a more complete corner man Deion. Five years after I finish this game, I want to be walking around the Hall of Fame with that yellow jacket on. I've been overlooked so much during my life, I want the attention." Whether Canton beckons him or not, Patriot Place finally welcomed him, inducting this intelligent and gifted performer in its own Hall of Fame in 2014.

66 Bruce Armstrong

Drafted by the Patriots in the first round in 1987 out of Louisville, Bruce Armstrong excelled as an offensive tackle in the midst of increasing futility for the franchise. The wonderful 1985 year had not heralded the commencement of a dynasty, and in the period between Raymond Berry ending his coaching career and Bill Parcells taking over the helm in 1993, the team sunk to arguably its worst period.

The team struggled to a 1–15 mark in 1990, and midway through another disaster two seasons later (about to lose their eighth straight game to open the season), Armstrong snapped his medial collateral ligament and both his posterior and anterior cruciate ligaments in his right knee. It might have ended his career, but instead presaged some of the more productive campaigns ahead of him. Reminiscing years later, the star tackle recalled "not even wanting to come out of the house because we were pretty much a point of ridicule. You go to the store or in the mall and you're not real proud of what you're doing. I'm a proud man. That really hurt."

Despite the club's lack of success, his peers took notice, as Armstrong was selected to six Pro Bowls starting in 1990. Although he played his first three seasons as a right tackle, he shifted to the much more prestigious left tackle position, where he played through the remainder of his career, one that stretched through 2000. Armstrong retained no illusions regarding the tasks required of him, believing that "You need unusual size but also unusual speed, which is not a usual combination. It's an oxymoron to say you want a quick guy who's 290, but that's what he'd better be."

The Parcells years rejuvenated him, providing Armstrong with his only opportunity to play in a Super Bowl. His 212 starts with New England is a franchise record, and he only trails John Hannah for total selections to the Pro Bowl as a Pat. A member of the Patriots' 50th Anniversary Team, Armstrong also has earned recognition as one of the two starting tackles on their All-Decade Teams for both the 1980s and the 1990s.

67 The Minutemen

Behind each end zone at Patriots home games stand about 10 men dressed in Minutemen garb, reenactors of that glorious period when Paul Revere rode around the Middlesex villages and towns warning the suburbanites that the forces of the British Empire were afoot. One man leads the group, and after a score the Minutemen raise their flintlock rifles, ejaculating a thunderous roar even though they only shoot blanks. An acrid and thick smoke then floats over the field, coincidentally most often invading the bench of the opposing team.

For those interested in joining, the militia require that one "must be a member of a noted reenactment group, belonging to the Continental Line, British Brigade, or B.A.R., first to learn safety, skills, and obtain the appropriate equipage. Be a member in good standing for a minimum of three years. Then you can request a spot within the End Zone Militia." The group is not for the faint of heart or for weekend warriors, a candidate must possess an underlying devotion to honoring and preserving the revolutionary heritage.

The End Zone Militia do not have any formal affiliation with the Patriots organization and they participate at other sporting venues, including events for the Boston Red Sox and the New England Revolution soccer team. They are ambassadors of a glorious past age, and beyond the sporting world, they dedicate themselves to inculcating others in the roots of our country.

68 Jim Nance

Syracuse University produced the finest running backs in the nation in the late 1950s and early 1960s, with such future professional stars as James Brown, Ernie Davis, Floyd Little, Larry Csonka, and Boston Patriots legend Jim Nance. Chosen by the Patriots in the 19th round, Jim started poorly for a poor team, averaging 2.9 yards in his rookie season as the team posted a 4–8–2 record for the year. No one ran well for the club that year with the

Butkus, Sayers, and Nance?

In the 1965 draft, the Chicago Bears had one of the finest first rounds in NFL history, choosing two future Hall of Famers in linebacker Dick Butkus with the third overall pick and back Gale Sayers with the next pick. The Bears did not have another opportunity to draft a player until the fourth round when they selected...Jim Nance. Although not picked until the 19th round of the AFL draft, Nance cast his lot with the upstart Boston team anyway, leading fantasy types to wonder how any team in the NFL could have stopped a Bears backfield of Sayers and Nance had Jim opted to play on Sundays at Wrigley Field.

exception of 35-year-old quarterback Babe Parilli, who gained 200 yards on 50 carries, many of which constituted life-saving dodges from enemy defenders.

Even as a player, Nance constantly battled to control his weight, and as any football card collector from the 1960s knew from reading the back of Jim's bubblegum card, he locked up his refrigerator the night before a game, in part to stay hungry while attacking opposing defenses. Coach Mike Holovak did not view the situation in such serendipitous terms, warning him during the 1965 season that a position switch to tackle was imminent.

Perplexed and perhaps hurt, Nance replied, "Mike, I don't want to be a tackle. I don't want to play the line." Holovak then finished reading the riot act, concluding, "Well, make up your mind. You're either a fullback or a tackle. You've got the talent for either. Decide." Nance dedicated himself to being a fullback.

By the next season the team and Nance reversed course, as the Pats went 8–4–2 in 1966 and Jim won the AFL MVP award. Chosen for his first Pro Bowl, Nance was the central reason for this change in fortune, rushing for 1,458 yards for a 4.9 average yards per carry, an AFL record. He also amassed 11 of the team's 17 rushing touchdowns. Speculating about this turnaround, one magazine writer felt that "Oddly, perhaps, what helped most to discipline Nance was his buying a place called Jim Nance's Lounge in Boston. The two jobs keep him too busy to eat. 'But the primary thing is that last year I wasn't serious,' says Nance. 'I had an ideal, easy life. Buying the place meant my employees had to rely on me, and I had to rely on them. If a person works for me, I expect him to do his job. I work for Holovak, and he expects me to do my job.'"

In one game, he tied a pro football record that had stood since 1934, rushing the ball on 38 occasions in a game against Oakland, and Nance did not nibble along the sidelines. He spent most of the time bursting through the center of the line. Nance accepted this role and its inherent limitations, once commenting, "I'm not a spectacular open-field runner. I'm supposed to plow through the line for as much yardage as I can grind out. And when I'm not doing that, I'm supposed to block."

Holovak noticed, later opining, "You have no idea what that man means to us. He does things that nobody notices. He'll always get his yardage, but what amazes me is his blocking. When he

Fullback Jim Nance twice led the AFL in rushing and was inducted into the Patriots Hall of Fame in 2009.

The Hammerlocking Halfback

Need any more evidence of the superior strength and athleticism of James Solomon Nance? How's this: he was the NCAA national wrestling champion in the heavyweight class in 1963 and 1965, losing only one match during his entire high school and college careers. Although Nance bypassed an almost certain invitation to the Olympics, he always believed that his wrestling prowess served him well as a professional running back, concluding, "It's good for my balance. It's good for the small cuts. And in wrestling, it's one guy against another, with nobody to help. I've got plenty of help on this team, of course, but the wrestling feeling has carried over. It's a personal thing. Those guys in the secondary are smaller than I am. They'll come in looking to tackle me head on, but after I've tagged them a couple of times they start closing their eyes or ducking their heads. Pretty soon they're swearing when they get up. Then they'll start turning their shoulders when they come at me, and I know I've got them."

doesn't carry the ball he protects everyone around him…. When they tried to blitz Parilli, he knocked Houston's safetyman right into the linebacker. I don't think I've ever seen a blocking back do that in this league."

Despite this promising season, the 1967 edition of the Boston Patriots limped to a 3–10–1 record, even though Nance gained another 1,216 yards on the ground and caught 22 passes. Nance again won all-star kudos, but he had begun to accumulate a massive amount of carries. The offense's overdependence on Nance became clear the next year as he only averaged 3.4 yards per carry on another awful Pats team.

Nance's final three years proved equally frustrating from a personal and team standpoint, as Carl Garrett increasingly became the featured back and Nance did not approximate his two excellent seasons of 1966–67. The team compiled 4–10, 2–12, and 6–8 records in those years, and at the end the club decided that Nance simply was not in their future plans.

In July 1972, New England tried to trade Nance to the Philadelphia Eagles for a fourth-round pick, a deal that did not materialize when the back refused his new assignment, seemingly spelling the end of his career. However, like Babe Parilli before him, Nance played out his string with the New York Jets in 1973, having taken a hiatus for a year after leaving the Pats. Although he only played in half the team's games that season, he did rush 18 times for 78 yards, his best average since his two finest previous efforts. This impressive cameo effort helped to elongate his career when the World Football League formed, a development that permitted him to excel for two final seasons for the Houston Texans and Shreveport Steamer. He totaled more than 2,000 yards in rushing for the short-lived league, making its all-time team and gaining the most yards on the ground.

Despite the nice conclusion to his professional career, Jim Nance is mostly remembered for his work with the Patriots, and his 5,323 career rushing yards has only been surpassed by Sam Cunningham in franchise history. No one else in AFL history ever had two seasons of rushing for more than 1,000 yards, and Nance has been posthumously inducted into the Patriots Hall of Fame.

69 Mike Holovak

An excellent athlete, Mike Holovak played back for Boston College in the early 1940s, coached by the legendary Frank Leahy before Leahy returned to his alma mater, Notre Dame. In 1942, Holovak was a consensus All-American (and later a College Hall of Famer), and like John F. Kennedy, he distinguished himself for valor in World War II for his service on a PT boat. When Holovak returned, naturally he played professional football.

Putting Things in Perspective

Poised to win a national championship in 1942, the Boston College Eagles lost their final game to the Holy Cross Crusaders, a crushing blow to co-captain Mike Holovak and his teammates, who had planned to celebrate that evening at the Cocoanut Grove, a popular downtown night club. In a tragic twist of fate, the loss prevented many of the young men from dying that night, as a fire swept through the venue that evening, killing 492 patrons.

And a damned good professional player he was. He had a decent rookie season in 1946 with the Rams, then flourished in his next two seasons with the Bears, taking orders from George Halas. Although featured backs Joe Osmanski, George Gulyanics, and George McAfee got most of the rushing attempts, Holovak made the most of his opportunities, averaging 5.5 yards per carry in 1947 and blasting for 7.6 yards a run in 1948.

Despite his prowess on the gridiron, Holovak's vocation lay in coaching young football players, beginning with his hiring at Boston College as a freshman coach in 1949, leading his charges to two undefeated seasons until he assumed the varsity head coaching role in late 1950. Over nine seasons at the Heights, Holovak led the Eagles to a cumulative 49–29–3 mark, and yet toward the end of his tenure the fans had turned on him, hooting him after each loss even though he had consistently fielded competitive teams.

He was fired from B.C., but as one door closed, another opportunity came to him, as he fortuitously landed with the Boston Patriots as a personnel director and assistant coach in the franchise's inaugural 1960 season. The team did not perform well that year for head coach Lou Saban—a talented leader who did not ingratiate himself with many of his players or with owner Billy Sullivan—so when the team staggered in early 1961, Sullivan sacked Saban and replaced him with Holovak. The second head coach in team history is still the coach with the second-most victories in franchise annals.

Disadvantaged by the 2–3 record he inherited from Saban, Holovak closed out the season with a 7–1–1 mark, aided by the addition of quarterback Babe Parilli and the shifting of personnel, such as Gino Cappelletti from defensive halfback to wide receiver. A keen talent evaluator, he led the Pats to a 9–4–1 record in 1962, and despite a seemingly mediocre 7–6–1 final season mark in 1963, he brought the club to its first championship game that year against the Chargers. Preceding that title match, the Pats had to win a tough playoff game against Buffalo, after which they simply did not seem to have any stamina left as San Diego blew them out in the AFL Championship Game. Despite this setback, in 1964 Holovak coached the team to another fine season (10–4).

The 1965 Patriots nearly reversed their fine performance from the previous campaign, throwing together a 4–8–2 disappointment. Help was on its way, as Jim Nance had played his rookie year and, due to some chiding and perceptive coaching, transformed himself soon after into one of the finest football players in America.

Roaring back in 1966, Nance gained 1,458 yards on the ground and a veteran core of Patriots restored the team, needing only to defeat the New York Jets in the final game to vie for the AFL title and thereafter, a potential spot in the first Super Bowl. As underrated today as he was overrated in his prime, Joe Namath led the upstart Jets to a 38–28 pasting of Boston, ending the season for Holovak and his men. Holovak earned his second Coach of the Year honors, but it served as a consolation prize in light of the team not reaching its goal.

The 1966 season proved a watershed year in franchise history because it exposed the management to scrutiny for some of its shortcomings as it concluded with a crash and burn. In *Violence Every Sunday*, a book Holovak co-authored later with Bill McSweeny, he owned up to one particular weakness. "I felt something else nagging at me. I was making an emotional mistake," he said. "There were three older players on the squad and they weren't a strength anymore. They were a weakness. I should have cut them and brought men up from the taxi squad. But they had been with me a long time and they were doing the best they could."

In short, Mike Holovak might have simply been too nice a man to head coach a professional football team. When the Patriots began ripping through opponents in the new millennium, older souls whose skills had begun to decline got cut. Holovak's reluctance to dump faded stars haunted him the next two seasons as the Pats staggered to 3–10–1 and 4–10 records. True, the team had aged, but in the three drafts from 1966 to 1968, the Patriots whiffed almost across the board, so even as older players departed, not enough skilled new players emerged. Perhaps some of those failings remain Holovak's responsibility as he continued to serve as a personnel director in addition to his coaching duties, too much work in a game that had become increasingly popular and complex. After the 1968 debacle, the club unwisely fired Holovak, ushering in the brief but disastrous Clive Rush regime.

Holovak hung around Boston briefly after his sacking, but then left to serve in various capacities in professional football in other cities, famously serving as a leader for one more game, subbing for Lou Holtz after he resigned as head coach for the Jets. He lost that one last contest, but Oilers owner Bud Adams must have always liked him from the old AFL days because he hired Holovak in 1981, where he served with distinction for almost 20 years.

Had Holovak insisted that Billy Sullivan hire a GM or personnel director in 1961, and had Holovak cut his players a year before they lost it rather than a season too late, he might have coached well into the 1970s, ultimately retiring as the man who brought the Patriots their first AFL or NFL title. But then he would not have been himself, a person remembered fondly by many fans as a man who coached some very good Boston teams in an era when Bill Russell and the Celtics ruled and the Red Sox and Bruins became great again.

175

70 Biggest Busts

Disappointment overtakes the better angels of our nature when evaluating the biggest busts in Patriots history, those collegiate gridiron greats who somehow lose a step after arriving in Foxboro. These are the "can't miss" prospects who, in fact, missed.

Traditionally, 1968 first-round draft choice Dennis Byrd, a defensive end from North Carolina State, has served as the main whipping boy for draftniks. The Patriots' website quotes Carey Brewbaker, his line coach at N.C. State, thusly: "[Byrd is] the best I've coached in 30 years and I had three All-Americans at Notre Dame…he's great at breaking double teams and above all…he will hit." Problem was, he hurt his right knee in his senior year in a game against Duke, and then tried to return to action too soon. Byrd had no business suiting up to play professional football. He did try to stick with the Patriots, but his career never had a chance. Looking back, Byrd now concedes, "I was never the same after the knee injury, and today I can hardly walk."

Some of the most noteworthy poor picks occurred when the Pats targeted offensive linemen, missing early with Karl Singer of Purdue with the third overall pick in the AFL draft in 1966. Singer played parts of three seasons before his spikes were hung up for him, a fate similar to a first-round faux pas committed over a quarter century later with Eugene Chung from Virginia Tech. Coach Bill Parcells, when asked why Chung did not play more, acidly stated something to the effect that coaches tend to start players who will help the coach win. Chung did not stay much longer, but he at least played a couple more years with other teams after his tenure at Foxboro ended.

Speaking of disappointments, let us consider the strange case of Ohio State linebacker Andy Katzenmoyer, a Butkus Award winner chosen in the first round in 1999. He hurt his neck in his rookie season and due to surgery played only part of his sophomore campaign. He exited training camp in 2001 due to concerns for his neck, and like Charlie on the MTA, he never returned. Luckily, that same year the Pats picked up a linebacker who played at OSU with Katzenmoyer, an émigré from the Pittsburgh Steelers named Mike Vrabel. Vrabel became one of the most popular and effective linebackers for the team, and as a spot tight end he caught 10 passes, all for touchdowns.

Receiver Ron Sellers comes close to being adjudged a bust. This tall and handsome receiver from Florida State, the sixth player chosen in the 1969 draft, played three years with the Pats and only five years in the NFL. What saves him is that he made a Pro Bowl his rookie season and played well in his second year. Still, no Stanley Morgan.

Gauging the difference between hype and performance, Ken "Game Day" Sims is our nominee for biggest bust the franchise ever chose. An absolute force as a defensive lineman at the University of Texas, Sims earned All-American selections twice and won the Lombardi Award his senior year. The Pats chose him with the first choice overall in the 1982 draft.

He won his moniker in the pros for reportedly stating, "I'll be there on game day," eschewing overexerting himself at practice. Unfortunately, he did not accomplish much on game day either, registering only 17 sacks in eight NFL seasons, only playing in all 16 games during the regular season once in his career. Implicated in early 1986 as one of the Pats' Super Bowl players with drug issues, Sims reportedly was arrested carrying cocaine on his person in 1990, an indiscretion that effectively ended his undistinguished career.

71 Not the Sweetest Hangover

Having improbably earned their first shot to participate in the Super Bowl, the 1985 Patriots almost immediately imploded two days later when the *Boston Globe* ran a story accusing the club of knowing during the regular season that several stars used drugs. Implicated in the scandal were Irving Fryar, Tony Collins, Stephen Starring, Roland James, Raymond Clayborn, and Kenneth Sims, and perhaps as many as six others.

The situation became unplumbed during the regular season, when head coach Raymond Berry supposedly became so disgusted with the lack of performance from many players that he threatened to resign unless many of them underwent drug testing. That seems like a reasonable request today, but at that time it marked a bold departure from practice. Union head Gene Upshaw complained, but the fait accomplit had already occurred.

The breaking of the story tarnished the incredible accomplishments of the team during the season, a year that the local fandom began to love the team as it had never done in the past, freeing it from seemingly fourth-place status in a town dominated by the Red Sox, the Celtics, and the Bruins.

"This is the worst thing that's happened to the game in years," Berry mused as the story broke. "The league office should never let those players get away with this."

While the team and the league and the union sorted matters out and threw bodies under the bus, fans wondered if the team had tanked in the Super Bowl due to drugs, and also rightfully began to worry about their favorite players. Fortunately, the club posted a strong 11–5 record the next season, losing narrowly to the Broncos in the playoffs, so many of the personnel matters had apparently worked out satisfactorily.

Or had they? Beginning in 1987, the club embarked on a steep decline that went virtually unchecked until Bill Parcells signed on six years later. Players who should have been superstars continued to underperform, and character guys like John Hannah retired, left the team, or fell prey to injuries or advancing age. Bill Belichick would never have coached some of these players, but Berry hung on to enough of them that he finally figuratively hanged himself.

Many of the players involved straightened out their lives at some point, while others either did not or took much longer to mature. The incident and the timing of the release of this story now stand as cruel epitaphs to an unlikely trip to the title game and the invigoration of interest in the local football club. The team suffered and soon the Patriots fell back into the fourth and last spot in the hearts of most New England sports fans.

An already beleaguered Berry and the club ownership had to now answer the critics on a number of levels: Why did the team not clearly and publicly crack down on the players during the season? Was the testing of their players during the season allowed under the league's collective bargaining agreement? Did the drug use continue and—gasp!—possibly lead to the team's destruction in the Super Bowl?

The only things that kept this story from becoming even larger was the fact that the entire country had just begun to mourn the doomed Space Shuttle *Challenger* crew, along with a much less honorable fact: that most of the accused players were stars, and star athletes, particularly then, got away with quite a lot. Indeed, each of the six accused players suited up with the club the next season.

72 A Real Cowboy

Onetime Patriots general manager Upton Bell fell in love with Duane Thomas, a Cowboys running back (and native of Dallas) who had gained 803 yards rushing in 1970. After that splendid rookie effort, Thomas entered into an undeclared war against virtually everyone in the Cowboys organization, including his teammates, essentially due to his dissatisfaction with his contract. Attempting to shoot his way out of town, Thomas accused Cowboys president Tex Schramm of being sick, demented, and dishonest, causing Schramm to retort, "That's not bad. He got two out of three."

Tom Landry saw a thing or two he did not like about Duane Thomas, and since he had two other quality backs in Walt Garrison and Calvin Hill, he gladly dumped Thomas when Bell and the Patriots came calling. The Pats parted with a draft pick and their own enigmatic back, Carl Garrett, the pet of head coach John Mazur.

Mazur did not get along with Bell and he cared for Thomas less, claiming insubordination almost immediately from his new player. The Patriots sought to void the deal, the NFL agreed, and back went Thomas to Dallas. Thomas sort of sorted out matters with the Cowboys, compiling a very respectable season's worth of statistics: 793 yards on the ground the next year, with an NFL-leading 11 rushing touchdowns. Famously, as his team celebrated its Super Bowl win at the conclusion of the 1971 season, interviewers had to essentially have Jim Brown interpret for Thomas in what should have been one of the most joyous moments of the young back's career.

He never played in Dallas again, as Landry shipped him off for good to the San Diego Chargers, who then cut him. Idled for 1972, he came back for two undistinguished years with the Redskins before checking out with one final season in the World

Football League. Had Mazur and the Patriots decided to put up with Thomas' ever-changing moods, they undoubtedly would have been rewarded with a stellar year from their running back for one season, and one season only. Thomas ended his career with barely more than 2,000 total yards rushing, an almost unbelievable feat given his prodigious gifts and great start in the NFL. In retrospect, he is a goofy footnote in Patriots history, the annals of which had several faux pas intermixed with occasional successes in those years before Bill Parcells came to rejuvenate them (and commit some faux pas of his own).

73 The Third Championship

Cincinnati Bengals running back Corey Dillon had endured a bad reputation during most of his NFL career, an unfair one largely because Dillon did not dislike the concept of team play; he disliked team ineptitude and the Bengals of that era simply did not win ballgames. That is not completely gospel—Corey certainly knew how to make a pain of himself—but Bill Belichick saw a winner and the Pats stole him from Cincy before the 2004 season. Dillon repaid this faith in him by gaining 1,635 yards rushing with his new team in that ensuing year.

Belichick did not cease tinkering with his team, letting Ty Law and Ted Washington walk away from the club on defense, as he added exciting new linemen Ty Warren and Vince Wilfork, not to mention a future star cornerback in Asante Samuel. The defense had its core, but the infusion of new talent, often overlooked, deflected any temptation for complacency in the shadow of so much recent success.

The players expected to win, an expectation shared by management, fans, and local media alike, but the confidence did not refract well off others. No longer the bright-eyed underdogs who had miraculously defeated the Rams' "Greatest Show on Turf," the Pats found themselves increasingly hated beyond the borders of New England. Having no choice, they invited the scorn.

Defeating the Colts in the opening game of the 2004 season helped vault the Patriots to a 6–0 start. Their one hiccup occurred when they faced the Pittsburgh Steelers, who dismantled them 34–20 in the eighth week of the season, as Ben Roethlisberger and Hines Ward torched them all game long, and then allowed Duce Staley and Jerome Bettis to roll all over them. Lesson in humility learned, New England did not lose again in the regular season except for a difficult-to-fathom loss to a poor Miami Dolphins team in December, a match marked more by Tom Brady being picked off an uncharacteristic four times. Supporters hoped it was a fluke in a meaningless tiff so close to the playoffs.

During the 1960s the greatest quarterback debate began and ended with a comparison between the Colts' John Unitas—who produced the most gaudy statistics—and the Packers' Bart Starr, who almost always won the championship ring. Similarly, in the new millennium, Peyton Manning almost always waxed Tom Brady in yearly quarterback ratings, but the Patriots quarterback more often spent the off-season visiting Disney World or the White House. In the 2004 playoffs, Manning again won MVP honors and faced a New England defense denuded of two of its key defenders, Richard Seymour and Ty Law, and yet Brady and company won again, this time by a 20–3 margin.

As a domed-stadium franchise, the Colts did not face enough inclement weather during the season, so when they came to Foxboro, they lacked the resiliency to stifle their opponents. Bill Belichick and offensive coordinator Charlie Weis devised a game control schematic, jamming running back "Clock Killin'" Corey

The Patriots' 24–21 victory over the Philadelphia Eagles in Super Bowl XXXIX earned them a third championship ring.

Dillon into the line all afternoon. It worked, with Dillon tabulating 144 yards for a 6.3 yards-per-carry average as his team maintained nearly a 2:1 time-of-possession edge over Indy during the game. Typically, Manning's passing stats exceeded those posted by Brady, but Peyton did not complete a pass for more than 18 yards.

"They didn't hurt us so much in the passing game other than on a couple critical third-down throws. Dillon and Faulk. That's where they hurt us," admitted Colts head coach Tony Dungy. The debate concerning which team possessed the better quarterback did not end that day, but the Colts' season did end, while the Pats earned the privilege of opposing the Pittsburgh Steelers the next week in the AFC Championship Game.

The Steelers had played nearly flawless ball all year, embarrassing the Pats and only stumbling once before the second season began. Pittsburgh still possessed the same healthy players on offense that had overrun New England at the end of October; on defense, linebacker James Farrior and safety Troy Polamalu led a similarly tough group. Their coach, Bill Cowher, was one of the few head coaches who matched up well against Belichick, and by virtue of their superior record, the Steelers hosted the Pats.

No matter; before halftime the Patriots had shot off to a 24–3 lead, culminating in a 41–27 victory and a ticket to their third Super Bowl appearance in four years. Dillon matched Jerome Bettis on the ground, but this time the Pats owned the sky, as Brady found receivers Deion Branch and David Givens at his leisure, with the long passes to Branch providing the telling blows. Roethlisberger coughed up three interceptions, Brady nary a one. Not one for gushing praise, Belichick succinctly but accurately appraised Brady, "There's no quarterback I'd rather have."

Safety Rodney Harrison made a key 87-yard interception off Roethlisberger, a timely swing as his touchdown prevented a certain Steelers score that would have reduced New England's lead to seven points. Instead, Harrison's ball-hawking extended his team's lead to 24–3. It's not that the Pats never looked back after that, but they no longer had to look back in anger, as they now had one game left to win, the Super Bowl against the Philadelphia Eagles.

During the overly long period of Super Bowl hype, an Eagles receiver kept shooting off his mouth, and strangely the din did not emanate from the usually loquacious Terrell Owens, who had sustained an injury serious enough to call his participation in the epic questionable at best. With or without him, star quarterback Donovan McNabb guided the offense and had a huge multi-warhead weapon at his disposal, running back Brian Westbrook, the Joe Morrison of his day, a player who did everything well.

Axiomatically, most Super Bowls devolve into dull affairs, with one team completely dominating its opponent, and by sometime in the second quarter, most home parties turn into just that—parties among friends, with few folks paying passing attention to the television. Not so for the Pats under Belichick, as his four trips to the dance all proved nail-biters, not nacho-biters, for the fans. Fittingly, the Pats and Eagles were tied at the end of each of the first three quarters and were deadlocked in a 14–14 tie entering the fourth.

Terrell Owens did play that afternoon, but the finest receiver on the gridiron was eventual game MVP Deion Branch, who snared 11 of Brady's passes for a Super Bowl record. Said fellow Pats' receiver David Givens, "[Branch] made some unbelievable catches and ran some great routes." On the ground, Dillon scored his team's final touchdown in the fourth quarter to give the Pats a 21–14 lead. When Adam Vinatieri chipped in later with a field goal, the lead appeared unassailable.

But then McNabb led his team downfield, albeit at an inscrutable snail's pace given the lack of time remaining in the game. Still, he found receiver Greg Lewis for a 30-yard touchdown pass to bring the Eagles within three points of the tie. The Patriots could not kill the clock, but their punter, Josh Miller, buried the Eagles on their own 4-yard line. McNabb threw an interception to Rodney Harrison (who else?) and the Patriots had their third championship in four years.

74 All World Francis

In a 1976 broadcast, the late Howard Cosell anointed Patriots tight end Russ Francis "All World," an appellation that stuck, though Foxboro's fans have mostly forgotten him. A first-round and 16th overall pick by the Patriots in 1975, he starred immediately as a rookie, catching 35 passes, a prodigious haul for a tight end in the 1970s.

Lending credence to the early accolades, assistant coach Ray Perkins broke down Francis' early efforts, opining, "I think he is

All-Around All World
During his high school career in Oregon, Russ Francis set a national record in the javelin, a mark that stood for 17 years.

the strongest blocking tight end in the league right now, and he thinks so, too. That's another thing he's got going for him. There is nothing he don't think he can do…. Russ is a very tall, flexible guy who can make good cuts, good tackles, and run patterns. He's also got a 137 IQ, no bad habits, and he's just super to work with. I think he's going to be a great ballplayer for a long time."

Francis' blocking—ably assisted by linemen such as John Hannah and Leon Gray—opened up ridiculous holes for the running backs to break through, a hallmark of those resurgent Pats squads of the late 1970s.

Everyone quickly agreed with Cosell and Perkins, as Francis garnered three straight Pro Bowl selections from 1976 through 1978, and yet he never truly starred in the league after that. He had become dissatisfied with the perceived stinginess of the Patriots and he was deeply affected after he witnessed Jack Tatum's paralyzing hit on Darryl Stingley. Very little escaped Francis' perception, and as a sensitive and intelligent soul, he always kept one eye on a life outside of the gridiron, a perspective responsible in part for his decision not to play in 1981.

His timeout only lasted a year, and after his sabbatical he joined the San Francisco 49ers for five full years and part of a sixth, surpassing his previous mark for receptions in a season with 44 in 1985. He played one game in New England in 1987 before concluding his career the next year as a Patriot. The team had to wait another few years before someone of Francis' caliber signed with them, and when he did, Ben Coates made most people forget about Russ Francis.

This is a most unfair development for the team's 1970 All-Decade tight end, an honor he undoubtedly would have replicated in the 1980s had he stayed with the team. Even in his final late-1980s incarnation, he started and distinguished himself as one of the greatest athletes and finest tight ends in club history.

75 Sentimental Pat

The Patriots stress family, and like every good family, it is important to know when the birds are ready to leave the nest. Like when the cap hit on a player outweighs his usefulness to the team, or as Nick Lowe once sang, "You gotta' be cruel to be kind."

Vince Wilfork has served the team for 11 years as one of the finest run stuffers in the NFL, chosen for five Pro Bowls along the journey, so after the team's fourth Super Bowl win the team naturally cuts him.

Because it was his time to go, and trying to make dispassionate decisions concerning personnel is the true Patriot Way.

Tired of Lawyer Milloy? Dump him and see him help lead the Buffalo Bills to the second greatest victory over a Belichick coached Pats team ever, 31–0, then play eight productive seasons in the NFL; but never get chosen to play in the Pro Bowl, something he had accomplished four times in New England. Similarly, Ty Law's career did not end when he left New England, but he only played in one more Pro Bowl thereafter.

Not all Patriots cuts are so unkind, some involve one- or two-year stop-gaps like Brian Cox and Ted Washington.

Richard Seymour, Willie McGinest, Joe Andruzzi, Ted Johnson, Adam Vinatieri, David Givens, Ty Warren, Logan Mankins, Wes Welker, Matt Cassel, Brandon Meriweather, Brandon Spikes, Brian Waters, BenJarvus Green-Ellis (or was it Jarvis Green): all

Pats who were turned out to pasture. Either by trade, not picking up options, cuts, not bidding against another team in free agency, it really does not matter. And that's just a partial list. Even Tom Brady's father thinks it will someday end poorly for his son.

Sometimes a Pat leaves voluntarily: Kevin Faulk, Tedy Bruschi, and Troy Brown showed how it can be done, but in each case it can be argued that they quit before they were fired. Matt Light might be the only Patriot who left a year early.

The Patriots have not always been correct in assessing a player's relative worth in keeping him on the squad. They let Asante Samuel walk, then he was chosen for three straight Pro Bowls.

But most of the time, when the Grim Reaper (and you know who he is) comes to you and asks for his playbook, heed not the spirit of Dylan Thomas to not go gently into that good night and to rage, rage against the dying of the light. Say the right things, drive out of Patriot Place without burning any rubber or bridges, secure in the knowledge that like Deion Branch or LeGarette Blount, some day you might be asked back to Foxboro. Where they hand out Super Bowl rings like Pez candy.

76 Missin' Sisson and Vinatieri

The New England Patriots scored often in well in the 1993 NFL draft, adding Drew Bledsoe, Chris Slade, Troy Brown, Vincent Brisby and Corwin Brown to their roster, but one pick simply did not produce results sufficient to keep himself with the club, particularly one run by then-coach Bill Parcells. With the first choice in the 5th round, the club selected place kicker Scott Sisson from Georgia Tech.

Hailed as "No Missin' Sisson," this member of the Georgia Tech Hall of Fame was told on draft day by Parcells half-jokingly that he better produce on the pro level. Unfortunately, his tenure with the club lasted only one year because the "No Missin'" part only pertained to extra point attempts where he established a perfect record. With field goals though, the adventure never ended, and by season's end he only made 53.8% of his attempts.

It is possible that many of his errant kicks probably emanated from his concern for his very sick relative, although Sisson would not have been the first college kicker whose college game did not translate to the NFL. No matter, Parcells had so lost faith in his kicker, that he replaced him with 37 year old Matt Bahr, who converted on all of his field goal tries. Bahr ended up staying with

Adam Vinatieri made some of the most important kicks in franchise history before joining the rival Indianapolis Colts in 2006.

Lucky Felix
Bill Parcells almost did not have Adam Vinatieri to kick around. Vinatieri's great-great grandfather Felix saddled up with George Custer's cavalry, but apparently was excused from accompanying the detachment that drove into Little Big Horn.

the team another two full seasons thereafter, but in New England, Sisson's luck had not so much run out, as it had never truly existed. Parcells provided the valedictory on Scott Sisson when a reporter asked the tactful coach if he thought Sisson had the right stuff to kick in the big time; Replied Tuna, "I don't necessarily think so."

Fortunately for Scott Sisson, he returned to the NFL in 1996 with the Minnesota Vikings, where he converted on over ¾ of his field goals, and although he did not play after that season, his exit at least was accompanied by a measure of dignity.

Once bitten and twice shy Bill Parcells hedged a bit with his next young kicker, trying out a free agent in 1996, this time an émigré from South Dakota State, a program nowhere near as heralded as that of Sisson's Georgia Tech Yellow Jackets (between Tech and New England, he had a stint with the Amsterdam Admirals). This time the Big Tuna's aim was true, as Adam Vinatieri has proceeded to compile one of the finest records for accuracy in NFL history, successfully making over 80% of his field goals and 98% of his extra points.

Heading into the 2015 season, Vinatieri sits in 16th place in NFL history for field goal percentage and fourth for field goals made. In his ten seasons with New England, he made two Pro Bowls and in those all-star seasons led the league in field goal percentage each time, making over 90% of his shots.

Much more than that, he made some of the most iconic kicks in franchise history, including his 48 yarder to clinch the team's first Super Bowl victory against St. Louis and his game-winning kick against Carolina for the title two years later. Very few sports fans have pictures of kickers on their sports rooms or offices, but thousands of Pats' fans have nailed pictures to their walls of Vinatieri making the tough kicks.

His most famous kick may have come against the Raiders in the famous "Snow Bowl" playoff game, when in hard-driving snow, he calmly tied the game and then won it in overtime with his clutch kicks in the midst of heavy snow. Vinatieri proved so clutch to the team, that it is not hard to believe that had he kicked for Ron Meyer's Pats against Miami in the famous 3–0 victory (also in heavy snow), he could have made that game winner without the help of Mark Henderson driving out in his snow plow and clearing the field. He was that good.

The good did not last with Vinatieri and the Pats, as he opted to join the Indianapolis Colts before the 2006 season. It was thought at the time that Adam's field goal percentages would improve over the already stellar heights obtained in New England due to the domed stadium in Indy, but through 2009 date, he has never made more than 90% of his field goals since he left. Maybe the attempts are too easy or maybe he simply is no Stephen Gostkowski.

He will never return to New England, but he will never be forgotten. Scott Sisson had a tough time in Foxboro, but "Automatic Adam" Vinatieri just kept scoring.

77 Earthquake

Perhaps the most obscure member of the Patriots Hall of Fame, Jim Lee Hunt is the only player other than Gino Cappelletti to have suited up for every Boston Patriots edition, ending his 11 years as a professional just before the team decided to claim all of

New England. Nicknamed "Earthquake," the Prairie View A&M product shied away from trying out for the NFL's Cardinals as a late-round draft choice to play in Boston, a huge boon to a new franchise choosing many of its players from what was behind Door No. 3.

In his lone career interception, he famously outran two pursuing Oilers running backs for almost 80 yards and a touchdown, quite a feat for a defensive tackle. His quickness contributed to his rare ability to both sack and create hurries from the tackle position, harrying opposing quarterbacks (no one kept that stat back then), but he specialized in inducing opponents to cough up the ball, leading the AFL in fumbles recovered in 1968.

A consistent performer, Hunt earned AFL all-star recognition after the 1961, 1966, 1967, and 1969 seasons as a member of the Patriots' fine front four, dubbed at the time "the Boston Pops." A member of the Patriots' All-Decade team for the 1960s, this popular tackle (and occasional defensive end) is one of only 15 Patriots elected to the club's Hall of Fame entering the 2011 season. Like his linemate and friend Bob Dee, he died too young, passing in 1975.

78 The Discordant Journey of Rommie Loudd

You almost have to divide the tale of Rommie Lee Loudd into three parts: an irrepressible rise for an African American in the face of prejudice; an extraordinarily sad story; and an inspiring redemptive parable. He started off well, destructively diverted his life and the lives of his victims, and then attempted to reverse course before he died in 1998 from complications from diabetes. Sadly, some stark incidents of staggeringly poor judgment made his existence much more one of sinning than sinned against.

An All-American at UCLA, the 49ers drafted Loudd late in the 1956 draft. Management did not see a whole lot that they liked, at least not enough to keep him on the roster. He may have played briefly for the Bears, but did not stick. Like so many other NFL rejects or miscalculations of talent, he caught on with the AFL's Chargers in 1960 and then played the next couple of campaigns in Boston as a linebacker, never starting, although he did intercept a few passes and returned a fumble back for a touchdown during his AFL years.

Despite his mediocre professional career, he demanded the attention of Patriots head coach Mike Holovak, who named him an assistant coach in 1966, making Loudd the AFL's first African American coach. Holovak loved the guy, a feeling shared by many in the organization, and Loudd later ascended to the position of personnel director. Even after Upton Bell became GM, Loudd stayed on in a related role.

While still working in the Patriots front office, Loudd embroidered ever brighter dreams for himself, musing aloud in 1972 about starting his own team, reasoning, "I can't say I have the inside track on a franchise, but I think I have the ability to get the inside track. I've played football, coached, and now hold a front office position. I've worked hard and kept my nose clean. With 25 years of experience in football, if I don't get a chance to head a team, well, they'll have denied me my Ph.D."

Loudd got his chance when E. Joseph Wheeler Jr., the owner of a proposed franchise in the new World Football League, decided to sell out his interest, with an Orlando group that Rommie helped form only too willing to rid him of his burden. "I was pushing interracial ownership. The NFL still does not have any black owners or general managers. Management is all white while 40 percent of the players are black," said Loudd, who was managing general partner at the time.

Of course, the World Football League tanked almost immediately, making those crazy and disorganized early years of the AFL appear like a paradigm of professionalism by comparison. By year's end Loudd had tried everything in an unsuccessful effort to ballast the club, even contacting officials in Atlanta and Tampa Bay in a vain attempt to relocate the team in a new environ.

Then it all caved in. Gravity began to bring down the trajectory of Loudd's life in that watershed year of 1974, as Rommie concocted a number of other fruitless gestures to reverse the fortunes of his club. Having finagled into existence the Florida Blazers, questions soon emerged concerning alleged financial improprieties by Loudd, and while some figures associated with this short-lived club later prospered, such as coach Jack Pardee, Loudd's life thereafter descended sharply.

Indicted in 1975 for conspiracy to deliver cocaine to an undercover agent, he later was convicted and sentenced to 14 years in prison, although he only served a small fraction of that time. Much more shocking, he served another jail term in an unrelated case in Los Angeles for sexually molesting a 12-year-old boy and a 13-year-old boy. Rommie Loudd had hit bottom, and then kept trying to drill deeper in determined fashion.

It did not end there, however, as Loudd became a minister in prison and hosted a television show while incarcerated. His conversion was evidently quite sincere, as he continued his ministry after he left jail and became a useful and productive member of society as an activist in Miami. Little was heard good or bad about Rommie Loudd, with the exception of his efforts to help ramp down the tensions during the Miami riots in 1980, until he died at age 64 in 1998.

Since he dropped off the radar, it is not known if Loudd had fully rehabilitated himself or if he reverted to his perverted or drug-pushing ways. He achieved many positive things early in life and made remarkable progress as a pioneer in face of the extremely tepid efforts of professional football in the 1960s and 1970s to meaningfully desegregate the coaching staffs and front offices of all of the teams. That he squandered his reputation with deviant behavior does not erase what he did for others, it only means that it completely ruined his legacy because of the grievous harm he did to others. It seemed at times that Rommie Loudd led multiple lives, but in reality no one does; he simply compartmentalized his existence as equal parts Dr. Jekyll, Mr. Hyde, and P.T. Barnum.

79 It's a Wonderful Life

It's a chicken-and-egg argument really: did future Patriots founder Billy Sullivan learn how to wheedle and cajole people due to his association as publicity director of Notre Dame football under notorious blusterer Frank Leahy, or was he born with the gift in Lowell in 1915? It matters little, because by the time Sullivan became famous, a sportswriter maintained that he "didn't just kiss the Blarney Stone, he swallowed the whole damn thing!"

He needed all of the nonsense in his arsenal when he boldly sought in 1959 to found an American Football League franchise in Boston with very little money, as he rubbed elbows with other owners such as the rich oilmen Hunts and prosperous hoteliers like the Hiltons. Billy had to scramble to pull together $25,000, with less than one-third of this amount coming from his own funds, but somehow he persuaded the other league founders into letting him into their club, thereby creating the Patriots. So threadbare was this team that Sullivan advised his players to sleep on top of the sheets in hotel rooms while on the road to save on housecleaning charges.

This penuriousness did not spring from a Scrooge-like mendacity, but rather from the irreducible fact that neither he nor the team had much money.

That said, do not believe for a moment that Billy Sullivan was anyone but the perfect person to bring a professional football franchise to Boston. His association with Frank Leahy provided him with a useful knowledge of big-time football in an era where the college game dwarfed the pro game in popularity. Leahy and sports information director Charlie Callahan (himself a Massachusetts native) knew that wins on the gridiron had to be followed with myth-making, and with Knute Rockne, the Four Horseman, and the Gipper as a foundation, they spread the gospel of Fighting Irish football across the land, with young Sullivan along for the ride.

Sullivan honed his skills as a publicity director with the Boston Braves and the Jimmy Fund, but when the Braves moved to Milwaukee, he stayed in the East and dreamt of another day, one in which he ran the show. He waited almost a decade, but as the pioneers of the proposed AFL gathered in the late 1950s, Boston stood little chance of landing a franchise. At that point, Sullivan's old mentor Leahy (now with the Los Angeles Chargers) stepped in and urged that Boston get its opportunity. Sullivan cobbled together some partners, posted the $25,000 entrance fee, and the Patriots were born. Billy Sullivan had done it.

Most fans possess a working knowledge concerning how the Patriots passed out of the Sullivans' hands piece by piece by the late 1980s, but few are aware of the fact that Billy Sullivan lost control of the team in the mid-1970s, when a faction briefly wrested control of the team away from him. Had Sullivan been treated better on his way out the door, he might not have been able to generate enough sympathy to give him enough shares to regain control. He did regain control and maybe gained too much, an effort that led him into litigation.

Sullivan hired capable family members to run the team, but he also brought in good football people like Bucko Kilroy, and by careful use of the draft the Patriots became a very competitive team from the 1970s through the mid-1980s. Of course, once it appeared that Sullivan had weathered the storm and had finally produced a consistent winner, he lost control of the team, with Michael Jackson of all people providing the coup de grace.

For critics of Billy Sullivan, the train wreck incompetence of the next owner, Victor Kiam, helped show most New Englanders how good they had had it with the Sullivans. Richard Johnson from the New England Sports Museum dubbed Billy Sullivan the "Happy Warrior," and while the founder of the Patriots has passed, he is remembered fondly as a member of the Patriots Hall of Fame.

80 Farewell, Fairbanks

Shelley Long should never have left *Cheers* and Chuck Fairbanks should never have left his head coaching position with the New England Patriots to become the coach of the Colorado Buffaloes. Like the true-life Diane Chambers, once Fairbanks left his very good job in Foxboro, he never experienced anywhere near as good of a second act again. Instead of everyone knowing his name, he became a historical footnote during his own lifetime.

It is not like this man could not lead a team. He had gradually wended his way through the collegiate ranks, with stops along the way at Arizona State, Houston, and Oklahoma as an assistant coach, before becoming the head coach at Oklahoma. Restoring the prestige of the Bud Wilkinson era, Fairbanks built the Sooners into one of the finest organizations in the nation before Patriots owner Billy Sullivan came a courtin'. Sullivan got his man in 1973, but he had to wrest him away from the Sooners and had to live with the fact that if Fairbanks departed from OSU, he might someday decide to scorn New England.

Then and now, words such as *enigmatic* and *mysterious* pepper descriptions of Fairbanks, but despite his apparent lack of color, he distinguished himself as one of the finest coaches in team history and surpassed all predecessors. He exhibited patience, enduring records in his first three seasons of 5–9, 7–7, and 3–11, and yet he knew how to build a team in his evaluation of talent and development of young players.

In 1973, John Hannah, Darryl Stingley, Sam Cunningham, and Ray Hamilton came aboard with linebackers Steve Nelson and Sam Hunt and running back Andy Johnson drafted the next year. Add tight end Russ Francis and quarterback Steve Grogan in

Déjà Vu

Chuck Fairbanks' departure from the Patriots has some parallels to the later travails of Bill Parcells. Both coaches seemingly ran aground at the very apex of their careers, crashing and burning before the final act, but to compare them too closely does a grave disservice to Parcells. Though Parcells spoiled the week before the Super Bowl and created an unneeded distraction (as his focus should have been on his team defeating the Packers), the Big Tuna had already led two Giants teams to Super Bowl titles. If coaching or team-assembling did not work out, he had experienced past success as a commentator as a fail-safe option, one he did not need as the Jets and later the Cowboys and Dolphins all desired his services. Fairbanks was really burning bridges as he planned his move to the University of Colorado, temporarily fired by Billy Sullivan and seemingly committing professional suicide as a professional-level coach. Although Bill McCartney later revived the Colorado football program, Fairbanks was dropping down to a program that traditionally served as a doormat to tougher Big Eight teams such as Oklahoma and Nebraska. Bill Parcells lived to fight again, but Chuck Fairbanks just faded away.

1975 and future Hall of Famer Mike Haynes, center Pete Brock, and safety Tim Fox in 1976, and Fairbanks had the nucleus of a powerhouse.

By 1976, Fairbanks had crafted a very strong and capable young team, a fact reflected in the Pat's 11–3 record that year. For the first time since the early Boston Patriots days, the club made the playoffs, losing to Oakland a week before Christmas, an early present to the Raiders if there ever was one.

The era of good feeling continued in 1977 with the club notching a 9–5 record, not quite good enough for postseason play, but clearly the Pats stood on the cusp of greatness. The next year, they seemingly achieved it, as the Patriots rang up an 11–4 record heading into their final game in Miami against the Dolphins.

Then the choo choo started veering off the tracks.

A booster from the University of Colorado approached Fairbanks with a lucrative offer to become the head football coach in Boulder. Fairbanks bit, asking Sullivan to let him out of the remaining years of his contract in New England, magnanimously offering to coach through the playoffs while simultaneously recruiting high school seniors for the Buffaloes.

Stunned, Sullivan tried to sack Fairbanks for the coach's rash decision. As the facts became clearer, Fairbanks had already in effect begun to serve two masters, recruiting for the Buffaloes while trying to outcoach Don Shula. Sullivan refused to allow Fairbanks to coach against the Dolphins.

In that final game, Ron Erhardt and Hank Bullough did their best as co-coaches, but the Pats went down to Miami and got hammered. The team still had the playoffs ahead, and the players and management manfully continued to venture into the vortex of their suspended situation in the days ahead. Of all things, Fairbanks came back to coach the team, marching them to a stiff loss to the Houston Oilers on New Year's Eve.

The new year's hangover commenced with the inevitable litigation involving the Patriots, Colorado, and Fairbanks. The local federal court was decidedly unsympathetic to Fairbanks, so the boosters came to his rescue with money for the Patriots and with Fairbanks backing off some of his demands. Fairbanks escaped to Colorado, where a regent stated, "My goal as a regent is to build a world-class university with a football program, not a world-class football program with a university...It appears that the athletic program is being run by a booster club rather than by a university."

81 Bucko

Bucko Kilroy broke into professional football in 1943 during the leather helmet era, eventually earning three Pro Bowl nods in his 13-year career. Despite his pedigree and his experience in a period of true smashmouth football, he did not end his career and then sit down on a couch and ruminate about how the game was once played.

Instead, he revolutionized how we look at it.

He coached for the Eagles, then ran player personnel for the Redskins in the early 1960s, shifting mid-decade to scout for the Dallas Cowboys. In that role, he helped the team become the dominant NFC franchise not only during his tenure there but also for several years after he left. When someone as large as Bucko jumps into the pond, the ripples are felt for years.

Smartly, Billy Sullivan recruited him to become the Pats' personnel director in 1971, and Bucko's keen senses led to rapid and lucrative dividends for his team. Take his 1973 draft, during which he brought rookies John Hannah, Ray Hamilton, Sam

Cunningham, and Darryl Stingley to Foxboro. While that draft was particularly fruitful, he also picked up many of the other collegians who became the foundation of the Patriots' resurgence in the 1970s right through the mid-1980s.

In all Bucko served in the NFL in some capacity for 64 years and with the Patriots he literally remained with them until the day he died as a scout in 2007. His influence did not end with the teams he was employed by, as he co-founded the college combine and also mentored many of the leading personnel directors and scouts in modern NFL history. He lived through the triumphs and occasional ebbs in New England's fortunes, surviving long enough to see three Lombardi Trophies in Foxboro, an enduring legacy of the remarkable Bucko Kilroy.

82. The Big Tuna Crashes and Burns His Way Into a Super Bowl

In retrospect, the relationship between coach Bill Parcells and team owner Bob Kraft had metastasized before the 1996 season began, in part because of the coach's inability to obtain a defensive lineman in the first round of that year's draft. Yet other factors seemed to divine that Parcells had painted an exit for himself at the conclusion of that season, in large part because he had coached the team for three years and had not rebuilt it into a champion yet.

Far from it, in fact, as the 1995 team missed the playoffs, meandering to a final 6–10 record and losing its last two games. Parcells perpetually projected the appearance of someone who habitually blurted out, "I don't need this," and he may have felt that he had done just about all he could to produce a winner. Patience never being a Parcells virtue, he somewhat justifiably may have felt his talents belonged elsewhere, either with another franchise that would permit him unfettered control of personnel or back as a television commentator.

Before the 1996 campaign, a disconsolate Parcells, in part dissatisfied by the Pats' lack of progress after his third year of coaching them, had amended his contract with Kraft. What each side agreed to became a matter of considerable controversy, but the coach at that point seemed exhausted and prepared to steer out of Foxboro after the 1996 season concluded.

Then a strange thing happened. After losing their first two games, the 1996 Pats only lost three more games, clinching a playoff berth and the right to vie for the divisional championship against the Steelers. The defense had improved, now a middle-of-the-pack unit rather than one of the worst, but the offense made the most significant strides. Drew Bledsoe was a very good quarterback, but he needed a surfeit of weapons to excel, and the team had drafted very wisely, over Parcells' objection. First-round selection Terry Glenn promptly set an NFL rookie reception record, and the Pats also picked up veteran receiver Shawn Jefferson. These players augmented a potentially potent offense, with Bledsoe, star back Curtis Martin, and all-galaxy tight end Ben Coates. Left tackle Bruce Armstrong anchored the line.

When the Power's Out

The power outage during the 1996 playoff game against the Jaguars was caused by a faulty fuse, the victim of too much power surging through during this very important game. Along with Gil Santos, Gino Cappelletti announced the game on the radio, having at one point to resort to telephones to get the story out to the live audience. Recalling the crazy early days of the franchise, Cappelletti was unimpressed by the shutdown of the game due to darkness, deadpanning, "When I used to play, it was darker than this."

The Pittsburgh Steelers had blasted their wild-card opponent, the Indianapolis Colts, by a score of 42–14 for the opportunity to play in New England. Ably coached by Bill Cowher, the Steelers had experimented a bit with Kordell Stewart at quarterback, but still relied on a very average Mike Tomczak behind center. Mostly, the team rose and fell based on the performance of star back Jerome Bettis, who had gained 1,431 yards on the ground during the regular season. Pittsburgh had a much better defense than the Pats, anchored by four strong linebackers and one of the greatest cornerbacks ever, Rod Woodson.

Unfortunately for Pittsburgh, Bettis was hurt and unable to produce at his peerless level once the playoff game began. Without the Bus, the Steelers stalled, producing only three points all afternoon. Pittsburgh seemed particularly confused on defense, a product of the foggy conditions in Foxboro that day plus some trickery by Bledsoe, who drove his opponent offside repeatedly due to a changed cadence count. The club had practiced it all week and even the New England players were drawn off trying to perfect this skulduggery. The Pats shot holes through a very good defense, and the 28–3 victory secured them a date against the Jacksonville Jaguars for the AFC championship.

Tom Coughlin, a head coach spawned from the same mold as Parcells, had formed a good team in Jacksonville (9–7 during the regular season) that would continue to improve in the future, centered around elusive quarterback Mark Brunell, a scrambler who actually outpaced his chief running backs that year, James Stewart and Natrone Means, in rushing yardage.

It was increasingly apparent that the Patriots had formed the nucleus of an opportunistic defense, a point later emphasized in the Pete Carroll years when the defense improved and the offense slid. Abundantly blessed with young players of their own in Ty Law, Lawyer Milloy, Ted Johnson, and Willie McGinest, the Pats possessed the antidote to Brunell and his brilliance, a smart team that knew where to play and who to hit.

It started right away with the Jags gaining no yards on their first drive, and when Jacksonville's punter tried to get rid of the ball, the Pats' Larry Whigham tackled him on his own 4-yard line. A couple of plays later, Curtis Martin blasted in for a touchdown. The game settled into a much less dramatic field-goal kicking contest for the rest of the half, with the Patriots ahead 13–3. One of the few breaks that the Jags got was when the stadium lights dimmed to about one-half potency midway through the second quarter, eventually causing an 11-minute game delay. Other than that, Brunell, Means, and Stewart were largely contained.

The third quarter might have been more entertaining without the restored lights as the teams traded territory until Jacksonville chipped in a field goal to reduce the Pats' lead to a touchdown. In the fourth, the Jags seemed to have the momentum as the Pats missed a field goal; Brunell then drove his team down to the Patriots' 5-yard line, largely on four well-placed and productive passes. It was at this point that Brunell received a proper introduction to Pats defensive back Willie "Big Play" Clay.

Brunell faded back and threw to his tight end, Derek Brown, for a sure touchdown and the tie. But the ball never got there, as Big Play lived up to his nickname and made the drive-killing interception. The New England defense kept victimizing the Jaguars. On a later drive, Stewart fumbled the ball and it was picked up by Otis Smith for another Pats touchdown. Tedy Bruschi intercepted another Brunell pass as New England advanced to the Super Bowl to face Brett Favre and the Green Bay Packers.

To that point, it was the high point of the Kraft era, and Parcells basked in the celebration after the game, kiddingly referring to Willie Clay as "Loose Change" Clay. Kraft beamed, "This is one of the great moment of my life," as the celebrations continued throughout the locker room and all around New England. While

New England had had to face an extremely formidable Bears team in its first Super Bowl appearance, on this occasion the team only had to beat Green Bay, a favored squad perhaps but no Monsters of the Midway.

No sooner had the era of good feelings in Foxboro commenced than Parcells (with assistance from his agent) began to cast a specter over the region. He had seethed all year because he did not get his defensive lineman in the draft and had to settle for Terry Glenn. His dissatisfaction hit the media in the interim between the AFC title game and the Super Bowl, and it threatened to derail his team in its pursuit of their final goal. Parcells should have been at an all-time high, but instead utilized much of this time to make his employer miserable. In doing so, Parcells also shifted the team's focus away from the one game remaining to the carnival atmosphere that Parcells created and fueled.

All Parcells had to say was that he enjoyed coaching the Patriots in 1996 and had decided to keep an open mind concerning his future, but instead his agent leaked that his client did not intend to return to the team. Instead of the upcoming Super Bowl match highlighting the team and its fans, Parcells took center stage, insincerely denying he had made up his mind while essentially letting his agent's comments stand. Days before the game, Kraft and Parcells staged an awkward press conference in which Kraft joked that he had just signed his coach to a 10-year contract running one of Kraft's businesses. No one laughed, and the whole pall cast upon the proceedings lingered to the start of the Super Bowl itself.

The Patriots probably lost the Super Bowl before they played it, although they actually led Green Bay 14–10 after the first quarter due to touchdown passes from Drew Bledsoe to Keith Byars and redoubtable Ben Coates. Unfortunately, the Packers owned the second quarter due to an 81-yard pass from Favre to Antonio Freeman, a two-yard touchdown run by Favre, and a Chris Jacke field goal.

Had Parcells chosen to concentrate on the game, he might have devised the perfect answer to Brett Favre, historically one of the greatest choke artists in the NFL playoffs. Instead, he permitted the self-styled "riverboat gambler" to chew up his team instead of turning over the ball and the game to the Pats.

And yet, despite Parcells' shenanigans, his team narrowed the gap in the third quarter to 27–21 as Curtis Martin ran the ball from 18 yards out for the club's third touchdown. Of course, Green Bay's Desmond Howard destroyed any Patriots momentum with a 99-yard kickoff return for a touchdown, and after the Packers converted for two points, the score read Green Bay 35, New England 21, and that is how the game ended.

Howard might have deflected some of the blame for the Patriots' loss from Parcells and Bledsoe (intercepted four times), but to his discredit, Parcells maimed his own team. Pouting all the way, Parcells did not fly back with his team to New England, opting to take another plane, one which landed in Providence, Rhode Island.

Almost immediately, the strongly suspected departure of Parcells took form, with NFL commissioner Paul Tagliabue enlisted to mediate the looming dispute between coach and team. Parcells maintained that his preseason amendment to his contract left him with a right to buy himself out of the contract, while Kraft argued that it meant that Parcells only could extricate himself from New England at the team's option. Tagliabue sided with Kraft, and the Patriots negotiated a stiff price with the Jets to make him New York's new head coach: the loss of draft choices. So Bill Parcells good-riddanced himself out of New England as the rivalry between the Patriots and the Jets entered one of its ugliest phases.

83 Johnny Rembert

Recently I was talking to one of the most fanatical of Patriots fans about Johnny Rembert, and this seasoned aficionado could not recall a single thing about the great retired linebacker. Every Patriots fan needs to know about Johnny Rembert, or if they have forgotten him, to be jogged into consciousness quickly. A fourth-round pick out of Clemson in 1983, Rembert excelled for 10 years, playing in a particularly peculiar period in club annals, ultimately serving with distinction under four head coaches. Whine all you want about busts from draft days past, the team received incredible value in this instance.

The failure to remember Rembert today reflects that during his entire career he played alongside Hall of Famer Andre Tippett, and also served with other well-known mates such as Steve Nelson and Vincent Brown. Under multiple coaches, he played both on the left and right as an inside linebacker and even played some outside linebacker, making him a bit of a jack of all trades. And yet, Rembert mastered them all.

Someone took notice of his consistent excellence, as he earned two Pro Bowl nominations in 1988 and 1989. Unfortunately, he never came close to playing a full season in the three years after his last Pro Bowl (his final season as a professional), a development that coincided with a plunge into the abyss for the franchise.

Here are some other defenders deserving of greater historical appreciation for their totality of work for the Patriots:

1. **Ronnie Lippett**
Counterintuitively, the New England Patriots scored magnificently with their later 1983 draftees (Rembert, Craig James in the seventh round) but did not fare well with some of the

earlier picks, such as first rounder Tony Eason and second rounder Darryal Wilson. Consistent with this development, the club cleared the table with their superb eighth-round selection, cornerback Ronnie Lippett from the University of Miami.

Unlike Rembert, who at least received some recognition during his career, Lippett never played in a Pro Bowl, and yet he rarely missed a game in eight years and intercepted 24 passes during that time, tied for eighth all-time in franchise history as of 2011. Similar to Rembert, Lippett had the "misfortune" of playing at a position where a superstar, in this instance Raymond Clayborn, lined up on the other side of the field.

One honor did not elude Lippett: selection to the Patriots' All-Decade team for the 1980s.

2. Tim Goad

Vince Wilfork epitomizes the current Patriots interior defensive lineman: big, intelligent, a gap-filler, and a very athletic man. Few play the position like Wilfork, but the Pats once had a nose tackle named Tim Goad who, despite his relative lack of size (usually playing at around 280 pounds), filled that position with dignity and determination. For seven years he steadily lined up, never missing a game until his final year with the club. After he left New England he suited up one year with the Browns under head coach Bill Belichick, and for a final season with the Ravens in the same spirit.

He did not play in a Pro Bowl, toiling generally for some woebegone Patriots teams and taking direction without complaint from four separate head coaches: Ray Berry, Rod Rust, Dick MacPherson, and Bill Parcells. Cruelly, just as the Big Tuna had begun to set the foundation for future Patriots greatness, Goad left the team, replaced by two new players who did not perform as well as he had. Tim Goad was missed.

3. Don Webb

A glaring weakness on the inaugural Boston Patriots, the defensive backfield profited enormously in its second year with the injection of a rookie from Iowa State named Don Webb. Almost an original Pat, he remained a fixture in the secondary throughout the 1960s and even saw action in his final year, 1971, in the team's next incarnation as the New England Patriots.

Webb filled in wherever needed as a starter, mastering his cornerback position as well as playing free safety and strong safety, and he only improved as he reached his 30th birthday in 1969, when he was chosen to his first Pro Bowl. Although he started playing in the club's second year of existence, he still stands 11th all time in interceptions more than 50 years into Patriots history.

4. Tony McGee

An undeservingly ignored player, "Mac the Sack" sacked opposing quarterbacks on 76 occasions in his eight years in New England as a defensive end. He also starred with the Bears for three years before coming to the Pats and for three years in Washington at the end of his career.

In college, he was one of the "Black 14" African American players tossed off of the University of Wyoming team because they wanted to wear black armbands during their game with BYU in opposition to a since-discarded Mormon practice and alleged taunting. He completed his collegiate career at Bishop College.

84 Pat vs. Elvis

At the end of the Eisenhower Administration, the Boston daily papers collectively still employed five sports page cartoonists, a group that produced some of the most wonderful sports art this side of LeRoy Nieman. At the *Boston Globe*, Phil Bissell more than capably performed the artwork, most famously on February 16, 1960, when his editor, Jerry Nason, informed him that the new AFL franchise had just christened itself the Boston Patriots. Nason ordered up a cartoon for the next day.

In 45 minutes, Bissell created one of the most enduring logos in American sports, Pat Patriot, so enduring that Pat refuses to die even after the official replacement of him by the Flying Elvis Patriot. (More on Elvis later.) Bissell placed a very determined colonial soldier in a three-point stance centering the football, with Pat's first words to the public being the auspicious "Now to make some history around here!" Bissell drew the figure with the idea that he would "beat the hell out of anyone who tries to stop him."

Contemporaneous with these developments, the Boston Patriots staged a promotional contest to design their first logo, but shortly after Bissell first drew him, Pat Patriot won over all contenders, reportedly because Billy Sullivan's young son Patrick liked him the best. Bissell received $25 for the cartoon and later learned that his logo had been given to the Patriots for their stationery, presumably without payment to Bissell. Fortunately team owner Billy Sullivan caught wind of this and summoned Bissell to his office and gave him considerably more money for the logo, and in fact for several years Phil drew the artwork for the team's game programs.

Oddly, although Pat had won the logo laurels, in Boston's inaugural 1960 season the club did not paste his likeness to the side of their helmets, opting instead to use a tricorn hat. Walter Pingree of Somerville, Massachusetts, submitted that design, and Sullivan heartily thanked him in a letter informing him of his successful entrant. Still, Pat did not relinquish his role as the resident logo, and by 1961 the helmet designers affixed his likeness, and not the lone tricorn hat, on the official gear.

Once ensconced as the logo, Pat did not remain unchanged over the seasons, as someone, not Bissell, replaced his wide-eyed look with a more grimacing stern stare. Pat survived an inconsistent set of campaigns for the team, surviving the Sullivan family and even Victor Kiam, but when James Busch Orthwein gained ownership, he not only hired Bill Parcells but also mothballed Pat Patriot.

Replacing Pat was the Flying Elvis Patriot logo, a swirling modernistic head of the Minuteman, eschewing the full-bodied and quite detailed look of Pat. Anyone could draw Elvis, and when the team started winning under Parcells, Pat seemingly got consigned to the dustbin of history as sort of an unlucky charm from past frustrating experiences.

Still, Pat refused to go quietly into the night. Very few people know who designed Flying Elvis, but the cheerful Phil Bissell helped keep his original creation alive. While the fans in the 1990s and the new century did not want their favorite team to return to past indignities, many of them retained a soft spot for Pat Patriot, reportedly a band that included later team owner Bob Kraft. Flying

Red State, Blue State

True nostalgists prefer the red uniforms of the old Boston Patriots over the blue ones that came to Foxboro with Flying Elvis, and with the exception of games featuring throwback ensembles, the red jerseys have remained mothballed. Unlike Pat Patriot, the red uniforms never should have been worn, because the colonial army that gained the country's independence wore blue uniforms, not the hated red of the British lobsterbacks.

Elvis held the field but Pat Patriot would live to fight future battles, still poised to beat the hell out of all comers.

Pat and Elvis coexist in an eBay type of world where any person's childhood from 1950 through 1970 can be re-created with reissues of G.I. Joe, Gumby and Pokey, and Barbie dolls. Many New England cars and trucks sport both the Elvis and Pat decals, and when the NFL orders teams to don throwback uniforms and gear, Pat returns for an encore on the team's helmet.

Pat has even made a resurrection of sorts, as Bissell designed all of the Patriots' program covers for the 2009 season, including the one for the January 10, 2010, playoff game against the Ravens, with his creation doling out abuse to the logos of the opposing clubs. And when the Patriots traveled to Detroit for the annual Thanksgiving Day game in 2010, they donned helmets with Pat on the sides. His original wide eyes have been lovingly restored, and 50 years later, Pat Patriot is determined to beat the hell out of anyone who tries to stop him.

Big D

Tom Brady personifies the Patriots' superb Super Bowl dominance with three titles between 2001 and 2004 and another in 2014, an oversimplification because during that span management had managed to assemble the finest defense in team history. Half of the defenders on the 50th Anniversary Team played on at least one edition of a championship squad (reflecting ambivalence between a 3-4 or a 4-3 scheme, the "team" consists of two tackles and two inside linebackers).

In 2001, Richard Seymour played end as a rookie, with another former first-round draft choice, Willie McGinest, anchoring a line with a number of veterans plucked from other organizations, including Bobby Hamilton and Anthony Pleasant. Two 33-year-old linebackers, Brian Cox and Roman Phifer, provided leadership for younger teammates Mike Vrabel, Tedy Bruschi, and Ted Johnson. Ty Law and Otis Smith started at corner while Tebucky Jones and Lawyer Milloy played safety.

An alloy of homegrown talent and prudent free-agent acquisitions accounted for 39 sacks and 22 interceptions, as the entire unit gave up 99 points fewer than the offense scored. They did not constitute a unit of all-time stars like the Packers of the 1960s or Pittsburgh's Steel Curtain defense; in fact, only Milloy and Law earned All-Pro nods. But the unit worked well together as an ensemble, with Cox providing toughness and former Jet Otis Smith (five interceptions for 181 yards returned) an intelligence that guided their younger mates.

The manifest strengths of the unit permitted the younger players to develop, while in the instance of Tebucky Jones, it helped wallpaper over a failed experiment at press corner. At safety, the quick and hard-hitting Jones played better, not at an All-Pro caliber but not at a level that made fans cringe and have nightmares about the return of Myron Guyton.

Oddly, the defense regressed dramatically in 2002, perhaps in part because the club did not sign up Cox or Smith, but that campaign proved vexing on a number of levels. Seemingly, some of the players believed that the championship was a fluke because they did not come close to contending, and too many games in a mediocre season devolved into nail biters.

Recognizing the value of tough veteran leadership, the Pats wisely signed up Ted Washington at nose tackle and Rodney Harrison at safety for 2003. A somewhat grumpy individual, Washington filled in spacious gaps, permitting Seymour to rack up eight sacks and to allow McGinest to make plays. Harrison was the type of player Patriots fans traditionally hated unless he played for their team, and his addition provided a key difference between a Super Bowl champion and a 9–7 team.

While some of the tinkering with additions and subtractions improved the team, linebackers Bruschi and Vrabel stepped up, with Vrabel registering 9.5 sacks. The club scuttled Milloy, but rookie Eugene Wilson substituted seamlessly at safety, with Tyrone Poole and Law filling out the backfield. The dumping of Milloy just before the 2003 opener looked potentially disastrous after Milloy's new team, the Bills, blew out the Pats in the opening game 31–0. Despite that clunker, the Pats' defense surrendered the fewest points in the NFL during the ensuing season. That 2003 defense may have been the finest one ever fielded in franchise annals, a massively aggressive reason for the club's restoration as recipients of the Lombardi Trophy.

The 2004 defensive unit was almost unconscionably stingy, sacrificing almost 180 fewer points than their offense accumulated, second in the NFL for fewest points allowed. By now Seymour had become an All-Pro lineman, but he had more than ample assistance with second-year player Ty Warren and rookie Vince Wilfork (whose presence at the nose permitted the team to let Washington walk). McGinest continued to play his hybrid defensive end/outside linebacker with Johnson and Bruschi starring at linebacker. Safeties Wilson and Harrison were joined by cornerbacks Ty Law and another young player, future star Asante Samuel. These defensive stars not only played hard on each play, but also often turned games around with picks or fumble recoveries as they vaulted the team to its third championship in five years.

86 Pete Carroll

After the disastrous call that ended Seattle's last chance to win the Super Bowl against the Patriots, the uncharitable suggested that Pete Carroll had finally done to the Seahawks what he had done to the Patriots years ago.

Sandwiched between two coaching geniuses, his three-year tenure as New England's head coach might otherwise be seen now as a transitional bridge between the dominating personalities and eras of Parcells and Belichick.

But for The Call.

Now and forevermore in Boston, he is part of the ages.

He seemed like such a blast of fresh air, after Bill Parcells had whined and wore out his welcome as the Big Tuna siphoned all of the joy out of his team being in the Super Bowl, even before his team lost. Early in training camp in the summer of 1997, star quarterback Drew Bledsoe commented that "My relationship with Pete is great. I can sit down and have a conversation with him and I can ask questions and get a straight answer. There's a lot of give-and-take, where before there was just a lot of take." Gone was the sarcastic and self-centered Parcells—in was a coach who would make things fun.

Unfortunately, in the three years that the more personable Pete Carroll coached in Foxboro, his teams declined, not all of it due to him; the general manager, Bobby Grier, struck out on drafts, with only one of his five first round picks in these three years becoming a productive professional. Terry Glenn's game regressed and Drew Bledsoe had reached the ceiling of his upside. Jets coach Parcells stole Curtis Martin and the heir to Martin in New England, Robert Edwards, was hurt after his rookie season in a freak postseason accident.

Shortly after the dawn of the millennium, Carroll was sacked and Belichick was hired as the new coach.

Carroll gained redemption, sort of, after being hired by USC as their new head coach. The fit seemed perfect, the amped and enthusiastic Carroll restored the program into the finest collegiate squad in the country. Then jumped to Seattle to coach the Seahawks, a step ahead of the sanctions incurred by the Trojans in the Reggie Bush fiasco. And people called Bill Belichick a cheater.

And yet Pete Carroll took a mediocre Seahawks team, cultivated the talent, and eventually guided it to its first Super Bowl victory. But that team had lost much of its power by the time it faced New England the next year in the Super Bowl. Golden Tate had left in free agency and the Patriots had picked off corner Brandon Browner. In mid-2014, the Seahawks rid themselves of Percy Harvin, making them more of a running team, dependent on the wheels of Russell Wilson and Marshawn Lynch.

Which utterly fails to explain why the Seahawks threw to the Patriots Malcolm Butler in their final offensive play of the season.

In the end, Pete Carroll is a very good coach, but he is not Bill Belichick. Few people are Bill Belichick—or Tom Brady for that matter. Most of the other six billion or so souls in the world are Pete Carrolls, me, and you. Without the Super Bowl ring.

87 Nick, We Hardly Knew Ye

Nick Buoniconti's reputation as an elite football player is staked almost entirely on his final seven professional seasons as a Miami Dolphin. Undeniably, he excelled in Miami; he was selected All-Pro once and to the Pro Bowl on three occasions, and led a young and underrated team to championships in 1972 and 1973. Still, he might have already played his finest games before the Patriots traded him away in 1969, a disastrous misstep.

A native of Springfield, Massachusetts, Nick did not grow up rooting for the Patriots because they did not yet exist, but he certainly knew about another local schoolboy gridiron star, Angelo Bertelli, the "Springfield Rifle." Nick's dreams of playing ball dimmed when he had all the cartilage in one of his knees removed during his junior season at Cathedral High, but he returned to earn the Corned Beef and Cabbage Award, bestowed upon the finest player in the western part of the state, en route to a scholarship to Notre Dame.

In South Bend, Buoniconti captained the 1961 team, playing on offense and defense, linebacker and guard, backing off much larger opponents from some of the finest programs in the country. He played for a poor coach on some mediocre teams, yet still earned All-American recognition that year and participated in the East-West Shrine Classic. His college coach, the woefully miscast Joe Kuharich, solemnly discouraged young Nick, opining, "I'm sorry Nick. You certainly played good football for us. But I don't think you're big enough to play pro football and because I don't I won't recommend you. It wouldn't be right." Condemned by his own coach, he evidently earned no respect from professional scouts who might have focused on the fact that Nick was not even 6'0", with some sources claiming he was as short as 5'9". Even though the NFL draft meandered through 20 rounds, the GMs ignored Buoniconti.

Cast aside by the NFL, the Patriots chose him in the 13th round of the 1962 AFL Draft, mainly through the machinations of Pats scout Joe McArdle, a tough Massachusetts native and former Notre Dame lineman himself. Oddly, Kuharich then approached team owner Billy Sullivan and strongly urged him to sign Buoniconti posthaste, speaking out of the other side of his craw, "Sign him.

I don't care who your middle linebacker is, Nick will take the job away from him." Warned Buoniconti's father, "Tell the other boys to watch out for Nick. He can get just as worked up in practice as he does in a game."

Early in his career he made few friends due to his intensity at practice, but that soon stopped once his teammates saw how he manhandled opponents and made his fellow defenders play better. It was claimed that Buoniconti in the early 1960s had to call a blitz for the defense on seven out of 10 plays to protect their weak secondary, but Nick himself developed a knack for intercepting passes, snaring 32 in his career, 24 of them coming during his seven years in Boston. As a Pat, he earned seven Pro Bowl nods.

The trade to Miami initially stunned the Massachusetts native who had devoted himself to the Boston Patriots, and he considered retiring and pursuing a career as a lawyer, an intelligent man who truly needed football less than his coaches needed him. And Miami needed him really badly, having finished its 1968 schedule at 5–8–1. Buoniconti cast his lot in with the Dolphins, and while that team had a rough 1969, Don Shula then came aboard and a very young and talented team gelled, even with a graybeard like Nick on the squad. The Dolphins won Super Bowl rings while the Patriots had to wait a few more decades before their players started wearing jewelry.

With the Patriots and Nick Buoniconti, the glass will be forever half-filled. Nick achieved his team goals more during the second stage of his career with the Dolphins, but he does not want for honors in Foxboro, chosen for the team's Hall of Fame in addition to making the 50th Anniversary Team.

Babe

For those old and nostalgic enough to have actual memories of the Boston Patriots, the long lofted passes from quarterback Babe Parilli to Gino Cappelletti hold a firm and unshakeable spot. In fact, only Cappelletti, Nick Buoniconti, and John Hannah were elected to the Patriots Hall of Fame before Parilli. Spawned from the quarterback-rich state of Pennsylvania, the "Rochester Rifle" more than met the demands of Bear Bryant, his head coach at the University of Kentucky. A two-time Heisman Trophy finalist, Babe led his team to a massive upset in the 1951 Sugar Bowl over Oklahoma.

After starring at Kentucky, the pre-Lombardi Packers chose him as the fourth player overall in the draft, quite a feat in an era when this selective service had 30 rounds. The only other quarterbacks picked in the first round in 1952 were Vanderbilt's Billy Wade and Boston University's Harry Agganis, the latter a future Red Sox phenom. In his first professional campaign, Parilli mainly spelled starter Tobin Rote, although he did handle the team's punting chores, once booming an attempt 63 yards. In his sophomore season, he sometimes assumed the starting role for a woeful 2–9–1 team, with only young receiver Billy Howton showing any promise. Parilli's punting role increasingly shifted to future Patriots head coach Clive Rush.

Parilli did not play the next two years, serving his country in a military installation in Rabat, Morocco, a stint memorable only for his taking leave on one occasion to see his grandmother for the first time in her home near Naples. He returned to play for Paul Brown and the Browns in 1956, unsatisfyingly part of a quarterback platoon with two former Notre Dame backs, Tommy O'Connell and George Ratterman, a situation that often caused Babe to break out in hives. His torment ended when Baltimore's linemen busted up Babe's shoulder on a play, terminating his season with prejudice and pain. Parilli returned to Green Bay in 1957 and 1958, not an optimal situation as Bart Starr clearly emerged as the leader of those perennial champion teams.

Parilli sat again in 1959 but he found another opportunity with the founding of the AFL, and while it is not widely publicized, he played for the Raiders in that inaugural season. Desperately seeking a quarterback, the Pats fleeced Oakland and after sharing his position again in 1961 with Butch Songin, new coach Mike Holovak finally settled on Parilli. Parilli later gratefully observed, "It was really the first time in my career that I didn't have to split the top job with someone. Mike Holovak was the first coach who gave me that opportunity, and I'll always be grateful to Mike for that."

Finally given the starting role, Parilli gifted Holovak with five straight fine seasons. Babe was slotted as an All-Star quarterback in 1963, 1964, and 1966, and bombed the record books with 3,465 passing yards and a 247.5 passing-yards-per-game average in 1964, huge totals for that time.

A member of the Boston Patriots from 1961 to 1967, quarterback Babe Parilli ended his career with more than 22,000 yards passing and 178 touchdowns.

Not Guilty

For those traditionalists who bemoan the prestigious drop in journalism since the introduction of the Internet, consider the unfair and distorted article by *Life* magazine in 1967, which smeared Babe Parilli in an irresponsible manner by trying to trump up guilt by association because he allegedly patronized a store rumored to be run by a suspected organized crime figure (get it?). Of course, many Patriots and thousands of other locals went there and the ill-conceived story died, though not before club representative and defensive captain Tommy Addison supported his teammate: "We, the players, think that Babe has been dealt a serious blow to his character...We stand behind Babe 100 percent on and off the field because he is the type of person that is beyond reproach as a quarterback or as an individual." Added team owner Billy Sullivan, "Babe is immensely popular with the players. I've been in professional sports for 32 years and I have never met a nicer man, a man with a better character than Babe. He'll sit for hours talking to little kids. I've never heard him swear. In some ways he reminds me more of a violinist than of an athlete. He's a gentle person." Mike Holovak perhaps stated it most aptly: "[Babe] is too much man."

By way of a brief aside and partial condemnation of fans devoted to statistics as the sole source of evaluating the particular talents of a football player, do not make the mistake of judging Parilli by his stats; he threw *a lot* of interceptions, some seasons more than touchdown passes. In *Sports Illustrated* articles in the mid-1960s, the scribes consistently refer to him as the greatest quarterback in the league, often citing his porous offensive line and slow and small receivers. That the Patriots fielded winning teams most years Parilli passed for them highlights his value and his ability to keep his team in games. Gushed an appreciative Coach Holovak, "Parilli knows exactly what he wants to do in every game."

Although San Diego defeated his Patriots for the 1963 AFL championship, Parilli ended his career in glory. In his last two seasons he backed up Joe Namath with the Jets (Parilli had been traded for a younger Mike Taliaferro in July 1968), winning a ring when his club upset the heavily favored Colts in the third Super Bowl.

89 Kevin and Ted

The next time you see a great football hit, particularly one of the prohibited helmet-to-helmet variety, pause for a moment to consider what might have just happened to your favorite player or his opponent.

In the third round of the 1992 draft, the Patriots chose running back Kevin Turner from the University of Alabama. He played little his first year, a 2–14 disaster in coach Dick MacPherson's last year, but he saw his role vastly expanded the next season with the arrival of a new head coach, Bill Parcells, and rookie quarterback Drew Bledsoe. In his second and third seasons as the club's starting fullback, he blocked much better than he ran, but as a receiver, he excelled as an outlet option for the young quarterback, catching 39 and 52 passes respectively.

Thereafter he played five more seasons with the Philadelphia Eagles before his career ended. "I know when I retired, they told me I had the spinal column of a 65-year-old man. Any other fullback or linebacker probably has the same thing," Turner said. The bad news got worse as he announced in August 2010 that he suffers from Lou Gehrig's Disease.

Medical research is beginning to link repeated trauma to the brain to a heightened risk of contracting ALS and also to other degenerative diseases. Facing his future as a man in his early forties, Turner observes, "Playing NFL football was a dream come true. I just never thought in 20 years I would be fighting for my life."

As Turner departed from New England, linebacker Ted Johnson joined the club, a second-round pick from the University of Colorado, then at its zenith as a major college football power. Unlike Turner, Johnson played his entire career with the Pats, earning three Super Bowl championship rings, with the third capping off a 10-year run with the club.

Johnson has also suffered due to multiple concussions, including memory loss. According to his doctor, he has demonstrated signs of early-onset Alzheimer's attributable to the damage to his brain.

Although Turner and Johnson never played on the same club, they both suffer from the lingering effects of injuries sustained on the gridiron. Hopefully some of the rules implemented to protect players will diminish the lasting effects of cheap hits, but some perfectly legal contact will unfortunately continue to cause permanent damage to the players whose replica jerseys you might wear.

So when your favorite player makes a great hit or manfully wobbles up after severe contact, think of the future that he might eventually face.

90 Nellie

Here's an interesting made-up statistic: the Patriots have the all-time record for middle linebackers who did not fit the mold for huge, powerful, and quick defenders, and yet every opponent would have loved to have had them on their team. Nick Buoniconti was the earliest exhibit of this phenomenon, but Steve Nelson, a fellow who likely never ran a 40-yard dash under five seconds, perhaps best personifies this type of player. Nick earned All-American honors at

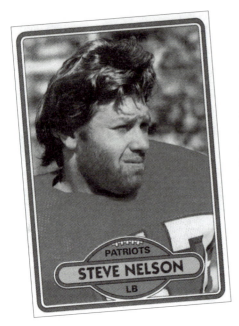

The Patriots' second first-round pick in the 1974 NFL Draft, linebacker Steve Nelson was inducted into the Patriots Hall of Fame in 1991.

Notre Dame, but Nellie came from Augsburg (where he suited up for an uncle, coach Edor Nelson) and North Dakota State, a huge recruiting oversight by every major college program but a boon to a rebuilding Patriots team that drafted him in 1974.

He did not even start out looking like a linebacker, drawing his first equipment in high school as a 5'4" quarterback for his father and head coach at Anoka High School in Minnesota. His sister was the family's finest sports star by consensus. Nelson transferred from Augsburg to North Dakota State after his freshman year in college, not a huge jump in the college pecking order, but most importantly

Doc & Nellie's

Steve Nelson once owned a popular restaurant with former teammate Bill Lenkaitis in Stoughton, Massachusetts, called Doc & Nellie's. It was a great place to meet friends, have a nice meal, and watch a game. Had it remained in existence, it would definitely be one of the top 100 things to know and things to do as a Patriots fan.

he dedicated himself to the goal of becoming the first player from his new school in more than 30 years to play professional football. Said Nellie later, "I'm sure most people were laughing at me behind my back. I could never run, and my size was only marginal at best. But I needed to direct my life into something positive."

Fortuitously for Nelson, the head coach of the Bisons was Ron Erhardt, not only a terrific little-school football coach but also a future New England Patriots assistant and later head coach. Once he moved to New England, Erhardt urged Patriots management to draft Nelson, and the club did the right thing.

His first head coach, Chuck Fairbanks, constantly urged Nellie to hit people, advice taken so much to heart that he started right away in New England. Two traits set him apart as a future star almost immediately: he read opposing defenses effectively and he played at a high level even when hurt. The ability to decipher an opposing offensive scheme more than compensated for any lack of speed. Concurred teammate and fellow backer Steve Zabel, "Steve is not overly big or overly fast but he is overly trained. His greatest ability is his reading ability."

A three-time Pro Bowl selection, Nelson has been named to the Patriots' All-Decade 1970s and 1980s teams and their 50th Anniversary Team.

91 Can We Have That One Back?

Although it's been said before, a brief mention of the worst trades in Patriots history has to include the 1969 deal that sent future Hall of Fame linebacker Nick Buoniconti to the Miami Dolphins for Kim Hammond and John Bramlett.

That's an obvious one, but in reviewing every such transaction in club annals, that deal stood in lots of bad company. Scratch the surface and you will find that New England swapped its first- and third-round picks in 1985 for the 49ers' first, second, and third choices. The Pats dropped down from No. 16 to No. 28 in the first round and selected lineman Trevor Matich, who had a long career in the NFL but did not work out with the Pats. Armed with the pick that the Pats relinquished to them, San Francisco chose wide receiver Jerry Rice. Ouch!

In 1987, New England erred by exchanging quarterback Rich Gannon for a fourth-round draft choice (used for receiver Sammy Martin) to the benefit of the Vikings. Not a fan of value picks? In 1990, the Pats lost out on Cortez Kennedy with their third overall pick, getting two first-rounders from Seattle in the persons of lineman Ray Agnew and linebacker Chris Singleton. To sweeten the deal, the Pats also let the Seahawks have a second-round pick, which deprived the Pats of choosing a player who might have, for instance, made up for the shortcomings of Agnew and Singleton.

Inauspiciously, the club's first trade might have been its worst. On New Year's Day in 1960, the Chargers obtained Ron Mix and in exchange the inaugural Boston Patriots received former Holy Cross quarterback Tommy Greene. Credit the Patriots front office for recognizing their lack of quarterback talent, but Greene was not the answer. The club had to wait a year until Babe Parilli joined the team and led his teammates for much of the ensuing decade.

Having drafted Mix out of USC, the Patriots clearly had little idea of the caliber of athlete that they had just secured the rights to. Mix proceeded to play right tackle for the Chargers throughout the decade, a perennial All-Pro selection and an eventual inductee into the Pro Football Hall of Fame. As an aspiring lawyer, Mix conceivably could have advised Billy Sullivan about the legal thickets the owner faced during the early era of the franchise. By way of partial consolation, Jon Morris, the center on the Patriots' 50th Anniversary Team, soon suited up for the team as Mix did on the other coast.

Even when they did keep a player past draft day, the Boston Patriots were still not immune to making a rash deal. During that first year they traded away a good back, Wray Carlton, to Buffalo for little in return.

In the age of free agency, it is limiting to think of poor transactions purely in terms of trades with other teams. In the new millennium, some of the Patriots' best personnel decisions occurred in letting a beloved lug leave the team in free agency. The Belichick-era Pats have prospered largely by correctly assessing when a player had begun to lose what made him special and then not extending an offer acceptable to him when he became a free agent. Bill Belichick and personnel director Scott Pioli became adept at bringing in a player with one more good year left and then letting him walk before the next camp opened.

They also sensed when signing that particular player at his price might throw the salary cap out of whack or otherwise unduly reward the service he provided to his teammates. In this last category, and by way of an exception of the Pats' prescience in this area, losing Asante Samuel crippled the team.

A Loyal Soldier

One of the Patriots' worst trades might be their most obscure one. On October 1, 1971, they traded former Pittsburgh Steelers running back Rocky Bleier back to Pittsburgh for safety Phil Clark. Bleier, a rare modern professional athlete who fought in the Vietnam War, returned badly wounded from that conflict. As a Steeler, he gained thousands of yards and helped lead fellow back Franco Harris to even more. Clark played two games for the Patriots as his career ended that fall. Most likely the trade constituted a favor to Steelers owner Dan Rooney, who wanted to keep Bleier on the roster while he recovered from his war wounds.

When the Pats cashiered Richard Seymour out of town to the Raiders, many fans cheered the move. The Patriots had specialized in getting rid of a star a year early rather than a year late, and Seymour had aged a bit, so he became expendable. The Raiders stunk and they had given up a first-round draft choice in 2011 to obtain Seymour, so it appeared that the Pats might get a high pick.

Unfortunately, Seymour still could play, and without him, the Pats had virtually no effective pass rush. The Raiders began to improve, so as they rose up the standings, the draft pick they had to relinquish fell all the way to No. 17.

92 See a Patriots Practice

Sounds too obvious, doesn't it? But for those of you who have not driven to Gillette Stadium in July and early August, you have truly deprived yourself.

The event is for everybody and the parking is free, so even fans from the nether reaches of Patriots Nation can drive and alleviate that concern. Droves of fans wearing the jerseys of their favorite players stroll to the practice fields, where bleacher seating and even some seating on the grassy hill by an end zone accommodates the guests. It's a great place to take a date, but it is also very family oriented, oftentimes with three generations camped out together. For the very young, there are plenty of moon walks astride the parking lot, and for the folks past their twenties, there are a plethora of Porta-Johns available for cranky kidneys.

This is Disney without the lines and expense. No one smokes in the stands, few swear, and even a fellow wearing a Notre Dame hat will not get abused by a Boston College fan. The views are terrific,

Know Before You Go

Other than not acting up, there are very few rules guiding the behavior of the spectators. Videos are prohibited, although many fans bring incredibly complex cameras and binoculars. Lather on sunscreen before arriving and have a great time. For archivists, if you look hard enough there is some Patriots practice film supposedly taken in 1960, probably taken by a home movie camera. A handful of children line the sideways as their heroes work out in penny jerseys, and afterward, the kids can get autographs. Good to know that some things do not change.

and after practice, it is easy for a youngster to get an autograph from one of the players. Older fans habitually fall in love each year with one Patriot, generally a late-round pick or free agent, and at times, their faith is paid back when that rookie makes the team.

Practice was not always such a great adventure, particularly when the club trained at the friendly confines of the East Boston field, jets lumbering overhead. The experience was certainly enhanced by the Parcells years at Bryant College in Smithfield, Rhode Island, though nirvana had yet to come. That is not a knock on the school in any way—it has fine accommodations for its needs as an educational institution and it served as a real boon for the extraordinarily loyal fandom in the Island State and the surrounding areas of Connecticut and Rhode Island. Yet it could not but pale in comparison with Gillette Stadium looming in the background, plus too many players jumped on carts and sped away, scarcely acknowledging the fans.

That has changed, with a considerable amount of the credit belonging to Tom Brady, who has a knack for recalling how he felt as a kid, graciously signing autograph after autograph with good cheer, serving as an ambassador for the team and a good example for his teammates.

93 Clive Rush

Brendan Boyd and Fred Harris once wrote a treasure titled *The Great American Baseball Card Flipping, Trading, and Bubble Gum Book* and warned that when naming a son, choose a name like Brick, something appropriate for the youngster who did not mind getting his jersey dirty. They particularly chided the parents of Foster Castleman, because "[o]f course a ballplayer with a name like this is never going to amount to anything. If you have a name like an orthodontist you're going to play like an orthodontist. The guy never really had a shot." In that vein, what were a couple of people named Rush thinking when they named their son Clive on Valentine's Day in 1931? And to worsen matters, they pronounced the name "Cleeve." Did they want their boy to grow up to be an English butler or a New York dandy?

Forget Bill Belichick, Bill Parcells, and Chuck Fairbanks for a moment; during considerable stretches in team history, Pats coaches have more often ranged from mediocre to poor. Defying description, Rush easily endured the most uncomfortable stint at the helm.

Rush had successfully served as offensive coordinator of the New York Jets and was responsible for developing Joe Namath into a Super Bowl–winning quarterback. In fact, Namath strongly endorsed Rush as a candidate for the Patriots head coaching position, a spot left vacant after the termination of Mike Holovak. The press immediately speculated after the sacking of Holovak that Fred Bruney or even Babe Parilli might next assume the helm, but the club focused on five other candidates: Rush, John Rauch, Ernie Stautner, Chuck Noll, and Florida State's Bill Peterson.

It has become almost sacred but inaccurate doctrine that team owner Billy Sullivan completely screwed up the decision by choosing Rush over Noll, then a Colts assistant coach (and later coach of four Super Bowl champion teams with the Steelers), an interesting tale since Noll accepted the Steelers' offer four days before Rush formally accepted the Pats' job. Sullivan may have preferred Rush over Noll, but he did not have much of a choice once Noll went to Pittsburgh.

Rush's tenure as the club's coach almost ended with the introduction of George Sauer Sr. as the team's new general manager on February 12, 1969, when an electric shock felled him after he grabbed a microphone. Sportswriter Jerry Nason wrote that Rush's "face suddenly contorted so that it resembled a purple prune, with a scream on his lips." Regaining his composure after someone pulled the electric cables out of the wall socket, Rush quipped, "I always heard the Boston press was tough, but I never knew how tough until now." This inauspicious start augured ill, and Rush experienced nothing but frustration during his brief tenure in New England. In the 1969 season the club posted an ugly 4–10 record. Rush's experiments included a "Black Power Defense" composed entirely of African American Patriots, which failed because he did not have enough African American players on defense to fill every defensive position, so he had to borrow players from the offense.

Tough or not, Rush excoriated the Boston knights of the keyboard in tones not heard since Ted Williams retired, even screaming at fans during a game. As the pressure mounted and the losses melded together, he became increasingly eccentric until he lost the faith of almost everyone in Boston.

Had Rush simply popped off against the media and some loud-mouthed fans, few would have noticed, but even observers who normally eschewed statistical analysis went agog when the club started off the 1969 season losing its first seven games. The record improved a bit as the Patriots won four of their last seven games, but they never defeated an opponent with a winning record, so although some hoped for the future, more astute observers saw a team with a miscast coach and very few stars.

In 1970, the wheels fell off completely and Rush permanently left the team in November due to health concerns. Oddly, Rush either became dizzy or experienced a racing heart rate and did not coach at the beginning of a game against the Buffalo Bills. He did return during the contest, one in which O.J. Simpson and the Bills trounced his charges, but he had effectively ended his tenure as head coach after the game when doctors began to examine him and Billy Sullivan suggested a leave of absence. The team's record stood pat at 1–6 (by year's end the Pats were last in the NFL in points scored and gave up more points than any other franchise) and Rush decided to resign, and even then it was unclear if he quit or was fired.

He coached a bit afterward, enjoying some success for one season as the head coach of the Merchant Marine Academy, but after his Patriots stint that chapter of his life essentially ended. Tragically, he died of a heart attack in 1980. Mostly forgotten now, Rush, to the extent he is recalled, is generally portrayed as a clownish figure, a most inapt description of a talented but often troubled man. He lacked the leadership skills to guide a team and did not possess the strength to endure reverses in fortune, traits not uncommon to many people. His travails in New England should be viewed in empathetic and compassionate terms. He was a fragile man in many ways, a competent assistant coach whose most blessed curse in life lay in becoming a head coach of a struggling franchise that did not have a Joe Namath to bail him out.

Years before Rush's death, the wonderful *Boston Globe* columnist Ray Fitzgerald delivered the most fitting requiem for this unfortunate soul: "This does not make the whole mess any less distasteful or the decline and fall of an imaginative but troubled man any less a personal tragedy. Sad is the only word for it."

94 Mosi Tatupu

Nineteenth-century New England cradled the Industrial Revolution, where small bends in the rivers spawned countless huge mills and factories. After World War II ended, thousands of factory jobs gradually disappeared, some to other parts of America and many to sweat shops overseas. Fortunately, high-tech work and service-related employment saved the region from morphing into a rust belt, a by-product of having some of the world's leading universities available to create new opportunities.

Despite their city having lost much of its manufacturing base, Boston sports fans never relinquished their devotion to the concept that the most favored players possessed a "lunch pail" mentality. If a player jumped after balls, played hurt, yelled just as loudly as any fan, and wore his heart on his sleeve, he became the ideal, hard-working laborer in an area that had largely sacrificed its blue-collar identity.

Several Patriots players exemplified these traditional virtues, including Andre Tippett, Tedy Bruschi, Troy Brown, John Hannah, and Kevin Faulk. The greatest of all may have been Mosi Tatupu.

Born in 1955 in the American Samoa, Mosiula Faasuka Tatupu played running back solidly at USC, and yet remained on the board in the 1978 draft until the Pats tabbed him in the eighth round. Having since drawn back the annual draft to seven rounds, in real terms Tatupu was essentially a free agent. For further perspective, the club chose such immortals as Bob Cryder, Matt Cavanaugh, Carlos Pennywell, Dwight Wheeler, Bill Matthews, Kem Coleman, Mike Hawkins, and Terry Falcon before him.

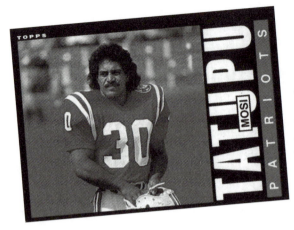

Special teams standout Mosi Tatupu was a fan favorite during his 13 years in New England. Tatupu passed away in 2010.

Having not garnered immediate respect, Tatupu played parts of three decades for the franchise, while most of those who preceded him in the pecking order had very attenuated careers with the team. Kem Coleman played as many games with the Patriots as legendary Red Sox broadcaster Ken Coleman did (zero). Doggedly and vigorously, Tatupu approached all assignments extended to him by his coaches and devloped into an excellent special teams player.

Tatupu performed quite well in the backfield as well. In 1983 he gained 578 yards rushing for a 5.5 yards-per-attempt average, an effort he nearly matched the following season when he ran for 553 yards. By 1986, however, the 31-year-old had begun to transition into the role by which he is best remembered, earning his lone Pro Bowl recognition as a special teams ace that year. He continued to thrive in that role through 1990, rounding out his career with one final season back in his old college home with the Los Angeles Rams.

A Tradition of Excellence

In college, Wes Welker won the Mosi Tatupu Award for his special teams play. Tatupu is a 1990s All-Decade Team selection as well as a 50th Anniversary Team choice for his special teams work. He is fondly remembered by his most fervent fans, "Mosi's Mooses."

Post-career, Tatupu did not remain in L.A. or return to Samoa, instead choosing to make suburban Boston his home. He continued to support local charities and coached for a local high school and a college. Like Ron Burton, he died too young, passing in 2010, but his legacy survives in the Mosi Tatupu Memorial Fund, which advances youth football in the American Samoa. Most of the old New England mills have been razed or converted into outlet malls, and sadly Mosi Tatupu too has passed. But the revered idol of the hard-working, thoroughly dedicated Boston athlete always has a place and serves as a steady source of inspiration to fans and athletes alike.

95 Jon Morris and Other Unsung Heroes

If Johnny Rembert and some similar players were unsung heroes on defense, a handful of offensive players should be known and appreciated by all Patriots fans, none more than center Jon Morris.

A Holy Cross Crusader, Jon Morris endeared himself to many New Englanders by turning down the opportunity to play for Vince Lombardi and the Green Bay Packers during their dynastic years. He started from 1964 through 1974, earning Pro Bowl selections his first seven years. After he left New England, he played three years with the Lions and one with the Bears.

Here are some more Pats deserving of our attention:

1. **Jim Whalen**

In the first five years of the Pats, two Boston College wide receivers, Jim Colclough and Art Graham, excelled for the team, so much so that at times they threatened to consign Gino Cappelletti strictly to kicking duties. And while these two ends deserve greater recognition for their efforts, a third B.C. product from this era, tight end Jim Whalen, merits a renewed historical perspective even more.

Playing in an era when tight ends were primarily blockers, he still snared 153 receptions in his five years with the Pats. In 1968, a year the team basically ran a quarterback-by-committee system, he caught 47 passes, nearly 30 more than any other teammate. Whalen earned All-Pro recognition, and yet strangely, the next season his total dropped to 16 catches under new head coach Clive Rush. (It is not uncommon to see the words *strange* or *strangely* in the same sentence as *Clive Rush*.)

Indeed, Whalen got the bum's rush after the 1969 season, traded out of town to the Denver Broncos for tight end Tom Beer. Essentially, the trade constituted a philosophical consideration of what a team wanted in the position: the Pats obtained the much larger Beer for his blocking prowess, as Beer only caught 25 passes the next three years while Whalen caught 36 in his first year with the Broncos.

2. Tom Yewcic

One is not a true Patriots fan until he or she learns more than a smattering about Tom Yewcic. A product of Michigan State, Tommy was drafted by the Steelers in the 1954 NFL Draft but gravitated toward a career as a professional baseball player, signed by the Detroit Tigers as a catcher that same year. He tenaciously held on to the diamond, earning exactly one at-bat with the team in 1957 but failing in his bid to get a hit.

His athleticism earned him an invitation to join Boston as a punter during the 1961 season, but since the AFL teams carried so few players, his versatility as a backup quarterback helped establish him as a valuable team member. As a rushing quarterback he gained 215 yards on 33 carries in 1962, and the next year he scurried for 161 yards on 22 runs. He remains today a fine raconteur of stories concerning the Boston Patriots.

3. Len St. Jean

Hailing from Northern Michigan, "Strongboy" Len St. Jean's Patriots career nearly dovetailed that of Jon Morris, as St. Jean played with the Pats from 1964 through 1973. Though he mainly played right guard, St. Jean also played some defensive line and registered the occasional sack.

St. Jean may have been the strongest player ever to play in New England, his Paul Bunyanesque heroics preceding him. As a youngster, he lived 22 miles away from his high school and often hitchhiked there, but on at least a couple of occasions he walked the entire route. He once secured work as a lumberjack. Even Chuck Norris has been known to whimper when Len St. Jean passes by him.

4. Craig James

This pick might surprise some. After all, former Patriots running back Craig James starred at SMU and with the Patriots and then seamlessly strolled into a long and distinguished career analyzing football on television. His national fame transcends his brief, relatively localized stardom in New England, and yet his feats remain largely unknown because too many football fans assume they already know them. That, and the fact that James' NFL career lasted all too briefly. While the manner of his departure from the league paled in juxtaposition to the fates of Darryl Stingley or even Robert Edwards, in many ways his tenure is a sad reflection on what might have been.

At SMU, he starred in the "Pony Express" backfield with Eric Dickerson in those heady days before that school received

Running back Craig James had a short but spectacular career with the Patriots from 1984 to 1988.

the NCAA's "death penalty." After SMU, James, the fourth-overall pick in the upstart USFL draft of 1982, signed on with the Washington Federals. In D.C., he gained 823 yards on the ground as a rookie and caught 40 passes out of the backfield. The sophomore jinx hit him the next year, as he suffered a season-ending knee injury after only 16 rushes.

Stealing a page from wily Celtics GM Red Auerbach, the Patriots had selected James as a seventh-round pick in the 1983 NFL Draft, banking on the long-term instability of the USFL. In one of the club's most underrated coups, the financially strapped Federals cut James after his injury, paving the way for his entrance into the NFL for the 1984 season. James rushed for 790 yards (4.9 yards per carry) and caught 22 passes in his first season in New England.

In 1985, he helped lead the Patriots to their first Super Bowl appearance, running for 1,227 yards with 27 receptions. On a personal level, he achieved his first and only Pro Bowl selection. During the team's AFC title game against Miami, James toted the rock for 105 yards.

Fresh from their first Super Bowl appearance, the Pats expected to contend at least through the decade, but the dream collapsed almost immediately after several of James' teammates were outed in the *Boston Globe* days later as alleged drug users. James was clean, but gained only 427 yards in 1986. Thanks to a knee injury, he only gained 25 yards in eight carries for the 1987 and 1988 seasons, and then his career was over.

The last person to cry for himself, James continues to distinguish himself with his preparation and astute analysis on television, so no one views the end of his career in the NFL in tragic terms. Often overlooked, the decline of his pro fortunes dovetailed with the swift decline of the Patriots in this era.

96 Bob Dee

An inaugural member of the Boston Patriots, Quincy native Bob Dee helped form a solid phalanx of Eastern Massachusetts products (either spawned from the Bay State or who attended college at B.C. or Holy Cross) who starred in the franchise's early years, a group distinguished by Jim Colclough, Art Graham, Jim Whalen, Jon Morris, and Joe Bellino.

Dee had attended Holy Cross and was the only player drafted in his round in the 1955 NFL Draft who made a team. He played two years with the Washington Redskins before returning to the Cross to help out with coaching. With the dawn of the AFL, he signed on as a defensive lineman with Boston. During one Pro Bowl, the game announcers broadcast live to the crowd the announcement of

A Medical Miracle

Bob Dee's brother-in-law, Catholic deacon Jack Sullivan, prayed to the late English convert and cardinal John Henry Newman so that his chronically bad back would not interfere with his vocation. Almost immediately, Sullivan's back problems disappeared. As a result, Newman was beatified, the first step toward sainthood, by Pope Benedict.

the birth of his second son; coincidentally, he learned of the birth of another son in a similar manner during another all-star appearance.

Credited with recovering a fumble for the first touchdown in AFL history during a 1960 exhibition game, his five recovered fumbles led the league in 1961. Like many players in the 1960s, Dee worked during the off-season, sometimes in real estate and at other times for the Hood Company, speaking at father-son banquets throughout the Commonwealth.

Despite the increasingly tense racial environment in Boston, he and Larry Eisenhauer socialized quite openly with his fellow linemates, African Americans Houston Antwine and Jim Hunt. They were often found after games at Fenway at the Elbowla Lounge.

At the conclusion of the 1967 season Dee retired to pursue other ventures, primarily cleaning up oil spills with his company Jet-Line Ventures. This gregarious and friendly man became quite ill with severe back pains during a job in Portsmouth, New Hampshire, in 1979, and he died shortly thereafter due to heart disease. He has subsequently been honored by the team as a 1960s All-Decade selection at defensive end, with final immortalization in the Patriots Hall of Fame.

97 James Busch Orthwein

James Busch Orthwein came close to becoming one of the most hated figures in New England sports history. The scion of a beer brewery fortune, Orthwein was a gentleman who purchased the Patriots in 1992 with the intention of moving them to St. Louis. He never hung around Boston much and always looked like one of the recently departed when photographed or when granting one of his rare interviews.

Almost by accident he became one of the pivotal figures in the eventual dynastic years of the club, in part because he wrested the franchise from its worst owner, Victor Kiam, and sold it in 1994 to Bob Kraft, its best owner. He also signed Bill Parcells to become the head coach, and while Parcells may have left the team four years later in an unfortunate manner, a new era of professionalism came to the operations of the region's football club.

More competent and cunning than Kiam, Orthwein shared one beguiling headache with Victor, the ownership of a franchise with no rights to the venue that his team played in. Wily as Orthwein may have been, Kraft waited him out and outsmarted him, leaving the St. Louis gentleman little choice but to sell to Kraft in 1994. Eventually Orthwein did play an instrumental role in bringing the Rams to St. Louis, so he certainly did well by his hometown and his civic devotion should be commended, especially since it did not come at the expense of New England.

Most New England Patriots fans have no chance of accumulating the amount of money that James Busch Orthwein amassed in his lifetime, but take solace that in the end, you received what he wanted most.

98 Kevin Faulk

In 1999, the Patriots did not, charitably speaking, draft with prescience. First pick Damien Woody has had a very productive NFL career but other first round choice Andy Katzenmoyer busted out all over. Despite this frustration, an appreciative soft parade of knowledgeable fans has since formed around the club's second round choice that year, running back Kevin Faulk out of LSU.

Faulk starred in college, a small but elusive back, and though some teams may have been deterred by his relative lack of size at 5'8" but the Patriots brain trust at that time perceived the back as a potential star, and at worst a very productive player.

Thriving in New England, Faulk personified the third down back in the NFL; not an every down back, but rather someone who could run and catch passes when called on. Faulk accumulated 3,607 yards rushing, but perhaps more importantly caught 431 passes, an impressive all-time statistic for most receivers in NFL history.

Faulk's usefulness did not end there. He returned 101 punts and 181 kickoffs in his career and scored 200 points, and no Patriot player has ever compiled more all-purpose yards than Kevin Faulk and quite possibly no one ever will.

That's not all. Despite his diminutive stature, he stood in to pick up blitzes on innumerable occasions, when another back might have scampered into the flats, as his quarterback lay flattened by an opposing lineman. Not Kevin Faulk, he absorbed the punishment to buy Tom Brady some additional time to find a receiver. On occasions, Faulk picked up the blitz and then slipped open for a catch.

Leading by Example

By 2010, only three players remained on the roster who had participated in the club's first three championships: Tom Brady, Matt Light and Faulk. In the second game of the 2010 season, against the rival Jets, Faulk left the game due to a torn ACL he sustained after a typically productive run. His season over, how did Kevin Faulk handle this adversity. In the first team meeting after the game, he was the first person who showed up.

Faulk's skill at a variety of tasks has not eluded the notice of Coach Belichick, who on one occasion ticked off the talents of his back: "Special teams, pass protection, running the ball, catching it, third downs, other downs...He's been a downfield receiver, third-down receiver, screens, draws. Even though he's not one of the highest play-time players, I think when he's in there he's very productive and he's one of the most respected players."

At the risk of offending strict constructionists in football fantasy leagues, Faulk also participated in some of the most key plays during the team's title runs in the early millennium, repeatedly contributing to extended scoring drives which separated the Patriots from a franchise of perennial good but disappointing contenders to champions. As appreciative teammate Matt Light once stated, "Whenever there's a big play to be made, there always seems to be a 33 at the end of it."

Coach Bill Belichick designed his dominant Patriots teams around one superstar, quarterback Tom Brady, and a number of other very good players who may never merit passing attention as potential Hall of Fame inductees. Faulk fits that mold and his very considerable contributions to his team has culminated in three Super Bowl championships in the first decade of the 21st century.

99 Upton Bell

Known by fans under the age of forty as a television and radio sports personality, Upton Bell, son of legendary NFL commissioner Bert Bell, joined the Patriots as a boy-wonder general manager in 1971 in the wake of the disastrous Clive Rush interregnum and its similarly listless aftermath. He had worked virtually his entire life in the game and had helped construct the fine Baltimore Colts teams of the mid- to late 1960s through his shrewd skills as a talent evaluator.

One of the most tantalizing what-ifs in team history lie in the unrealized possibility that had Bell been permitted to take all the steps he wished, the Patriots might have won a Super Bowl in the 1970s. Two central obstacles impeded him: his dislike for head coach John Mazur and the bare cupboard left for him both in existing personnel and available draft choices. His issues with Mazur commanded much attention, as the two men basically embraced each other in a mutual dance of death. Mathematically, Bell calculated that one of them must go, when in fact both of them could go.

The 1971 Patriots had little veteran talent around which to build, but Bell drafted wisely, choosing Jim Plunkett and Julius Adams with the first two picks. When the Rams later soured on Plunkett's favorite target in college, Randy Vataha, Bell astutely added the receiver to the roster to the benefit of the club for several years thereafter. Little appreciated before or since, thereafter the team only had fifth, sixth, and ninth picks in the first 10 rounds (the league drafted through the 17th round then) and received very little of value in these later rounds. Bell had restored hope to New England, as the team improved from 2–12 to 6–8, and Mazur saved his job with a final win thanks to a Plunkett-to-Vataha heave against Baltimore.

In 1972, the team did not possess a first-round pick and only received value in defensive back Ron Bolton, the death knell for a group dependent on building through youth. The team fell to 3–11, and while Mazur walked the plank early in the season, so too did Bell in the end. After a brief dalliance with the World Football League, Bell never helped run a football team again.

Bell erred in his assessment of Duane Thomas, a back he briefly picked up in a trade with Dallas, and he should have always had the authority to fire Mazur. The GM job in New England had become a bit of a hot box under owner Billy Sullivan, so it is difficult to assess the club's ultimate fate had Bell stayed on and had unfettered control of the personnel decisions. We will never know.

100 Myra

Legend has it that when Bob and Myra Kraft first met it apparently was the closest to love at first sight there is, and the Brandeis co-ed wound up marrying the man from Columbia. More well known, Bob Kraft became an early fan of the Patriots, buying season's tickets over Myra's objections, and taking their four sons to the game, a good apprenticeship for their own future service for the franchise. Haltingly, Myra learned the game of football and has been a presence at the games during the Kraft ownership, sharing her family's love for the team and its sport.

She also served as its conscience, instrumental in shaping the type of organization the Patriots embody, from management to players to game time employees.

Most notably, she distinguished herself in the field of philanthropy, both in her work as the President and a Director of the

New England Patriots Charitable Foundation and in her involvement in numerous boards and other offices. She assisted cultural charities certainly, but also had a knack for divining those charities often overlooked and in most need of support, to continue their missions.

For example, when the Boys and Girls Clubs of Boston struggled, she took notice and began her efforts to restore that organization. She rarely spoke in public, permitting her husband or one of her sons to talk about the team, but Myra Kraft is and shall always remain the guardian angel of the Patriots franchise.

Acknowledgments

I would like to thank profusely the staffs at the Professional Football Hall of Fame and the Sports Museum. Richard Johnson at the Sports Museum was a huge help when I encountered detours in the road. The New England Patriots organization was extremely helpful, particularly Dan Kraft and Stacey James. Stacey kept an appointment and gave me an hour of his time right after the club had traded Randy Moss, true grace under pressure. Brockton's Jack McCormick provided a wealth of information. Pat Sullivan is one of the nicest people you will ever want to know, and he gave me a lot of time and very useful and candid information. Phil Bissell provided some very useful historical information, and as Phil would put it, occasionally hysterical information. The Patriots players of the past that I spoke to were all generous with their time, not to mention friendly and professional. Thanks to Lori Hubbard and Billy Hubbard for editing assistance. I relied on pro-football-reference.com for much of my statistical research, and deliberately used the term Pro Bowl even to refer to AFL all-star games for convenience.

Much love to Lori, Billy, and Caroline Hubbard.

Sources

Larry Fox, *The New England Patriots: Triumph and Tragedy* (New York: Atheneum: 1979).

Sean Glennon, *The Good, the Bad, & the Ugly: Heart-Pounding, Jaw-Dropping and Gut-Wrenching Moments from New England Patriots History*, (Chicago: Triumph Books, 2008).

Michael Holley, *Patriot Reign: Bill Belichick, the Coaches, and the Players who Built a Champion*, (New York: Harper-Collins Publishers, Inc., 2004).

Mike Holovak and Bill McSweeney, *Violence Every Sunday: The Story of a Professional Football Coach*, (New York: Coward-McCann, Inc., 1967).

Bob Hyldburg, *Total Patriots: The Definitive Encyclopedia of the World-Class Franchise*, (Chicago: Triumph Books, 2009).

George McGuane, *The New England Patriots: A Pictorial History*, (Virginia Beach: JCP Corp. of Virginia, 1980).